INTEGRATED POLLUTION CONTROL

Integrated Pollution Control

Change and Continuity in the UK Industrial
Pollution Policy Network

ADRIAN SMITH

*Studies
in
Green Research*

Aldershot • Brookfield USA • Singapore • Sydney

Published by
Ashgate Publishing Limited
Gower House
Croft Road
Aldershot
Hants GU11 3HR
England

Ashgate Publishing Company
Old Post Road
Brookfield
Vermont 05036
USA

British Library Cataloguing in Publication Data

Smith, Adrian
　Integrated pollution control : change and continuity
　in the UK industrial pollution policy network. -
　(Studies in green research)
　1.Pollution - Government policy - Great Britain
　2.Pollutants - Government policy -Great Britain 3.Factory
　and trade waste - Environmental aspects - Government policy
　- Great Britain
　I.Title
　363.7'37'0941

Library of Congress Catalog Card Number: 96-79947

ISBN 1 85972 597 X

Printed in Great Britain by The Ipswich Book Company, Suffolk

Contents

List of figures

List of tables

Foreword

The introduction of the Integrated Pollution Control system was to have been one of the most radical innovations in UK environmental policy for a generation. The 1990 Environmental Protection Act brought changes in both the regulatory principles underlying industrial pollution control and the institutional means for applying them.

The goals were ambitious: to sweep away parallel regulatory systems and bring complex industrial processes under the control of a single regulator; to regulate discharges to different environmental media within the same framework so as to achieve the best solution for the environment as a whole; and to make the UK's system more compatible with the evolving style of European Union environmental policy. The motives for instituting this change were complex and apparently contradictory in some respects. The need for change was recognised by all interested parties, including business, environmental groups and government itself. One goal was to provide the means to implement a more ambitious environmental policy. Another, ironically, was to pursue a deregulatory agenda by providing a regulatory 'one stop shop' and cutting the red-tape involved in securing the authorisation for industrial processes. The motive was to make it easier to implement European initiatives, yet it would preserve the distinctive style of British regulation.

This book makes it clear, as in many other areas of public life, that policy was for all practical purposes made as it was implemented. The institutional and technological complexities of applying abstract regulatory principles posed immense challenges. These challenges were most easily met by those who had the necessary technical expertise and who were closest to implementation on the ground - that is industry itself and the staff of HM Inspectorate of Pollution (HMIP). Understaffed and overwhelmed by the task of bringing thousands of processes within the new system over a four year period, HMIP inevitably had to rely very much on the co-operation of industry. Inevitably, the traditional style of UK pollution control began to re-emerge. Decisions were based on case-by-case pragmatism rather than the application of generic principles and standard rules; the discretion of individual site inspectors began to play a more important role; and the process of decision-making became less transparent to external observers.

Electricity generation and chemicals manufacture engendered particularly high levels of controversy during the implementation of Integrated Pollution Control. While the power sector debate related to the context of privatisation and the specific nature of background European legislation, the chemical industry controversies raised more generic issues. Indeed the traditional British pragmatism which re-emerged can be attributed almost directly to the experience of authorising organic chemicals processes.

That experience is the subject of this book. The book makes two distinct contributions. First, it provides an authoritative account of how UK Integrated Pollution Control came about and how it was implemented. By using organic chemicals as the case study, the author is able to highlight the key debates which underpinned the implementation process. Through interviews with all of the key players and through detailed examination of the documentation that greater openness has allowed into the public domain, the author is able to analyse in detail the ebb and flow of the debates which have characterised the Integrated Pollution Control policy initiative.

Secondly, the book provides a useful addition to the literature on policy networks theory. The case study provides powerful evidence that the membership of networks and the relationships between actors can be of critical importance in determining policy outcomes. In this case, a very tight network consisting of industry and regulators put in place a system of pollution control which is rather different from that envisaged by the original architects.

To that extent, the book is invaluable. But the debate about the style of industrial pollution control is not yet over. The European Union's new framework Directive on Integrated Pollution Prevention and Control leans heavily on the UK system of Integrated Pollution Control - or at least the system as originally conceived. A new set of policy issues will arise as the Directive is given effect in individual Member States and more specific 'daughter' Directives are developed. This process could follow the British route - aspiring to pollution prevention through pragmatic assessment on a case-by-case basis - or the alternative approach of specifying process requirements in ever more detail. Implementation will be at least as complex as that of IPC in the UK.

This is the final contribution of the book. The analysis of the implementation process for Integrated Pollution Control in the UK provides very obvious clues about the issues and debates that will arise as future measures are proposed and implemented. Implementation and policy network concepts will prove just as relevant and useful then as they have done in this book.

Professor Jim Skea
Director
ESRC Global Environmental Change Programme

Preface

As the title suggests, this book is not so much concerned with the science of pollution, nor with the technologies for controlling it, but rather with the social and political processes by which levels of pollution are established. In particular, this book examines how industrial pollution is regulated in the UK.

There are over 100,000 industrial chemicals in commercial use worldwide. Another 500 to 1,000 new chemicals are added to that list each year. The US National Academy of Science has written that toxicity information for a majority of these chemicals is absent, whilst for the remainder it is minimal. Indeed, there are serious gaps and uncertainties (perhaps chaotically inherent) in our knowledge of the effects of industrial chemicals on ecosystems.

Poisoning due to organic mercury, ozone depletion from organohalogens, the acidifying effects of oxides of sulphur and nitrogen, the enhanced global warming attributable to anthropogenic carbon emissions, the carcinogenic properties of volatile organic compounds, the toxicity of dioxins, the hormone disrupting effects of xeno-oestrogens, and so on all testify to the fact that industrial releases can be threatening. Calls are made increasingly for a precautionary approach to dumping wastes into the environment: given that the suspected effects could be so pervasive or catastrophic, it might be wiser to act in advance of incontrovertible proof of scientific cause-and-effect.

Even if we could become perfectly informed about the health and ecological effects of industrial releases, pollution control would retain a political dimension. This is because value judgements are inevitable. Exactly which deleterious effects does society accept as tolerable, given the various benefits arising from different types of industrial production, and which intolerable? Establishing answers to this sort of question involves competing interests - some sections of society will be less concerned about given release levels than others, for a variety of reasons. Some sections are able to assert their values as those which set the tolerable and intolerable levels of pollution for society as a whole. The freedom to drive large, fast cars as opposed to the freedom to breathe clean air and play in the streets, for example.

Through the detailed analysis of the origins and practice of Integrated Pollution Control, this book seeks to provide an understanding into the political process by which releases from British industry are regulated. How are the levels of industrial release, which we all have to live with, actually set? And by whom? Hopefully, the insights provided into that process here might help those who find current levels intolerable to improve conditions for us all, and to stop industry from being so wasteful. Dumping millions of tonnes of by-product into the environment is a testament to the inelegance of much contemporary design in production engineering.

This book began life as a DPhil thesis undertaken at the Science Policy Research Unit at the University of Sussex between October 1992 and July 1996. Much of the material which went into that thesis is presented in this book largely unaltered. But don't let that put you off reading the following pages. The case of Integrated Pollution Control is an illuminating example of how elements in industry dilute and frustrate even the limited ambitions of regulators wishing to provide some protection for our environment.

Though responsibility for this book is mine, considerable credit is due to my supervisor, Professor Jim Skea. It was his patient supervision of my DPhil which made the book possible. The value of his advice, comments and encouragement cannot be overstated. Other staff at the Science Policy Research Unit contributed with comments and stimulating discussion during the DPhil process, particularly Steve Sorrell, Frans Berkhaut and Sonja Boehmer-Christiansen.

In addition, thanks go to those people who volunteered their time to be interviewed as part of my research. Others searched out and sent me documents. The assistance of these individuals from industry, government, environment groups, and the civil service has been invaluable.

Finally, many friends provided floors to kip on during my travels around the country, made necessary by interviews and data gathering. Their hospitality turned what could have been a dreary and tiring experience into a fun and exhausting experience! Along with friends in Brighton, they also provided me with the encouragement to keep going, whilst at the same time keeping me sane from too much involvement in the minutiae of industrial pollution regulation. The DPhil project and this book have been as much a test of motivation and stamina than of intellect, which is why credit for its production is theirs. Thanks.

Adrian Smith
Brighton
October 1996

List of abbreviations

BAT	Best Available Techniques
BATNEEC	Best Available Techniques Not Entailing Excessive Cost
BOD	Biological Oxygen Demand
BPEO	Best Practicable Environmental Option
BPM	Best Practicable Means
CBI	Confederation of British Industry
CEGB	Central Electricity Generating Board
CIA	Chemical Industries Association
CIGN	Chief Inspector's Guidance Note
COD	Chemical Oxygen Demand
COPA	Control of Pollution Act
DEmp	Department of Employment
DoE	Department of the Environment
DTi	Department of Trade and Industry
EC	European Community
EMS	Environmental Management System
ENDS	Environmental Data Services
EU	European Union
HMIP	Her Majesty's Inspectorate of Pollution
HoC	House of Commons
HSC/E	Health and Safety Commission/Executive
HWI	Hazardous Waste Inspectorate
IAPI	Industrial Air Pollution Inspectorate
ICI	Imperial Chemical Industries
IEHO	Institute of Environmental Health Officers
IPC	Integrated Pollution Control
IPPC	Integrated Pollution Prevention and Control
LA	Local Authority

MAFF	Ministry of Agriculture, Fisheries and Food
NAO	National Audit Office
NEDC-SOSG	National Economic Development Council-Specialised Organics Sector Group
NEEC	Not Entailing Excessive Cost
NGO	Non-governmental organisation
NII	Nuclear Installations Inspectorate
NRA	National Rivers Authority
NSCA	National Society for Clean Air and Environmental Protection
RCEP	Royal Commission on Environmental Pollution
RCI	Radiochemical Inspectorate
RTZ	Rio Tinto Zinc
SI	Statutory Instrument
SOMER	Specialised Organics Manufacturers Eastern Region
SS	Suspended Solids
STP	Standard Temperature and Pressure
TUC	Trades Union Congress
UK	United Kingdom
US EPA	United States' Environmental Protection Agency
VOC	Volatile Organic Compound

1 Introduction

The significance of Integrated Pollution Control (IPC)

Britain is credited with establishing one of the world's first environment agencies (McCormick, 1991, p.9). The Alkali Inspectorate was created in 1863 initially to regulate emissions from processes in the chemical industry.[1] Indeed, it is the organic chemical industry which is the case study industrial sector for this book's analysis into integrated pollution control.

More recently, Britain has been criticised for dragging its feet over environmental issues. In the mid-1980s a lack of specific air pollution standards, relaxed discharge consents, the dumping of industrial wastes in the North Sea and radioactivity in the Irish Sea, the co-disposal of domestic and toxic wastes in landfills, reluctance to sign an international Protocol designed to curtail sulphur emissions, and so on provided environmental critics with ammunition to dub Britain the 'Dirty Man of Europe' (Rose, 1990, pp.1-8; Boehmer-Christiansen and Skea, 1991, pp.210-217).

Yet by the end of the 1980s British Ministers were claiming Britain to be in the environmental vanguard of Europe. An important element in this was the government's new system for the Integrated Pollution Control (IPC) of industrial releases, introduced in the Environmental Protection Act, 1990. Ministers used this new system of regulation to dispel the government's reputation for environmental procrastination:

We have already taken the lead in Europe in preparing an integrated pollution control system. Integrated pollution control is the way legislation on environmental protection will develop across Europe in the 1990s.
(Environment Minister Virginia Bottomley, Parliamentary Written Answers, Column 646, 22nd March 1989)

1

This will be the first system of integrated pollution control in Europe. We are ahead of the field. Other countries, particularly in the Community, are turning their attention to this question of the integrated nature of pollution control. They will, I believe, be impressed by the advantages of our approach.
(Secretary of State for the Environment Chris Patten, Parliamentary Debates, Column 35, 15th January 1990)

IPC was the government's flagship legislative measure, controlling releases from some 5,000 of the country's most polluting industrial processes. 'IPC was heralded as a sophisticated regime that would ensure the use of the "best practicable environmental option" and drive the uptake of cleaner technologies. Another key aim was to introduce greater transparency and public accountability to the control of industrial pollution' (Allott, 1994, p.ix). Ostensibly, IPC was introduced in the UK as a more effective means for controlling releases from industrial processes. By seeking to simultaneously control releases to air, water and land, IPC overcomes the problems associated with single medium pollution controls.

In the past, pollution policy focused upon industrial releases to land, air and water in separation, with little regard for the other two environmental media. The separate controls placed upon industrial operations were administered by different regulators. This fragmented approach could have a perverse effect. Single medium regulations controlling releases to air, for instance, could lead to an increase in discharges to water. For example, some types of 'end-of-pipe' pollution control equipment used to scrub pollutants from air emissions result in a polluted aqueous solution instead, which still presents a disposal problem. With no overall strategy, single-medium controls can simply shunt polluting releases from one environmental medium to another, according to whichever offers the path of least regulatory resistance.

Arguments for a more integrated approach to pollution control were not new. The problem had been noted by the Royal Commission on Environmental Pollution (RCEP) in 1976. This respected body of experts recommended that integrated pollution controls be introduced and administered by a single regulator (RCEP, 1976). But as Albert Weale points out, 'successful pursuit of environmental policy depends not only on the intellectual cogency of the arguments advanced in its favour but also on the circumstances within which it is developed' (1992, p.136). Environmentally rational policy ideas are not taken up automatically. So why did the government introduce IPC in 1990?

One view is that IPC was part of a shift in UK environmental policy in the late 1980s (Jordan, 1993, p.411). Gray (1995, p.1) suggests that some commentators saw Mrs Thatcher's 1988 'green speech' to the Royal Society as

2

an important marker in this fundamental shift (see also McCormick, 1991, pp.58-68). Policy was now more transparent, accountable, formal, interventionist, legalistic, centralised and strategic. Others saw Thatcher's speech as little more than populist rhetoric, capitalising upon an episode of increased green consciousness amongst the electorate (Gray, 1995, p.2; Ward and Samways, 1992). Environmental policy would continue along its secretive, elitist, informal, voluntaristic, consensual, devolved and incrementalist path (Gray, 1995, p.1; Vogel, 1986, pp.70-106). One review of the evidence concluded that whilst some measures have improved environmental protection, usually driven by the European Union (EU), they do not amount to a fundamental shift in government policy (Gray, 1995, p.10). Other reviews have been more critical, concluding that recent initiatives such as IPC amount to little more than symbolic window dressing (Ward and Samways, 1992). Indeed, it is unclear if all the commitments made by the government since the late 1980s will be achieved, such as targets for domestic recycling (DoE, 1996).

This book presents a detailed analysis of the IPC policy process. A 'policy process' is defined as the 'series of patterns of related decisions to which many circumstances and personal, group, and organisational influences have contributed' (Hogwood and Gunn, 1984, p.23). The IPC policy process led to the government switching away from single medium air pollution controls and into IPC. It spans the whole series of decisions and non-decisions which led eventually to IPC controls on individual industrial processes. This policy process began with the creation of an 'integration' policy issue by the RCEP in 1976, which was ignored by government and finally rejected by them in 1982. The IPC policy process then includes the government's policy reversal: its formulation of IPC policy and passing of legislation in 1990. It culminates in Her Majesty's Inspectorate of Pollution's (HMIP - the public body appointed as IPC regulator) regulation of releases from individual industrial processes within the IPC legal framework. This book can be conceived as an empirical test within the debate concerning the 'greening' or otherwise of our government - IPC is taken to be an element of pollution policy which is in turn a sub-set of environmental policy.

Earlier studies by O'Riordan and Weale (1989) and Jordan (1993) suggest IPC does present evidence of a shift in UK environmental policy. They saw the traditional UK approach, involving site-by-site administrative discretion in interpreting loosely defined legal principles, being replaced by formal emissions standards, set centrally. O'Riordan and Weale claimed that 'No longer can the British hide behind plant-specific emission controls linked to broad, non-statutory, environmental quality targets' (1989, p.291). For Jordan, IPC fitted an 'emerging style' which 'is likely to be more transparent, increasingly formalised and structured, participative, timetabled and more

3

strictly enforced; [and] the administrative structures are likely to be more centralised, integrated and possibly more technocratic and managerial' (1993, p.411). Both studies viewed Europe as a driving force behind these changes. O'Riordan and Weale argued a process of 'purposive adaptation' was occurring in the late 1980s, whereby a more formal European approach was having to be accommodated by the informal British tradition (1989, p.292). Pearce and Brisson (1993, p.39) believed a more formal, sector-wide, systematic approach to standard setting was essential for IPC; any return to the traditional 'case-by-case' approach would be a 'retrogressive step'.

This book improves upon these earlier studies thanks to the passing of a few years of IPC implementation. It argues the formality forecast above has proved to be ambiguous at best. A formal, arms' length approach to regulation, out of step with the British tradition, was adopted by HMIP not long after publication of the O'Riordan and Weale paper. But difficulties in its application led to informally set, plant-specific emission controls, albeit within more formal and transparent procedures than earlier regulatory regimes. Many features traditional to domestic environmental policy (such as site-by-site discretion, and informally set standards) persist with IPC; in this policy sector at least, there has been no fundamental shift.

Two motivations prompted the book. The first was indeed the apparent clash between the policy innovations claimed for IPC on its introduction and the criticised UK tradition in environmental policy: why did the secretive 'Dirty Man' introduce 'transparent and accountable' IPC? Second, as an important element of overall environmental policy, just how fundamental a shift in pollution policy is IPC?

Given the above two motivations, two questions frame the book: (1) why did the government introduce IPC?; and following on from this, (2) how has IPC been implemented? The book uses a recent developments in the public policy literature to analyse the IPC policy process and to provide answers to these two questions. This theoretical development is the policy networks concept. It analyses the complex interactions between policy actors, which advocates believe to be the defining characteristic of modern policy making (chapter 2).

The second of the above two questions has several elements to it. First, how does IPC compare with the pollution control regime it superseded? In other words, is there evidence of a fundamental shift in policy? IPC focuses upon individual industrial processes when controlling pollution, in common with the industrial air pollution regulatory regime it replaced. Both pollution regimes have used a permitting system for the control of emissions from selected industrial processes. An industrial process cannot operate without a permit. Certain conditions (usually release limits) must be met before the permit is issued to industrial operators by the regulator. For these reasons this book compares IPC with the air regime in order to ascertain how policy has changed.

The second element to the 'how' research question concerns the way standards of pollution control are set under IPC. Who is involved? Why are they included and others excluded? How do these actors set pollution control standards? And in relation to policy change, how does this approach compare with the air regime? These are all issues related to IPC implementation.

The final 'how' element concerns IPC's impact in terms of policy output. Ideally this could be assessed by measuring the extent to which IPC is reducing industrial releases and improving our environment. However, assessing the environmental impact of regulations is not straightforward. Other factors, such as reduced economic activity or changes in economic structure, can bring about greater changes in pollution than a new regulatory regime (Vogel, 1986, p.147; DoE, 1996, p.23). For instance, Skea (1995) argues the UK is meeting its international acid emission commitments primarily through the technological implications of electricity privatisation. The adoption of less polluting technologies can be motivated by multiple factors, in which disentangling the influence of regulation can be complex.

There is also a more immediate impediment to an emissions assessment of the policy output of IPC. The fact is that prior to IPC the Alkali Inspectorate, the public body responsible for regulating air emissions, did not maintain records of emissions from the industrial processes it regulated. It is not possible to compare emissions under the air regime with emissions recorded under IPC. Nor is it possible to assess trends in releases under IPC given its relatively brief existence to date.[2] An alternative assessment of IPC's policy output has to be made. The approach taken here is to compare the actual actions required of industry by HMIP with HMIP's initial aspirations for IPC.

In summary, determining how IPC has been implemented requires comparison with the previous air regime, analysing how control standards are set, and assessing policy output. An analysis of these aspects of IPC's implementation, in conjunction with the initial question concerning IPC's origin, forms the backbone of this book.

Assuming critics of Britain's environmental policy are correct, then the argument underlying this book must be that IPC was introduced primarily for reasons other than a 'greened' government seeking a fundamental shift in pollution policy. A corollary of this view is that IPC's implementation will have suffered a lack of political support: IPC should present little evidence of a fundamental shift, particularly in the way pollution control standards are established and implemented. The literature on environmental policy repeatedly notes the EU source of many domestic policy measures (for example, Haigh and Lanigan, 1995; Haigh, 1989; O'Riordan, 1988, pp.40-42).

Given the Ministerial claims for IPC, it is somewhat ironic that its origins can be found in the EU.

Industrial pollution regulation as a policy issue

Pollution regulation is the act of limiting releases, usually set by a public body given the authority by government to issue commands to industrial operators to control their process releases. It is HMIP which has responsibility for regulating industrial processes under IPC legislation. The series of influences and decisions by which pollution controls are set is the regulatory process. This book tends to refer to it as a policy process - see above - because regulatory processes are a sub-set of policy processes. The difference being that regulatory processes culminate in a regulation limiting an activity. Policy processes include processes which culminate in different types of policy output: 'regulatory', 'distributive' (e.g. public works), and 'redistributive' (e.g. welfare benefits) (Lowi, 1972 cited in Hargrove, 1983, p.283). The following chapter begins by exploring regulatory and policy processes in more detail.

Pollution as a phenomenon can be defined as the release of a substance into the environment in quantities or concentrations greater than can be coped with by the cleansing and recycling capacity of nature (Weale, 1992, p.3; Crump, 1991, p.201); Martin Holdgate, former Chief Scientist at the DoE, described pollution as damage to targets in the environment (1979).

But pollution is as much socially defined as it is scientifically. The physical limits regulating (quantitatively and qualitatively) what can be released from industrial processes effectively sets the levels at which polluting activity begins (Hawkins, 1984, p.23). These physical limits reflect the decisions of policy actors. They mediate scientific evidence and political pressures. Regulating pollution is an issue for public policy owing to its characteristics, elaborated by Weale and summarised here (1992, p.5-9):

1   A clean environment is a public good in the sense that, relative to a particular set of affected parties, it is enjoyed by all individuals. If a member of a community takes steps to reduce their polluting releases into that community, then the whole community benefits.

2   Pollution is often the by-product of legitimate activities within society.[3]

3   The identification and control of pollution involves a large core of scientific and technical interpretation.

4   The effects of pollution can be spatially and temporally pervasive. Long-term impacts can affect future generations who are often under-represented in policy-making arenas. Equally, long-distance impacts can affect populations far removed from national or local policy-making arenas.

5   Pollution cuts across established policy sectors, being a problem associated with transport, energy, agriculture, trade and industry.

With the environment being a public good, pollution regulation has traditionally been a responsibility for governments (see Fischer, Dornbusch and Schmalensee, 1988, p.66 for discussion of public goods and government provision). That pollution is a by-product of activities considered otherwise legitimate means governments have to circumscribe the nature of those activities rather than outlaw them. So, for instance, chemical manufacturing sites may be required to install effluent treatment plant for by-products rather than shut down all production.

So industrial pollution regulation requires a balance to be struck between the freedom with which a production activity is allowed to continue and the severity with which it is circumscribed in order to limit polluting by-products. There are a variety of types of pollution control which seek to limit either the quantity or the impact of the polluting by-product (see Haigh, 1989, pp.13-20). Exposure standards, environmental quality standards, emission standards, technology-based standards, product standards and so on can all be used to limit levels of pollution.

Whichever type of standard is adopted, setting levels is often considered the domain of the technical experts in the regulatory bodies (Davies and Davies, 1975, p.184). The DoE, for instance, defers IPC standard setting to its experts at HMIP. Scientists can uncover the effects on certain targets of certain pollutants at certain levels; and technical expertise can devise chemical, biological and physical pollution prevention or control measures. But an element of value judgement is needed to decide which pollution effects society wishes to tolerate or avoid (see Blowers, 1984); 'while we may be able to define what level of environmental quality is necessary for particular uses, the definition of what constitutes pollution is dependant on the public's decision as to what uses it wants to make of its environment' (Davies and Davies, 1975, p.4).

Thus setting standards which limit pollution to a certain level involves both scientific and value[4] judgements. The exercise retains an inherently political dimension, as different groups seek to assert their values for adoption by government as the value determining the degree of environmental protection

7

and hence level of regulation.[5] Part of this book's task is to characterise how standards are adopted for IPC.

The IPC regulatory framework

Both IPC and the earlier air regime share characteristics with respect to the focus of attention when controlling pollution (the industrial process), and the means for controlling the pollution (issuing a permit before the process can operate). A comparison between the characteristics of the two regimes is an element of the analysis into how IPC has been implemented. Therefore a detailed elaboration of the two regimes is inappropriate here. Nevertheless, it is important to explain the basics of IPC in order to facilitate the forthcoming analysis.[6]

IPC utilises technology-based pollution standards. That is, emission limits are set for industrial processes on the basis of the performance that can be achieved using the best pollution control techniques. The standards derived in this way are mitigated by the cost associated with pollution controls. For the air regime the guiding principle was for controlled processes to use the 'best practicable means' to limit pollution. Under IPC the 'best available techniques not entailing excessive cost' must be used to control pollution.

At the heart of the IPC system is an application-authorisation permitting procedure. Process operators have to apply for an authorisation in order to legally operate their process. Operating a process without authorisation is an offence, as is transgressing the pollution control conditions written into the authorisation by HMIP. This is the regulatory framework set up by government legislation and within which HMIP operates.

It is HMIP which issues authorisations and sets the pollution control conditions for the process ('the regulation'). Those conditions must follow two statutory principles enshrined in IPC legislation. Operators must show in their application that the process is the Best Practicable Environmental Option (BPEO) for balancing releases to all three environmental media; and that they are pursuing the Best Available Techniques Not Entailing Excessive Cost (BATNEEC) to control those releases. Authorisations contain release limits (based upon BATNEEC for the type of process); they can include other conditions, such as maintenance of plant, and they include Improvement Programmes which timetable how the existing process will upgrade to meet the higher standards associated with new processes. Authorisations can be modified on request of either the regulator or the operator, with any justifiable alterations written into a Variation Notice.

The types of process regulated under IPC are known as 'prescribed processes'. They are prescribed by government Statutory Instrument, and cover the most complex and polluting industrial processes in England and

8

Wales.[7] IPC was phased in over a six year period after its legislative introduction in 1990. The regulator responsible for administering IPC, HMIP, had been created by the government in 1987 as a unitary pollution regulator. Thus HMIP's creation is an important element to IPC's introduction since it was at this juncture that the government decided upon integrated pollution controls. Analysing why IPC was introduced rests upon explaining HMIP's creation.

A major innovation under IPC legislation was the provision of a public register containing operator applications, corresponding HMIP authorisations, and other records such as process release data and variation notices. This advance has enabled this book to analyse IPC implementation in considerable detail.[8] The air regime had no such publicly available documentary record. Elements of IPC such as this have certainly brought unprecedented transparency to pollution regulation and as such have enabled the analysis necessary for this book. The book's presentation of it's IPC policy process analysis is mapped out below.

The structure of the book

Whilst IPC follows regulatory principles defined by statute (BATNEEC and BPEO), the law defers to the regulator their interpretation into specific regulatory standards. Only a limited understanding can be gained from study of the IPC legal framework. Analysis will have to draw upon the public register, interviews with participants, and documentary records in order to construct the full picture. Answering the 'why' and 'how' research questions will require study of the whole process which led to IPC's introduction and saw through its implementation. This introductory chapter began by pointing out Weale's observation that environmental knowledge alone is insufficient to drive policy (1992, p.136). In this respect, this IPC case study should contribute towards a clearer understanding of the process of making environmental policy, and provide some evidence of whether or not there has been a fundamental shift in domestic environmental policy since the late 1980s.

The IPC policy process is sketched out below in Figure 1.1. For heuristic purposes it has been broken down into three stages: the creation of a policy issue; formulation of IPC policy; and implementation of that policy. Stages in a policy process will be discussed more fully in chapter 2. Here the objective is to signpost the route taken by the book, which presents the analysis in chronological order. This seems most appropriate given the book's task is an explanation of the process by which IPC arose and has been implemented.

Analysis of the first stage focuses upon the characteristics of the pre-IPC industrial air pollution control regime and examines criticisms of it. The intellectual case for integrated reform arose after a spell of public criticism of

9

the air regime in the early 1970s. However, it was not until the 1980s that reforms took place. IPC policy formulation revolved around reforming the principles which regulation had to follow. How transparent should the regulations be? Should standards be uniformly applied or tailored to individual circumstance? How should these standards be set (BPM or BATNEEC)? What regulatory duties are required? How should these be divided between regulator and regulated? As pointed out in the preceding section, IPC defers to the implementation stage the setting of regulatory standards in accordance with the regulatory principles introduced at the formulation stage.

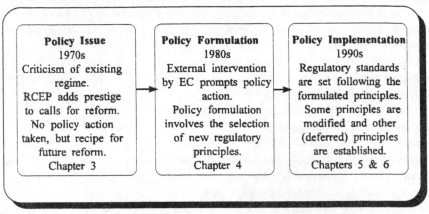

Figure 1.1 The IPC policy process

Chapter 2 develops an analytical framework for interpreting the empirical evidence gathered for the book. Even though this book's subject matter is regulation, theories of regulation are not used in the analysis. This is due to this book's interest in the whole IPC policy process. Different elements of the regulation literature tend to focus exclusively upon aspects of regulation, such as its creation or its enforcement, but not the whole process; or theories are relevant to specific regulatory contexts, such as business regulation in America, and are inappropriate for transposition to other contexts.

Given that the second of the two questions concerning this book relates to the implementation of IPC, it seems natural to examine the literature on implementation studies for analytical help. Again this literature does not extend over the whole policy process. This is something concluded in the literature itself. Policy formulation (why the IPC regulatory framework was introduced) and policy implementation (how that framework has been put into effect) have to be studied as a complex continuum.

Some writers in both the regulation literature and the implementation literature recognised that analytical approaches should focus upon the interactions of actors seeking to influence decisions over the policy process. This is the territory of policy networks, the main body of background theory comprising this book's analytical framework. Policy networks are a recent development in the analysis of public policy (Hogwood, 1995, p.65-66). The preceding literature is used in chapter 2 as a justifying introduction for the use of policy networks, with some lessons concerning implementation being carried through from that literature. Using this combination of implementation studies and policy networks, and drawing upon other studies into IPC, five hypotheses are generated at the end of chapter 2 with respect to IPC's origins and implementation. The remainder of the book tests these theoretically informed hypotheses against actual events, and thus the utility of the theory introduced in chapter 2 can be assessed. This is done in the concluding chapter, chapter 7.

Chapter 3 contains an analysis of the industrial air pollution control regime which preceded IPC. It includes a discussion of the unsuccessful calls for pollution policy reform in the early 1970s. The reformers did nevertheless prompt the RCEP investigation into the issue of air pollution. Their 1976 report alerted government to the environmental benefits of an integrated approach to the control of industrial releases. However, it was not until the 1980s that reforms took place and IPC was introduced. In chapter 4 the events of the 1980s which led to the creation of HMIP and IPC's introduction are analysed. The chapter points out how HMIP and IPC appeared at the time to signal a shift toward more formal regulation. Analysts at that time were interpreting events as representing a fundamental shift in environmental policy (see for example O'Riordan and Weale, 1989; Jordan, 1993).

Much of the material used in the above two chapters draws upon secondary sources. That is, research done by others or interpretations of events contemporary to that time. This has been complemented by my own research in the form of interviews with participants in those events, and documents generated during the policy process (government consultation papers, for example). However, it is in the remaining two chapters that the majority of my own research is presented. Detailed interviews and examination of IPC documents has enabled a thorough analysis of IPC implementation to be presented in these chapters. A policy network analysis of IPC, particularly in the sense of covering the entire policy process, is without precedent and consequently a revised understanding of IPC is achieved.

The empirical material for this book draws upon 48 interviews conducted with participants and observers of the IPC policy process, including civil servants, industrialists and environmentalists. Access to such individuals, some working at high policy levels, was secured with the understanding that comments would remain non-attributable. Their participation in research means the book presents considerable insights into the policy process.

11

Interviews were backed up with detailed analysis of a wide variety of documentary evidence both generated by the IPC policy process (for example, trade association internal memos) and commentary upon the policy process (for example, press reports).

In chapter 5, HMIP's derivation of BATNEEC pollution standards for organic chemical processes is analysed. The organic chemical industry was chosen as a case study primarily because it is the largest sector regulated under IPC[9] and because its implementation of IPC fell within the timetable of this study. In addition, the primary environmental problem facing the chemicals sector is industrial pollution.[10] The organic chemical sector is maintained as a case study in chapter 6, which considers the site-level implementation of IPC. This chapter analyses how individual HMIP Inspectors negotiated IPC authorisation conditions with individual process operators. The focus upon concrete cases also makes chapter 6 the appropriate point to conduct an assessment of IPC policy output and to compare IPC with the air regime analysed in chapter 3.

IPC's policy output, the actions of operators and inspectors, has been measured through a content analysis of the IPC public register. For instance, the analysis measures the proportion of operators who included in their applications an environmental assessment of their process releases, as requested by HMIP for all applications. By contrasting HMIP's initial application requirements with what was actually delivered by operators (as measured by the content analysis) some idea of IPC's implementation deficit can be gained. The content analysis examined applications and authorisations for 60 per cent of the organic chemical operators regulated under IPC. All these operators were regulated under the preceding air pollution regime. They were not new to pollution regulation, and so a direct comparison between the two regimes (air and IPC) can be maintained. Further elaboration of the analysis and its results are presented in chapter 6.

Logical inferences (in contrast to statistical inferences) can be drawn from the organic chemicals sector about the implementation of IPC amongst industry in general (Platt, 1988, p.18; Mitchell, 1983, pp.198-200). The validity of any industry wide inferences have been confirmed by checking against other studies of IPC (for example, Allott, 1994; Lyons, 1992) and against reports in the press (for example, ENDS Report).

In the concluding chapter, the analysis is reflected upon in order to consider the changes and continuities IPC has brought to industrial pollution regulation. The utility of policy networks for analyses of the policy process is also discussed. The penultimate element of the chapter looks to the future of IPC. In April 1996 the government joined HMIP with the National Rivers Authority (NRA) and regional waste regulatory authorities (WRAs) to form a new Environment Agency. How will IPC fair under the new Agency? Another potential influence upon IPC's future is an EU Directive on Integrated Pollution Prevention and Control (IPPC). To what extent, if any, will this alter IPC? Given the insights into the dynamics of industrial pollution regulation learnt over the course of the book, it appears unlikely that these two events will alter IPC radically. Drawing upon lessons learnt from features of IPC policy process chapter 7 finishes by making some policy recommendations into how regulation could be altered in order to strengthen the protection of our environment. However, future developments and my prescriptions for policy change are more a final footnote to the book's central objective: an analysis of the IPC policy process from the 1970s into the 1990s. If there is one lesson to be learnt from this study, it is that environmental policy can only be as effective as its implementation. Those seeking improved environmental policy should keep an eye on the devil in the detailed agreements between those involved in the site-level activation of such policy.

Notes

1   The types of industrial process scheduled for regulation expanded over the years.

2   The Chemical Release Inventory for processes regulated under IPC has only two or three years release data.

3   Or, more precisely, activities considered legitimate by influential elements of society.

4   Some environmental economists wish to collapse the way society values the environment into an apolitical, financial cost-benefit exercise; but the theoretical and practical potential for a mechanical determination of desirable use remains contentious (Adams, 1996, p.2). 'Attempting to encapsulate environmental quality in a monetary value is like trying to measure the width of a temperature, or devine the velocity of love' (Stirling, 1993, p.101).

5   Individuals, industrial firms and so on may choose to protect the environment further, but this book is concerned with the public level of protection as arrived at through the regulatory process.

6   For a more detailed introduction to the IPC system see DoE (1993).

7   A system of IPC also exists in Scotland and N. Ireland but are regulated by other bodies. This book uses Britain or the UK for shorthand when

really it refers only to England and Wales. Apologies to people in Scotland and N. Ireland.

8   Allott (1994) is the only other study of the public register. This was less detailed and not rooted in any theoretical or historical context.

9   By April 1995 over 621 organic chemical processes had been authorised under IPC; the next largest tranche of processes was the 252 combustion processes (out of a total of 1728 authorised processes) (HMIP, 1995a, p.133).

10   For other industrial sectors industrial pollution is not the sole environmental issue. These sectors have other environmental problems which could confuse or diffuse analysis of IPC. The environmental issues associated with the waste disposal sector are those primarily of resource use, landfill, contaminated land and leaching. Pesticide production also involves environmental problems other than industrial pollution: agricultural practice; safety in use; and surface run-off. The power sector is tied up with the aftermath of electricity supply privatisation and the 'dash for gas'. In other words, other sectors have more diffuse environmental policy issues which leak into other environmental policy sectors.

2 A policy network approach to analysing IPC

Introduction

This book is concerned with the IPC policy process. In the introductory chapter the research task was framed as two questions: why did the government introduce IPC; and how has IPC been implemented? Analysis of IPC implementation will hopefully demonstrate how pollution control standards are set and enable an assessment of IPC's output to be made. In addition, comparison must be made between the implementation of IPC and practices under the preceding air pollution regime. This is necessary in order to ascertain the nature and extent of any changes that have taken place in industrial pollution policy.

So the scope of this study sweeps from IPC's pre-history (the air regime) through events and decisions leading to the introduction of IPC, and on to IPC implementation. In this chapter general characteristics of policy processes identified in the literature are discussed. The aim of this chapter is to identify and introduce an analytical framework which can span and explain the entire policy process. The policy networks concept is considered appropriate because its focus on the interactions between policy actors allows analysis to track along the policy process (Hanf and O'Toole, 1992). The selection of this analytical framework has to be justified. Hence it is arrived at following a rejection of the regulation literature (for the purposes of this study) and after a few lessons (and similarities) have been drawn from the implementation studies literature.

IPC is a regulatory regime, so it would indeed seem natural to use theories from the regulation literature for analysing IPC. However, the regulation literature often tends to consider only discrete elements of the entire regulatory process. Individual theories of regulation tend to cover isolated elements of the whole process, such as the creation of a regulatory framework or its enforcement, but not both. Moreover, some theories presented in the literature can, arguably, be specific to the types of regulation upon which they were based, such as the 'capture' theory of economic regulation. Applying those theories to different types of regulation or in different contexts may be inappropriate. This study needs an analytical framework which has the flexibility to explain the whole IPC policy process. Thus this chapters next two sections begin by examining the regulatory/policy process whilst arguing theories of regulation are inappropriate for its study. This is not a lone assertion, a collection of studies into regulation concluded that analysts should adopt an approach akin to policy networks (Hancher and Moran, 1989).

The IPC legal framework leaves considerable standard setting discretion to HMIP. Interpretation of the BATNEEC and BPEO regulatory principles is deferred until the implementation of IPC, and this will have a significant impact on IPC's output. This chapter goes on to propose that the implementation studies literature can provide lessons for analysis of this important element of the IPC policy process. This literature is examined to see if it provides any help for the analysis of how IPC has been implemented. The literature demonstrates the considerable influence implementation can have on policy output and serves to illustrate the complexities of modern policy making. Emerging from this literature was an opinion, shared here, that 'implementation' needs to be situated and understood within the whole policy process. Moreover, some of the conclusions from implementation studies concerning the interactions that take place between policy actors can be found in the policy networks literature, due to a shared intellectual heritage in inter-organsational studies. Once again study of the literature points towards policy networks as a suitable analytical framework.

By-passing theories of regulation as insufficient for analysis of the whole policy process, and via implementation studies (which are concerned with the latter stages of policy processes), this chapter finally arrives at the policy networks literature, which forms the main body of background theory for this book. Modern policy problems, such as industrial pollution, are so complex that policy actors seeking a solution often find themselves interdependent upon the resources of others (such as knowledge, finance, legal authority or organisational capacity). The basic premise from policy networks is that this resource interdependency brings actors together into policy network arrangements, and that these constrain and influence the policy process. Thus policy networks are clusters of resource interdependent policy actors (Rhodes, 1988, p.77). The focus of this literature is the different types of policy network (conditions of interaction between policy actors), and how these affect the policy process.

So the IPC policy process will be analysed by studying the shifting resource interdependencies and policy networks associated with industrial pollution

16

policy. The final section of the chapter takes the lessons from other IPC studies, introduced throughout the chapter, and generates five hypotheses using lessons from implementation studies and the policy networks concept. The background theory suggests IPC was introduced after changes forced upon an industrial air pollution policy network. The distribution of resources between HMIP and industry necessary to set IPC regulations implies the latter has had an influential role in an IPC policy network that has formed during IPC's implementation. The implementation studies literature suggests IPC's impact on industrial pollution has been dampened at the implementation stage. Industry was influential in this dampening effect owing to the resources it could marshall and their significance to the implementation of IPC.

What is regulation?

Regulation is not a new phenomenon. Students of regulation cite regimes such as the fourteenth century Royal Edict on the burning of sea coal in London (Rhodes, 1981, p.123), or the ancient Sumerian tablets which contain rules governing food prices (Francis, 1993, p.259). Indeed, Hancher and Moran believe regulation to be virtually a defining feature of any system of social organisation (1989, p.271).

The term regulation, though widely used, is not often defined (Mitnick, 1980, p.1). Mitnick develops a definition from a concept of interference, 'Regulation is the public administrative policing of private activity with respect to a rule prescribed in the public interest' (1980, p.7).

This definition implies regulations serve the public interest[1], which is contentious amongst some theorists of regulation who see regulations as either 'captured' by the regulated (Stigler, 1971) or the outcome of interest group contestation (Wilson, 1980). Francis (1993, pp.1-2) borrows from Stone (1982) to define regulation as state intervention which constrains private activity. More importantly, he points out a key characteristic of regulation: 'Much in regulation suggests ambiguity, for the working assumption behind state intervention through regulation is that the product or activity at issue should be both permitted and constrained. Regulation is best understood as a midpoint between prohibition and the complete absence of state involvement' (Francis, 1993, p.6).

This book also defines regulation as the publicly administered constraint of private activity, but argues the degree of constraint can actually lie on a continuum of 'points' between non-intervention and prohibition. So for example, limited IPC regulation would be the deemed authorisation of prescribed processes as they stood. More severe regulation would refuse to authorise prescribed processes (and hence prevent them from operating) until they met improved pollution control standards, more strict than those currently practised by the process operator. This notion of a regulatory continuum is illustrated in Figure 2.1 below.

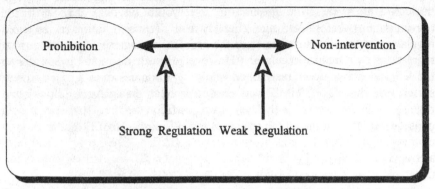

Figure 2.1 Regulation as the constraint of an activity

The regulation literature

Regulatory controls, such as IPC authorisations, emerge from a regulatory process involving decisions which identify issues for which regulation is felt necessary, formulates a regulatory framework, and sets standards of constraint - see below. Unfortunately, much of the literature on regulation fails to explicitly position itself at any point or points in that process (Mitnick, 1980, p.79; Schuck, 1981, p.721). In addition, theories of regulation - how standards are set, whose interest they operate in, why regulatory frameworks originate in the first instance, and so on - can sometimes be specific to the type of regulation upon which they are based, which means they have to be transposed with caution.

Stigler (1971) argued that regulations were captured 'by the industry and designed and operated primarily for its benefit'. Rent seeking firms encourage and manipulate regulations as barriers to competition or to guarantee profits. This capture theory is grounded in economic regulation. Schuck (1981, pp.705-708) argues that capture theory does not account for the rise of social regulation[2] in the 1970s (including environmental protection).

Schuck's point also raises the need for the judicious application of general regulatory theories to specific empirical cases. Explanations offered up for general consumption can sometimes fail because they are too rooted in their original context. Had capture theory, for instance, been grounded in environmental regulation a different conclusion might have been reached; such as conceptualising it as cost minimising firms successfully managing a favourable pace and direction to the general environmental improvements demanded by others. That is, capture has not arisen from the outset for rent seeking motives, as suggested by Stigler.

Bernstein (1955) focused upon regulatory agencies, suggesting they go through a life cycle: from 'generation', into 'youth' (vigour), onto 'maturity' (devitalisation), before 'old age' (debility and decline). Bernstein believed regulatory capture occurred later in the process, during the administration of regulations by a mature regulator. However, Bernstein's model is specific to the US and draws upon analysis of whole new regimes over a much longer period than this study. HMIP was created from an amalgamation of existing regulatory bodies, each with their own tradition. The Bernstein model consequently fails to match the reality of the IPC case. HMIP went through a confidence crisis shortly after its creation (O'Riordan, 1989, p.115), and later attempts at a vigorous, 'arms' length' approach to regulation were soon unceremoniously dropped (Allott, 1993, p.ix).

There have also been theories of regulatory enforcement (for example, Diver, 1980; Viscusi and Zeckhauser, 1979) and a political economy of monitoring and inspection (Hemenway, 1985). The point though is that few take full account of the whole regulatory process. So whilst single regulatory theories, such as agency life cycle, can be empirically rejected, this book rejects using the regulation literature because it tends to focus on a few regulatory events rather than the whole regulatory process.

The regulatory process as policy process

So far this discussion has not really defined the regulatory process beyond being a series of influences and decisions leading to a regulation; it has also been linked to the wider group of policy processes. What specifically do these processes involve? A 'full theory must ... explain how regulation is proposed, formally considered and approved, put into effect, administered, has impact, is evaluated, and is altered' (Mitnick, 1980, p.80). Schuck (1981, p.716) posits a series of events in the regulatory process which need explaining:

1   The appearance of a regulatory issue on the political agenda.

2   The ability for that issue to attain sufficient priority for recognition and resolution by the political system.

3   The adoption of a proposed solution in a particular form (regulatory framework).

4   The subsequent 'institutionalisation' of the proposal in a 'legislative or administrative milieu'.

19

5   The staffing patterns for the regulatory programme.

6   Substantial decisions resulting from the regulatory activities.

7   The evolution (and occasional demise) of the regulations.

The case for an integrated reform of UK industrial pollution control was first mooted by the Royal Commission on Environmental Pollution (RCEP) in 1976 (O'Riordan and Weale, 1989, p.284; Owens, 1989, pp.170-171). However, the issue did not become sufficiently salient until the mid-1980s. A series of 'interacting sources' prompted the political system to create HMIP in 1987 (Owens, 1989, pp.184-5), and to provide a legislative framework for IPC in 1990. However, substantial decisions concerning regulatory standards were deferred to HMIP (Jordan, 1993, p.410). Ultimately it is the negotiation of authorisation conditions with the operator which finally determines the 'regulation'. All of these events form the regulatory process under analysis in this book.

The regulation's position on the regulatory continuum (Figure 2.1) emerges through 'an intensely political' regulatory process (Bernstein, 1955, pp.278-9) involving different actors attempting to exert influence. The regulatory process spans a range of events: from creating[3] an issue warranting intervention through to enforcement of intervening controls - illustrated schematically in Figure 2.2 below. It accords with the history of this IPC case study, beginning with the RCEP's recommendations following criticism of the old industrial air pollution regulatory regime (Ashby and Anderson, 1981, p.133), through to the site-level implementation of IPC regulations.

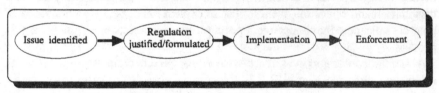

Figure 2.2 Schematic of the regulatory process

This book argues that the IPC regulatory process can be understood as a type of policy process, just as a programme for the construction of social housing is a type of policy process (see also Mitnick, 1981, p.79). So it is no surprise that definitions of the policy process are similar to the above elaboration of the regulatory process.

The policy process proceeds from the appearance of issues, to the assimilation of issues into the political agenda, a prioritising of those issues and setting objectives, examining options for resolving an issue, the implementation of preferred options, the evaluation of policy outcomes, and the termination or succession of a policy (Hogwood and Gunn, 1984, p.24). This is an ideal conceptualisation and, like the schematic in Figure 2.2, is too linear. In reality policy emerges and feeds back in ways different to the formal distinctions suggested in the figure (Ham and Hill, 1993, p.12). Indeed, not all policy problems proceed toward the generation of solutions (Bachrach and Baratz, 1970) or are even allowed to become issues in the first place (Lukes, 1974). Nonetheless, breaking the process into a series of events does serve as a useful heuristic, providing labels with which to situate events and enabling study of the policy process.

Studying IPC as a policy process implies the broader policy studies literature can be used legitimately for studying regulation. A collection of studies into economic regulation in European countries drew some conclusions about how best to study regulation which are very similar to the central tenets of the policy networks literature (Hancher and Moran, 1989). 'The critical question for the analyst of the European regulatory scene is not to assume "capture", but rather to understand the nature of this shared [regulatory] space: the rules of admission, the relations between occupants, and the variations introduced by differences in markets and issue arenas' (1989, p.271). This 'encourages us not only to examine relations between those who enjoy inclusion, but also to examine the characteristics of the excluded' (1989, p.277). 'The most important parties are bound together in relations of exchange and interdependence' (1989, p.287). Hancher and Moran found that regulation involves resource interdependent actors; that is, policy networks. The distribution and relevance of these resources determines which actors are most able to influence the policy/regulatory process and at which points in that process.

A similar conclusion was reached in the implementation studies literature (Ham and Hill, 1993, p.110). But the same criteria continue to apply for selecting an appropriate analytical framework: it must be applicable to the IPC case and have sufficient scope to analyse the whole policy process. The implementation studies literature fails in this last respect, relating as it does to only the final stages of the policy process. Nevertheless, study and theorising on implementation led to some important conclusions concerning the nature of the overall policy process and how best to study it. Implementation is important for IPC - where regulation involves considerable HMIP discretion to set standards within a legislative framework carrying vague statutory principles (BATNEEC and BPEO) - and implies this stage will have a significant impact upon policy output. Thus the implementation studies literature can inform analysis. So before leaping to a discussion of policy networks it is worth considering studies into implementation.

Implementation studies

The growth in implementation studies begun in the 1970s was not exclusive to issues of regulation - though studies into the implementation of regulations did follow (for example Hanf and Downing, 1983; Knoepfel and Weidner, 1982).

> A study of implementation is a study of change: how it occurs, possibly how it may be induced. It is also a study of the micro-structure of political life: how organisations outside and inside the political system conduct their affairs and interact with each other; what motivates them to act in the way that they do, and what might motivate them to act differently.
> (Jenkins, 1978, cited in Younis and Davidson, 1990, p.5)

Williams (1980) believed implementation studies had 'a healthy eclecticism' which 'has yielded a relatively rich knowledge base in a fairly brief time'. 'Also, the researchers have started with what they perceived as the right questions and moved toward them with the techniques that seem most appropriate, rather than reformulating questions to fit dominant methodology or theory' (1980). Implementation was the 'missing link' connecting policy formulation to evaluation of policy outcomes (Hargrove, 1975; and Younis and Davidson, 1990). Such a conceptualisation was consolidated by early theorists such as Pressman and Wildavsky (1973), who took a 'top-down' approach to implementation analysis. Like an 'If... Then...' computer algorithm, policy formulation is the 'If', setting initial conditions by passing legislation and securing funds. Implementation is the 'Then' of ensuing actions leading to outcomes (1973, p.xv).

In practice, finding a clear division in the policy-action dichotomy proves difficult (Barrett and Fudge, 1981). Lipsky (1980), in a study of various US federal agents (teachers; police officers; legal aid lawyers; and social workers), described how these 'street-level bureaucrats' had sufficient discretion to alter policy at the same time as implementing it. A 'bottom-up' critique of top-down models emerged.

The top-down approach to implementation studies

The top-down approach assumes policy is formulated at the 'top' by decision-makers, then this is translated into instructions for administrators at the 'bottom' who will act to achieve the top's policy objectives. This view would look for evidence of IPC standards, or the methodology for setting

22

them, being formulated and controlled by legislators or HMIP's central executive (at the top) for administration by field Inspectors (at the bottom).

Pressman and Wildavsky (1973) believed policy objectives set by formulators are realised through an implementation chain, and so the problematique for 'implementation ... is the ability to forge subsequent links in the causal chain so as to obtain the desired results (1973, p.xiv). In a similar vein, Van Meter and Van Horn (1975, p.445) see implementation as '[t]hose actions by public or private individuals (or groups) that are directed at the achievement of objectives set forth in prior policy decisions'.

Implementation becomes an exercise in administering rules. The specificity of rules and the provision of resources are central factors in the top-down approach (Mountjoy and O'Toole, 1979, p.466). Implementation is the management and co-ordination of resources (by the 'top') to ensure that these rules are put into action (at the 'bottom'). This does not always go to plan. Policy can fail because it is badly designed and/or because it is badly implemented.

A clear demarcation is assumed between policy formulation and its implementation. 'Implementers, having been given funds and authority, are responsible for achieving the objectives of the policy maker' (Younis, 1990, p.6). Thus much of the top-down literature is concerned with how bureaucracies are managed and how complex systems administered, using an organisational theory focus (Dunsire, 1978), and tending to prescribe 'good practice', as suggested by Hood: 'One way of analysing implementation problems is to begin by thinking about what 'perfect administration' would be like, comparable to the way in which economists employ the model of perfect competition. Perfect administration could be defined as a condition in which 'external' elements of resource availability and political acceptability combine with 'administration' to produce perfect policy implementation' (1976, p.6).

Ham and Hill (1993, p.101) summarise top-down prescriptions:

1   The nature of the policy - see that it is unambiguous.

2   The implementation structure - keep links in the chain to a minimum.

3   The prevention of outside interference.

4   Control over implementing actors.

So the top-down approach to implementation studies characterises policy as 'the property of policy-makers at the 'top'' (Ham and Hill, 1993, p.101). Implementation is a hierarchical process whereby the purposive management, co-ordination, and co-operation of actors ensures actions are taken to meet defined policy objectives. However, the top-down approach is not without its critics. Younis and Davidson (1990, p.12) argue that 'through its emphasis on lines of hierarchical control, [the top-down approach] suffers from the serious disadvantage of omitting the reality of policy modification or distortion at the hands of policy implementers'.

The top-down model of implementation does not sit easily with the conclusions of other studies into IPC. O'Riordan and Weale believe IPC 'is clearly not a process of rational reform, in which a clear set of operating procedures leads to a structural alteration that provides the necessary conditions for new policies and standards of performance' (1989, p.292). Jordan notes that IPC's introduction to the UK 'has been haphazard, incremental and protracted, and is still only partially completed' (1993, p. 405).

Bottom-up approaches to implementation studies

Though grouped together under the 'bottom-up' banner, the work discussed under this heading is diverse, reflecting a dissatisfaction with 'top down' prescriptions. The common thread weaving bottom-up approaches together is recognition that the 'bottom' influences policy output. Power relations and conflicting interests are no less important during policy implementation than formulation. This can also limit options available to policy makers at the top. Often, implementation of new policies is the responsibility of pre-existing agencies. The agency structure and skill resources might be insufficient for the job (Marsh and Rhodes, 1992a).

'Where policy stops and implementation starts depends on where you are standing and which way you are looking' (Barrett and Fudge, 1981, p.11). Barrett and Fudge's perspective is that policy objectives are often (and sometimes deliberately) ambiguous, that implementation requires consensus, control, and compliance between actors, and that this makes implementation a political rather than managerial issue (1981).

Writers in the top-down school also recognised negotiation as important in establishing the implementation 'chain'; but this is assumed to take place with the top exercising its authority over other actors to relinquish some of their objectives. Barrett and Fudge (1981) credit the 'bottom' with more equal standing, taking part in the effective formulation of policy through their role as implementers, 'the policy-action relationship needs to be considered in a political context and as an interactive and negotiative process taking place over time between those seeking to put policy into effect and those upon whom action depends'.

Even greater emphasis is put on the bottom by Lipsky (1980). Lipsky believes policy is effectively made by 'street-level bureaucracies' at the sharp end (1980, p.xi). These street-level bureaucrats possess some decision-making capacity - circumscription by policy formulators at the top is limited. The reason for this limitation is twofold:

1   The complexity of the task cannot be reduced to programmatic formulations.

2   The tasks are carried out in situations with a human dimension, calling for sensitive observation and judgement rather than detached, rational decision-making.

Thus Lipsky argues 'that the decisions of street-level bureaucrats, the routines they establish and the devices they invent to cope with uncertainties and work pressures, effectively become the public policies they carry out' (1980, p.xii). This is more than the structural hindrance of working conditions, since street-level bureaucrats will pursue or distort policies to make 'their organisational life more consistent with their own preferences and commitments' (Lipsky, 1980, p.xi). Lipsky believes the agency of those at the front line of implementation to be important.

Indeed, Elmore (1980) takes the implementation front line as a starting point for policy design. He suggests a 'backward mapping' approach, which involves '"backward reasoning" from the individual and organisational choices that are the hub of the problem to which policy is addressed, to the rules, procedures and structures that have the closest proximity to those choices, to the policy instruments available to affect those things, and hence to feasible policy objectives' (Elmore, 1980, p.109). The bottom-up approach becomes action centred, attempting 'to find a conceptualisation that reflects better the empirical evidence of the complexity and dynamics of the interactions between individuals and groups seeking to put policy into effect, those upon whom action depends and those whose interests are affected when change is proposed' (Barrett and Hill, 1980, p.19 quoted in Ham and Hill, 1993, p.109).

Recognising these interactions, some students began using interorganisational concepts to capture the complex realities of implementation (Hjern and Porter, 1981, p.220). The structure and nature of actor interactions during implementation became a key analytical concern (see also Hjern and Hull, 1982). It is only after understanding how these 'implementation structures' are developed, maintained and adapted that interventions can improve implementation (Thrasher, 1983). Implementation structures are maintained through resource exchange and power dependency relationships between actors (Hjern and Porter, 1981, p.220). In this respect they mirror conceptualisations in the policy networks literature (see Hanf and O'Toole, 1992).

Hanf (1982) developed the implementation structure approach for an analysis of the implementation of environmental regulations. A 'regulatory structure' evolves, consisting of actors bargaining with one another. The constellation of actors involved in the implementation structure is empirically determined. Consequently the regulatory output can only be discerned from studying the 'pattern of interdependencies' through which actors negotiate controls; and output 'cannot be assumed to follow directly from the policies articulated in the substantive regulations' (Hanf, 1982, p.163). This implementation structure is embedded in the influential macro-level socio-economic order. Taking this view suggests analysis of IPC should focus upon the interactions of implementing policy actors more than examining the legislation or official guidelines. These are all themes prevalent in the policy networks literature, the difference being one of analytical focus. Policy networks are broader in scope, with the potential to reach along the whole policy process, and are consequently more appropriate to this IPC study.

So the significance of the bottom-up implementation literature is that it brings to our attention the possibility that policy making is not necessarily exclusive to the 'top' formulating decision makers. However, some students had to be reminded that the 'top' still had some significance and that complete rejection of the authority of (accountable) policy formulators might be unwise. Marsh and Rhodes (1992a, p.6) caution overestimation of street-level discretion - legal, financial and organisational constraints exist. Thus it remains important to explain the origins of the bargaining game by which many bottom-up theorists characterise the implementation process. HMIP may have considerable discretion over IPC implementation, but it still has to operate within a regulatory framework codified by the legislation. Moreover, the switch from single-medium controls to 'integrated' controls, as well as the creation of HMIP itself, form an important element of the research task. The pattern and nature of interdependencies throughout the policy process in all its complexity has to be understood (Younis and Davidson, 1990, p.12).

A return to the policy process

By delving into the later stages of the policy process many new insights were made. Policy formulation and policy implementation are not as distinct as once thought, but more a complex, inter-related continuum. Sabatier (1986, p.23-24) suggests reasons why an implementation deficit[4] could appear between initial policy aspirations and actual policy output, not all of them attributable to policy implementation:

1   Ambiguous or inconsistent objectives.

2   Weak causal theory.

3   Inadequate resources or inappropriate policy instruments for implementation.

4   Discretion of street-level bureaucrats.

5   Lack of support from relevant interest groups and public bodies.

6   Shifting socio-economic contexts which can erode political support or break down the causal theory.

Implementation deficit reflects the realities of the policy process in action.

[That] reality ... is not of imperfect control but of action as a continuous process of interaction with a changing and changeable policy, a complex interaction structure, an outside world which must interfere with implementation because government action is, and is designed to, impinge upon it, and implementing actors who are inherently difficult to control. Analysis is best focused upon the levels at which this is occurring, since it is not so much creating implementation deficiency as recreating policy.
(Ham and Hill, 1993, p.110)

Earlier studies into IPC implementation suggest a deficit has arisen between the regulator's initial objectives and the actual outcome (Allott, 1993; Lyons, 1992). This deficit has been measured at the site-level and confirms forecasts made by earlier analysts who focused upon the (lack of) resources provided for IPC implementation by the 'top' (particularly for the operationalisation of BPEO) (O'Riordan, 1989, p.120; Owens, 1989, p.194).

Contrary to top-down prescriptions, Ham and Hill (1993, pp.107-108) provide a number of reasons why policy formulation may be ambiguous deliberately and its concretisation left until implementation:

1   Because conflicts cannot be resolved during the policy-making stage.

2   Because it is regarded as necessary to let key decisions be made when all the facts are available to implementers.

3   Because it is believed that implementers (professionals, for example) are better equipped to make the key decisions than anyone else.

4   Because little is known in advance of the actual impact of the measures.

27

5   Because it is recognised that day-to-day decisions will have to involve negotiation and compromise with powerful groups.

6   Because it is considered politically inexpedient to try to resolve the conflicts.

All of these are relevant to the IPC policy process. Hargrove (1983) believed unresolved disputes about the degree of regulation are handed down to the bureaucracy by the legislature - such as the stringency of emission standards operationalising BATNEEC. In the face of opposition from those it regulates, the regulatory body may then either dilute the intentions of the law or seek to mobilise (diffuse) support for tough regulations. If the bureaucrats and the regulated cannot resolve disputes, then the Courts can become drawn into the implementation process. Any such legal adjudication can subsequently 'define the contours of the agency's regulatory discretion' over future decisions (Schuck, 1981, p.722). Thus in various ways the implementation process becomes a continuation of the formulation process, involving negotiation and bargaining between multiple, resource interdependent actors.

Acting in the opposite direction, research by Knoepfel and Weidner (1982) into different pollution control strategies found evidence of implementing actors' increasing interest in policy formulation as a means of achieving implementation regimes and outputs favourable to them. 'The factual interdependence of both processes makes it necessary for empirical studies to form a complete picture of actors and interests for the total policy area. It is therefore necessary that behaviour of 'related' actors be analysed throughout the entire policy process ... Whoever wishes to have more than a peripheral influence upon the implementation process, can seldom avoid extending his activities to the phase of programme formulation' (1982, p.90).

Owens argues such pre-emptive involvement in policy formulation was one element in the creation of HMIP. British industry began lobbying for pollution control reform in the mid-1980s. This was a defensive measure against the imposition of 'irrational' standards from the European Community. Industry wished to maintain the British tradition of accessible (to it's interests) standard setting procedures which ensured their participation (Owens, 1989, p.187).

Hanf and O'Toole, both with a history of studying implementation, are right in expressing the need for 'the linking of research on policy formulation with policy implementation' (1992, p.164). Given the conception of the regulatory process presented in this book, as one type of policy process journeying from the appearance of an issue on the public agenda through to implementation and enforcement, it seems that it would indeed be more fruitful to see this process as a complex continuum. The previous sections' excursion into implementation studies has confirmed this.

Terminology such as 'process' can suggest a linear model but this perception should be avoided. It is important to bear in mind that public policy is not so much a chain of events as an historical process of decisions which can feedback between 'levels' of decision making. The 'formulation' of the (statutory) IPC regulatory framework has undergone several amending re-formulations in the light of 'implementation' experience.[5] In this book terms such as policy 'formulation' and 'implementation' will inevitably be used to denote the formal roles of actors in the regulatory process, but without making *a priori* assumptions concerning their relative influence on the policy process. As Ham and Hill put it, '[t]here is something of a seamless web here, though it may be ... that it is possible to identify some decisions which are more fundamental for determining the major issues than others' (1993, p.107). Policy networks are a suitable conceptual device for such an analysis and, following a study of the literature, can help provide hypotheses in answer to the research questions framing this book: why did IPC come about; and how has it been implemented?

Policy networks

Studies into implementation have confirmed the many political scientists who deny 'the descriptive accuracy of classical or Downsian models of democratic theory that emphasise unitary policy making by parliamentary majorities legitimated through general elections, and hierarchical implementation under the control of politically accountable ministers or chief executives' (Scharpf, 1991, pp.7-8). Policy output emerges from the complex interactions of actors in the policy process.

The policy networks literature recognises these complexities (Hanf and O'Toole, 1992, p.165; Bressers, O'Toole and Richardson, 1995, p.5; Hanf, 1978, p.12; Kassim, 1994, p.19; Kenis and Schneider, 1991, pp.34-36; Mills and Saward, 1994, p.79) - though it is attempting nothing new in explaining these interactions. 'Looking at theories of political processes, the main distinguishing feature concerns the pattern of actor involvement' (Richardson, Maloney and Rudig, 1992, p.158).

Other models of policy making exist, such as pluralism[6] and corporatism[7]; but policy networks move beyond these approaches by recognising that different patterns of interaction exist in different policy sectors or in the same policy sector over time (Marsh and Rhodes, 1992b, pp.2-4). Previous models have tended to be exclusive, trying to find one or other dominant policy making style: corporatist, pluralist and so on.[8] Policy networks are able to accommodate different patterns of policy making, but these are not assumed at the outset. Rather, policy networks provide an analytical tool for interpreting and explaining interactions which are discovered empirically (Wilks and Wright, 1991, p.326).

Over the following pages the policy networks approach is elaborated and discussed. The term policy network has arisen throughout this chapter, usually accompanied by allusions to resource interdependent policy actors. The next sub-section pauses to reflect what is actually meant by the term policy network. Discussion then turns to the levels of analysis to which the policy networks concept is applicable (that is, policy areas, sectors, sub-sectors, or even single policy issues). The discussion argues policy networks can help in analyses at more than one policy level, and that this flexibility lends the concept to this study of the IPC policy process. Having established this, the discussion turns to the mechanics of policy networks. Central to this is the power dependency theory of resource interdependence which binds policy network members together. Policy network members evolve rules of the game and have shared appreciative systems which regulate conduct toward one another and determines the inclusion or exclusion of other policy actors. The final two sub-sections respectively discuss the different types of policy network that can exist and the dynamics under which policy networks change. Thus the objective of this section is to provide a working knowledge of the policy networks concept which will allow hypotheses to be generated for the IPC policy process in the final section of this chapter.

What is a policy network?

Policy networks arise around policy issues or in policy sectors/sub-sectors. It is the scale, nature and pattern of interactions which define a policy network and which distinguishes different types of network. Rhodes (1988, p.77) adapts a definition by Benson (1980) for policy networks. A policy network is 'a complex of organisations connected to each other by resource dependencies and distinguished from other complexes by breaks in the structure of resource dependencies' (Benson, 1980, p.148). Benson was redirecting interorganisational theory toward a study of policy sectors when he coined this definition.

Interorganisational theory focuses upon the controlling structures between organisations whose divided labour needs co-ordinating in order to meet an objective. The theory assumes a determinant relationship between the interorganisational structure and its likely success in meeting the objective. Thus the problematic of interorganisational theory is to discover the relations between structure and outcome under specified conditions (Benson, 1980, p.142). Elements of the policy networks literature are concerned with links between policy networks and policy outcome (Marsh and Rhodes, 1992b;

Mills and Saward, 1994; Bressers, O'Toole and Richardson, 1995). The literature suggests policy networks have an influence on outcomes, being 'political structures which both constrain and facilitate policy actors and policy outcomes' (Rhodes and Marsh, 1994, p.9).

A different approach to defining the policy networks concept is taken by Kenis and Schneider (1991). They define them by elaborating upon their function rather than their constitution.

Policy networks are new forms of government which reflect a changed relationship between state and society. Their emergence is a result of the dominance of organised actors in policy making, the fragmentation of the state, the blurring of boundaries between the public and the private, etc. Policy networks typically deal with policy problems which involve complex political, economic and technical task and resource interdependencies, and therefore presuppose a significant amount of expertise and other specialised and dispersed resources.
(Kenis and Schneider, 1991, p.41)

Analysts such as Kenis and Schneider (1991), Scharpf (1991), and Hanf (1978) conceive policy networks as special types of government-interest group arrangement. For them, European academics with a background in interorganisational studies, policy networks are more concrete policy devices than the abstract conceptualisation suggested in the British literature. They tend to invoke policy networks as the emerging predominance of informal, decentralised and horizontal relations between organisations in the policy process, replacing the older regime of formal, hierarchical and vertical relations[9] (see, for example, Hanf and O'Toole, 1992). These networks are seen as purposive, managerial arrangements, carrying a similar prescriptiveness to Elmore's (1980) bottom-up approach to policy implementation. This is in contrast to other (British) uses of policy networks, which tend to be more abstract in the sense that they are a conceptual device for modelling different patterns of resource interdependence between actors in (or excluded from) the policy process.

The same observation has been made by Mol (1995, p.63), who drew a distinction between 'steering-prescriptive' models and 'analytical-descriptive' models (see also Bressers and Richardson, 1994, p.215). It is this latter policy network perspective which is taken here. IPC is the negotiated outcome of resource interdependent policy actors, and therefore the policy process can be analysed using a policy networks perspective.

31

When talking about level of analysis it is important to distinguish between conceptual levels and empirical levels of analysis. On the conceptual level, Rhodes (1986, p.16) defined policy networks as a meso-level concept since they are concerned with the network structure of resource interdependent policy actors (see also Mol, 1995, p.67). This is in contrast to micro-level concepts concerned with individual policy actors and their resources; and in contrast to macro-level concepts, which are concerned with questions concerning the distribution of power within society (Marsh and Rhodes, 1992b, p.1). These levels are not mutually exclusive. They are simply different levels of abstraction which can all benefit explanation.

The other issue concerning level of analysis is to which empirical level of analysis is the policy network concept relevant? Are policy networks suited to characterising national styles of policy making, as Richardson and Jordan (1979) suggest? Or is it best suited to policy sectors (Rhodes, 1988), or sub-sectors (Benson, 1980)? Before answering this it is necessary to be clear what is meant by the various policy levels, and to do this Wilks and Wright's model is adopted (who consider policy networks to be a concept appropriate to the policy sub-sector and below) - see Table 2.1 below.

Table 2.1
The different policy levels surrounding industrial pollution control

Policy level	Aspect relevant to IPC
Policy area	Environment
Policy sector	Industrial pollution
Policy sub-sector	Integrated Pollution Control
Policy issue	e.g. BATNEEC standards for new plant

Source: adapted from Wilks and Wright (1987)

The suggestions in the paragraph above confuse conceptual levels (i.e. micro-, meso-, and macro-) with empirical levels of study. An analysis of the outcome of a particular policy issue (a low empirical level) could, for instance, draw upon macro-level concepts such as a Marxist emphasis on the tension between social legitimation and capital accumulation (a high conceptual level). It is nevertheless more likely that explaining the outcome of a policy issue will draw upon micro-level concepts in the form of interests and their resources. Policy networks, could be invoked since this meso-level concept both constrains and facilitates the influence of those interests within network 'rules of the game'.

So policy networks can occur at more or less every policy level (Smith, 1993, p.65; Marsh and Rhodes, 1992b, p.254): from the European level (Peterson, 1994), down to technical policy issues (Cunningham, 1992). This book uses this advantage of the policy network concept to understand the IPC policy process as it shifts between policy levels. IPC emerged from the late 1980s, a period of heightened political interest in the environmental policy area generally (McCormick, 1991). Moreover, it had to conform with the requirements of EC Directives concerning industrial pollution (O'Riordan, 1989, p.117), making apparent just how analysis must shift between policy levels (Table 2.1).

Much of the policy networks literature agrees that when individuals act they do so in the role of organisation representative (Van Waarden, 1992, p.33). Kaufman (1986, p.16) points out that individuals act in three frames of reference. The first frame is that of the individual as a person, the second is as the organisational representative, and the third frame of reference is that of the interaction in which the individual is participating. Hanf and O' Toole cite Kaufman to suggest that networks therefore have an emergent quality, individuals 'do not, in the first instance, act as individuals but rather as members of an organisational unit ... the interaction will have a history that is in part defined in terms of the relationships among the organisations involved' (1992, p.176).

It is Kaufman's second and third frames which are prevalent in the networks literature. Individuals enjoy access to a network because of their organisational role, '[p]rivate citizens rarely have a significant legitimate role in the formulation and implementation of regulatory policy' (Hancher and Moran, 1989, p.286). Bressers, O' Toole and Richardson suggest that 'the behaviour of the individuals within networks is likely to be shaped heavily by the institutional arrangements that drive the perspective of the actors and the composition of the network' (1994, p.6). This book follows the 'network convention' by treating policy actors in terms of their organisation and their relationship with the policy network.

Power dependency theory and policy networks

A policy network is constituted from the pattern of resource interdependencies between policy actors. Resource interdependence means organisations have to bargain with one another if they are to secure policy outcomes.

Issues of public policy which are perceived by the key players to affect their interests provoke relationships. In seeking to influence the outcomes to

33

those issues, key players interact ... The relationships are relationships of mutual but asymmetric dependence. Each player's room for 'decisional manoeuvre' on an issue is constrained by the material and intellectual resources available to him, appropriate to that issue and which he is prepared to use, and by those possessed by other players, who may perceive their own interests differently.
(Wilks and Wright, 1987, pp.4-5)

The unit of analysis is the resulting policy network itself. 'These organisations are embedded in a particular set of relationships, the structure of which constrains the options open to them as well as the kinds of behaviour they can engage in ... the pattern of linkages and interactions as a whole should be taken as the unit of analysis' (Hanf and O' Toole, 1992, p.169). Studies have used policy networks for comparative studies in policy making (between countries and between policy sectors) and for longitudinal studies (of a policy process or changes to a policy sector) (Marin and Mayntz, 1991, p.13).

A policy network analysis of the IPC policy process must relate events and outputs along that process to the network of resource interdependencies between policy actors. Policy actors' possession of different resources of varying relevance to the process at different times will shape the policy network and affect the policy process.[10]

Either implicitly (for example, Bressers, O' Toole and Richardson, 1995) or explicitly (for example, Rhodes, 1986; Wilks and Wright, 1987), policy network students use power dependence theory as the basis for underpinning actor interactions. Some students have used exchange theory to examine interactions between policy actors (e.g. Read, 1989); but Bressers, O' Toole and Richardson (1995, p.4) suggest there are theoretical differences between power dependence theory and exchange theory, though they do not elaborate these differences.

Put in a dichotomous fashion, the difference is between: theorists who see 'exchange' as a source of voluntary interaction, with both organisations realising their goals co-operatively in a positive-sum game; and advocates of 'dependency', who say exchange ignores relations involving coercion, domination and conflict in zero-sum games (Aldrich, 1979, p.267). '[Exchange] relations are formed when members of two or more organisations perceive mutual benefits from interacting ... [power dependency] relationships are formed when the motivated party is powerful enough to force or induce the other to interact' (Hjern and Porter, 1981, p.220).

Baldwin (1978) points out the dichotomy is really a conceptual difference and that real world interactive relationships often involve an element of both. He shows how many conflictual, 'power dependency' relations can in fact involve some co-operative 'exchange' (even warfare). Kenis and Schneider

34

(1991) argue that co-operation is needed particularly in situations where the necessary resource is information, especially 'tacit knowledge'. 'Nobody can be forced to provide intangible information. Implementation processes which depend on the mobilisation of such resources cannot be governed by hierarchical command-and-control relations' (1991, p.43). This has relevance to IPC.

Owens noted that implementing IPC would require 'familiarity with industrial processes, identification of all sources of waste, understanding of pollution pathways (including transfer of pollutants from one medium to another), and analysis of dose-effect relationships in the environment. Information at some or all of these stages is bound to be inadequate' (1989, p.194). Lacking this information, HMIP is open to challenge over the accuracy of its regulatory decisions. Consequently, 'pollution control standards will reflect, at least to some extent, political judgements and industrial lobbying pressures, as well as technical feasibility and costs' (Lyons, 1992, p.15). So HMIP's authority appears to some extent to be dependent upon the information provided by industry. Jordan (1993, p.421) suggested that the 'self-policing' this implied could only be relied upon in relationships of 'trusting co-operation and mutual respect'.

Pure conflict and pure co-operation are rare polar extremes for relationships often involving elements of both at various levels of conceptualisation (Baldwin, 1978, p.1232). Exchange and power dependency can occur in the same network (Hjern and Porter, 1981, p.220); though others see the kind of relationship (positive-sum or zero-sum) as a characteristic distinguishing different networks (Smith, 1993, p.63; Mol, 1995, p.69). This book follows Baldwin's general conclusion that exchange relationships can be considered a sub-set of power dependency relations, distinguished by the use of positive sanctions or lacking zero-sum characteristics.

A central policy network proposition is that a government, wishing to achieve a policy objective with a minimum of conflict, needs the assistance and co-operation of other groups (Mol, 1995, pp.65-66; Smith, 1993, p.59). 'Government can exchange access to the policy process for co-operation and thus establish a policy network' (Smith, 1993, p.59). Rhodes (1981, pp.98-99; 1986, p.16; 1988, p.42) writes that this 'power dependence framework' contains five propositions:

1   Any organisation is dependent upon other organisations for resources.

2   In order to achieve their goals, the organisations have to exchange resources.

3   Although decision-making within the organisation is constrained by other organisations, the dominant coalition retains some discretion. The appreciative system of the dominant coalition influences which relationships are seen as a problem and which resources will be sought.

4   The dominant coalition employs strategies within known rules of the game to regulate the process of exchange.

5   Variations in the degree of discretion are a product of the goals and the relative power potential of the interacting organisations. This relative power potential is a product of the resources of each organisation, of the rules of the game and of the process of exchange between organisations.

Some policy actors may have an array of resource attributes such that they form the 'dominant coalition' or policy network. 'The perceptions of the dominant coalition will influence the choice of goals, the definition of the problem and the identification of needed resources' (Rhodes, 1986, p.18). The policy network exerts a dominant appreciative system, understood by Rhodes (1986, p.18, after Vickers, 1965) as 'that combination of factual and value judgements which describe the state of the world or reality'. Thus groups which raise problems or propose solutions at odds with the appreciative system are excluded from the policy network (Smith, 1993, p.62).

Under IPC's preceding air regime, the Inspectorate and industry considered air pollution control a purely technical matter over which they would use their discretion to resolve problems collaboratively and confidentially, free from the interference of others (O'Riordan and Weale, 1989; Vogel, 1986). This appreciative system meant that local community groups were excluded from the policy network, unable to discover the control standards imposed on local processes (Frankel, 1974). In the 1980s, EC prescriptions for pollution control were seen as a challenge to this appreciative system (Owens, 1989, p.187).

A policy network's rules of the game guides members' behaviour toward one another and influences the way they deploy resources (Mol, 1995, p.71). Van Waarden saw the rules of the game reflecting and influencing actors' perceptions, attitudes, interests, social and knowledge/professional background (1992, p.36). That is the rules of the game and appreciative system are related. Table 2.2 draws on some of the contrasting cases used by Van Waarden to illustrate appreciative systems and rules of the game.

The rules of the game are seen as limiting the process of negotiation between network members, in addition to guiding their behaviour to one another (Wilks and Wright, 1987, p.305). Identifiable rules of the game include: mutuality (that is, an expectation of mutual benefits from participation); being consulted

36

on issues; maintaining confidentiality within the network; the use of legal remedy as a last resort; and so on (see Wilks and Wright, 1987; Mol, 1995, p.71).

Table 2.2
Some opposing rules of the game

Network relations understood as adversarial, expectation of opportunism by others. Negotiation between mutually recognised conflicting interests.	Search for consensus, accommodation and appeasement.
Acceptance of following narrow particularistic self-interest.	Shared sense of public interest and general welfare.
Politicisation.	Mutual understanding to de-politicise issues.
Secrecy.	Openness.
Ideological disputes.	Rationalist pragmatism.

Source: Van Waarden (1992)

Studies into IPC suggest HMIP initially attempted to alter the rules of the game by which pollution would be controlled. Jordan found 'senior HMIP staff have announced that the agency intends to re-define its operational relationship with industry: in the future, it was suggested, the relationship will be less cosy, more structured and conducted more at "arms' length"' (1993, p.415). O'Riordan and Weale (1989, p.278) agreed that the confidential and collaborative approach of the air regime was shifting toward more transparent and accountable structured relations under IPC. O'Riordan and Weale saw the British tradition having to adapt to EC formalism, the 'Europeanization of British regulatory practice' (1989, p.293). However, other studies find evidence that this unilateral attempt by HMIP to alter the rules of the game has failed (Allott, 1994, p.ix), and that a 're-born spirit of co-operation is now emerging' with industry (Jordan, 1993, p.424). Analysis will have to consider what appear to be shifting rules of the game.

Various strategies are open to policy actors concerning the types of relationship they seek with others. For instance, a policy actor could seek insulation from other actors' influence in an area. Alternatively, policy actors might adopt a strategy whereby they seek to penetrate a policy area. Other strategies include mutual adaptation between policy actors in an area, or their

37

agreed co-operation on an issue (Grant, Paterson and Whitston, 1988; Mol, 1995, p.71).

Rhodes (1986, p.17) identified five resources central to the interaction that takes place between network members. These resources are:

1   Authority: The mandatory and discretionary right to carry out certain duties and functions.

2   Money: The financial resources to fund objectives.

3   Political legitimacy: Access to public decision making structures, and the right to build public support.

4   Information: The possession of data, and control over its collection or dissemination.

5   Organisation: Possession of 'people, skills, land, buildings, material and equipment and hence the ability to act directly rather than through intermediaries'.

Mol (1995, p.71) agrees that legal (1), economic (2) and information (4) resources warrant analytical attention. Actors with an interest in the policy process 'manoeuvre for advantage, deploying the resources they control to maximise their influence over outcomes, and trying to avoid (where they can) becoming dependent on the other 'player' ' (Rhodes, 1986, p.18). The nature of the bargaining, for example if it is routine compared with sporadic, positive-sum or zero-sum, is a distinguishing characteristic of the policy network.

However, there can be persistent asymmetries in the relationships, bargaining is not between equals and exchange of resources need not be voluntary (cf. Aldrich, 1979, p.267). For instance, Weale points out that one 'problem with all environmental regulation is that the knowledge of the public authorities lags behind technological innovation. Those responsible for potentially polluting substances are characteristically in a better position to appreciate what new controls can be applied than are the public authorities' (1992, p.177). These 'asymmetries of information' are 'a pervasive feature of the regulatory process' (Weale, 1992, p.178). Such asymmetries may have enabled industry to challenge HMIP's authority when it attempted to shift the rules of the game.

In summary, at the heart of the policy networks concept is the notion that resource interdependent policy actors deploy, withhold and exchange resources in order to influence decisions during the policy process. Policy network analysis examines the relations between policy actors, uncovers the dominant appreciative system, seeks the rules of the game and strategies employed, and considers the resource interdependencies which structure the interaction (or exclusion) arising in a policy process or sector.

Each policy actor has objectives, with resource attributes and needs for those ends. The ability for policy actors to influence decisions through resource manipulation implies resources are a source of power.[11] Thus policy networks enable a distinction to be drawn between formal power (e.g. that of HMIP for the statutory control of pollution) and effective power (i.e. who most influences the degree of pollution control).

Power derives not just from the resources an actor possesses but also from the way they are deployed (Smith, 1993, p.59). It is important to bear in mind the different types of resource interdependency that can exist. Scharpf (1978) defines three classes of resource relationship in decreasing order of power potential: unilateral dependence; mutual dependence; and mutual independence.[12] HMIP and operators appear to be in a position of mutual dependency, with the former needing information (in order to establish BATNEEC standards, for instance) and the latter an IPC authorisation (in order to continue operating their process). But setting standards in authorisations cannot take place until HMIP has sufficient information from operators - something which appears not to have happened with initial operator IPC applications (Allott, 1994). So this mutual dependency has a sequence to it which suggests industry could have some power over the policy process.

Organisations can endeavour to modify the nature of the resource relationship in order to increase their power potential, either as a means to exert influence or to increase autonomy.[13] This can be done either by increasing other actors' dependence upon your resources, or by seeking alternative sources for a resource upon which you are dependent (Scharpf, 1978, p.359). 'The general picture conveyed is one of decision makers attempting to manage their environments as well as their organisations' (Aldrich, 1979, p.267).

A limitation is the opportunity cost involved in modifying one's resources in order to make an influence attempt or to reduce susceptibility to others' influence attempts. HMIP needed a considerable information base for it to implement IPC (Owens, 1989, p.194), but was suffering from insufficient organisational resources (for example, manpower) to meet this task (O'Riordan, 1989, p.119). Thus speculation can be raised concerning the inhibitive opportunity cost for HMIP to gather regulatory information independently and how its dependency upon industry in this respect strengthened the latter's influence.

Read (1989, p.86) points out that behaviour can be based on perceived as much as real resource interdependencies. Hanf and O' Toole (1992, p.173) agree, suggesting actors react on their perceptions of the actions, motives and so on of other actors. British industrial leaders, for instance, perceived EC environmental controls as 'irrational', prompting their support for a DoE based regulator (HMIP) able to argue the British case in Europe (Owens, 1989, p.187).

Read also points out that 'resources are not mutually exclusive; to conceptualise power dependence in this manner recognises that groups and government depend on each other, although the degree and direction of dependence differs according to the circumstances' (1989, p.32). This raises the issue of 'scope' of resource attributes and dependencies. 'Since people perform different activities, it is quite possible - and highly probable - that A's power over B will be limited to certain dimension's of B's behaviour' (Baldwin, 1978, p.1235). A policy actor may have the scope to be a power holder in certain circumstances, but a power subject under different circumstances: 'mutual but asymmetric dependence'.

Policy network dimensions and characteristics

Policy networks can vary in a number of respects. Different policy networks can be characterised along 'dimensions' which reflect their properties. Many dimensions and typologies have been suggested in the literature. For example, Van Waarden (1992) suggested networks can vary along seven dimensions, containing a total of thirty seven sub-categories, which define a network as one of eleven types! With such variety it is important to have criteria for assessing the analytical suitability of different types of proposed dimension.

Policy networks must be characterised with at least one dimension which holds explanatory promise (Bressers and O' Toole, 1994, p.203). Therefore the first criterion for selecting dimensions is that at least one of them should, potentially, indicate affects upon the policy process. A second criterion for selecting network dimensions is that they should be amenable to empirical research, something Van Waarden was criticised for failing (Jordan and Schubert, 1992, p.17). The final selection criterion avoids dimensions whose variable is in fact a policy actor variable and not a property of the policy network itself. Dowding (1995) emphasises this distinction, but even he acknowledges that it 'should not be overdrawn. The power of members is dependent upon the powers of other members given the relationship between them. Similarly the type of relationship members have will be dependent upon their resources' (1995, p.153). Dowding uses the distinction critically, to simply remind us that explanations utilising policy networks should do just that. These criteria allow a more systematic selection of dimensions from the multitude in the literature.[14]

Some common network dimensions meeting the criterion are: *membership* (its extent, and interests/functions); *resource distribution* (combination and employment of resources amongst actors); and *integration* (the rules of the game, appreciative system, degree of consensus, and intensity of relations[15]).

The degree of network integration is the most ubiquitous dimension in the literature (Bressers and O'Toole, 1994, p.203). 'The structures of policy networks can then be compared according to the level of integration. On a simple 'high-low' scale, those which are highly integrated are characterised by the stability of the relationships of their members, the continuity of a highly restrictive membership, the interdependence within the network, based on the members' shared responsibility for the delivery of a service, and the insulation from other networks. Those networks which are weakly integrated tend to have a much larger number of members with a limited degree of organisational interdependence; they are loose, atomistic, and often inchoate structures' (Wilks and Wright, 1987, pp.301-2). Marsh and Rhodes (1992b) labelled these high- and low-integration networks 'policy communities' and 'issue networks'.[16] Their characterisation of these two polar types[17] is elaborated in Table 2.3.

Policy community membership is often small and exclusive, exhibiting a high degree of continuity and consensus over the network's appreciative system and rules of the game. Conversely, issue network memberships can be large and shifting. 'Any direct material interest is often secondary to intellectual or emotional commitment ... The price of buying into one or another [issue] network is watching, reading, talking about, and trying to act on particular policy problems' (Heclo, 1978, p.102). The saliency of the issue network is related to that of the issue: each can raise the profile of the other.

Being highly integrated and consensual, policy communities tend to de-politicise issues and exclude groups with challenging views (Smith, 1993, p.63). Conflicting views are more likely in issue networks. Smith argues that where government departments are in conflict over responsibility for an issue then an issue network can arise (1993, p.63). Each department will draw groups into an evolving network for support, with the issue becoming politicised.

In policy communities the resource interdependency tends to be based upon exchange. Consequently interaction involves negotiation and bargaining over policy direction in positive-sum games. Resource distribution within issue networks is less equal and so interaction is at best consultative, between the powerful and lobbyists in zero-sum games (Mol, 1995, p.69; Smith, 1993, p.64). Overt criticism and demonstration is absent from policy communities (Smith, 1993, p.61), yet can be useful measures for issue network members to take.

Table 2.3
**Types of policy network: the characteristics of policy communities and
issue networks**

Dimension	Policy Community	Issue Network
1. Membership		
(a) Number of participants	Very limited number, some groups consciously excluded.	Large.
(b) Type of interest	Economic or professional interests dominate.	Encompasses range of affected interests.
2. Integration		
(a) Frequency of interaction.	Frequent, high quality, interaction of all groups on all matters related to policy issue.	Contacts fluctuate in frequency and intensity.
(b) Continuity	Membership, values and outcomes persistent over time.	Access fluctuates significantly.
(c) Consensus	All participants share basic values and accept the legitimacy of the outcome.	A measure of agreement exists but conflict is ever present.
3. Resources		
(a) Distribution of resources (within network).	All participants have resources, basic relationship is an exchange relationship.	Some participants may have resources, but they are limited and basic relationship is consultative.
(b) Distribution of resources (within participating organisations).	Hierarchical, leaders can deliver members.	Varied and variable distribution and capacity to regulate members.
4. Power	There is a balance of power between members. Although one group may dominate, it must be a positive sum game if community is to persist.	Unequal powers, reflects unequal resources and unequal access. It is a zero sum game.

Source: Marsh and Rhodes (1992b)

Conceptually, policy community and issue network are ideal types on a continuum of possible networks: 'It is important to stress the diagnostic role of this typology. Inevitably, no policy area will conform exactly to either list of characteristics; hence the need to retain the term 'policy networks' as a generic description. It is equally important to focus on trends in a given area: to explore the extent to which it is becoming more or less integrated or an interest more or less dominant' (Rhodes and Marsh, 1992, p.187). The three network dimensions - membership, resource distribution, and integration - facilitate observation of changes to the network over time and examination of any related changes to the policy process (Bressers, O'Toole and Richardson, 1994, p.13).

Indeed, some studies have characterised networks as a 'core' of tightly knit, exclusive and consensual actors surrounded by a 'periphery' of actors whose relationship to one another is more akin to an issue network (Read, 1992; Bressers, Huitema, and Kuks, 1994; Rudig and Kraemer, 1994; Heilman, Johnson, Morris and O'Toole, 1994; Maloney and Richardson, 1994; Bressers and O' Toole, 1994, p.199; Mills, 1992; Smith, 1993). So there can be degrees of exclusion from a policy network.

The dynamic of policy networks

Distinction must be drawn between two types of policy change, something not always done in the policy networks literature. Policy change consists of changes to policy output (including procedures) and/or changes to the policy network. How the two types of change relate is important for this book, since analysis wishes to explain the IPC policy process by focusing upon the dynamic of policy networks.

The fact that industrial air pollution policy output was so secretive led to the emergence of a vocal issue network in the early 1970s, critical about lack of public access to pollution standards (see Ashby and Anderson, 1981, pp.136-140). So policy output appears to influence policy networks by provoking non-members to take an interest in the network. Equally though, the policy network influences the policy output. The reason for so much air pollution secrecy was the long tradition of trustful co-operation and collaboration (Vogel, 1986) of a policy community of operators and air Inspectors. So the influence is two way, though the particular direction or dominant current remains an empirical question. The policy networks literature maintains networks influence outputs, without establishing any clear patterns (Bressers and Richardson, 1994, p.213) beyond their conservative affect (Rhodes and Marsh, 1992, p.193).

The policy networks literature, particularly for policy communities, emphasises the stability, continuity and conservative affect they have on policy (Smith, 1993, p.97). 'The existence of a policy network, or more particularly a policy community, constrains the policy agenda and shapes the policy outcomes ... Of course, there has been policy change, both in the shape of the policy networks and in the policy outcomes, but the existence of a policy network or policy community acts as a major constraint upon the degree of policy change' (Rhodes and Marsh, 1992, pp.197-8). But policy change does occur (the switch from air controls to IPC, for example) and needs explaining.

There are two sources of change to policy networks: endogenous; and exogenous. Both can have a concomitant impact on policy output. Endogenous sources of change arise within the policy network itself - amongst its membership. Policy actors take steps to modify the array of resource attributes which they can marshal. Consequently the pattern and intensity of resource interdependencies (and the policy network) will shift. Indeed, the membership of the policy network can alter following resource building or the obsolescence of a resource to a policy issue or (sub-)sector (Read, 1992).

Endogenously driven radical change is rare owing to the routinised relationships which constitute policy networks (especially policy communities). Promoting continuity and stability, 'they foster incremental outcomes, thereby favouring the status quo or the existing balance of interests in the network' (Rhodes and Marsh, 1992, p.193). Policy output is unlikely to change considerably if it is the domain of a policy community. Issue networks are more likely to generate substantial shifts owing to the lack of any strong consensus, fluctuating interaction and the fluidity and diversity of membership (see Bressers and O'Toole, 1994, pp.211-212). Often issue networks ring a policy community core, so even influence from the issue network is mediated by the policy community.

This conservatism would suggest that the creation of HMIP and formulation of IPC was the product of something more akin to issue network arrangements than the decision of a policy community. The long history and tradition the literature attributes to the preceding air pollution regime (Vogel, 1986; Ashby and Anderson, 1981; Hill, 1982; Weait, 1989; Hutter, 1986) suggest it fitted the policy community model (chapter 3). The policy network literature suggests the switch to IPC did not arise from within this policy community but by some sort of disruptive issue network.

Policy communities can respond to and even anticipate peripheral changes (Read, 1992; Saward, 1992); 'contextual and sometimes anticipatory effects of the broader network structure can be seen in the strategies and actions of those in the core' (Bressers and O'Toole, 1994, p.200). The late 1980s saw growth in public awareness and concern for environmental issues. This context affected many policy communities within the British environmental policy area.

Apparently endogenous sources of change can be pre-emptive reactions to changes in the policy network periphery. For example, the Chemical Industries Association established its Responsible Care programme following the prominence of environmental concern on the public agenda and the industry's poor image in the late 1980s (Liardet, 1991). The programme aimed to

44

convince the public that the chemical sector was environmentally responsible (a legitimacy resource) and included the 'aim of limiting state intervention to a level that is acceptable to the industry' (Simmons and Wynne, 1993, p.205).

External demands can force networks to become more communicative and to consult 'external' actors, 'actors that to some degree become thereby part of the network' (Bressers and O' Toole, 1994, p.205). Limited accommodation of some actors into a policy community is more likely to maintain the level of influence enjoyed by original members than is a complete break-down into pluralistic arrangements (Smith, 1993, p.54). So changes in a network's environment can be internalised in two ways, either through building new resources or through including new (interdependent) members possessing those resources. The core policy community practices a 'dynamic conservatism'. Rhodes and Marsh (1994, p.14) argue that shifts in resource patterns in a network are 'most commonly in response to changes external to the subsystem'.

So the real motors of network transformation are situated in the external economic, political, institutional and cultural environment (Mol, 1995, p.70). Smith (1993, pp.91-97) and Rhodes and Marsh (1992, p.193) identify similar types of exogenous change which propel changes to policy networks:

1   Economic or market change is the first type of exogenous change. Operators in sectors in recession were routinely treated more leniently by the air Inspectorate, and allowed to delay upgrading their air pollution controls (Health and Safety Executive, 1979; Hill, 1982).

2   Ideology, can have influence. The decision to create HMIP was finally made after a Cabinet Office Efficiency Scrutiny concluded that a unified Inspectorate could deliver deregulatory benefits (in step with Government ideology) as well as integrated environmental benefits (Owens, 1989, p.85; O'Riordan and Weale, 1989, p.288).

3   Changes in knowledge and technology make up the third exogenous source of change. For example, new technologies can bring with them new professional and economic interests which pose a challenge to the existing network order. Equally, new techniques such as environmental assessment methodologies can extend the scope of a network's function.

4   Finally, new institutional arrangements can impinge upon policy networks. A prime example is the emergence of the European Union as a source of environmental policy making and how this can constrain and disrupt domestic policy networks, such as UK air pollution control. In such cases, 'sporadic interventionists' can puncture or by-pass the policy

network and directly influence the policy process or policy issue (Richardson, Maloney and Rudig, 1992). In turn, this can have repercussions for the make up of the policy network (Atkinson and Coleman, 1989, pp.60-66).

So whilst there are two possible sources of change to a policy network, only exogenous sources carry with them the potential for significant change. Exogenously driven change tends to disrupt the dynamic conservatism of policy networks. 'In other words, policy change is not just a function of endogenous factors (that is, the pattern of resource dependencies) but also of exogenous factors (for example, the changing national government environment)' (Rhodes and Marsh, 1994, p.9). This suggests an analysis into reason(s) for the IPC regime must include an examination of its context and of policy actors not normally associated with industrial pollution policy networks (such as the Cabinet Office Efficiency Unit).

This discussion of change has concentrated upon factors driving policy network transformations. This is because the relationship between policy network and policy process under different conditions is recognised as a grey area in the literature; with no real pattern beyond policy networks' conservative, incremental affect (Rhodes and Marsh, 1992, pp.197-98; Bressers and O'Toole, 1994, p.213). The policy process involves interacting policy actors throughout its procession - that is why policy networks were chosen for an analytical framework. This book's framing questions concerning the origin and practice of IPC (chapter 1) will benefit from a policy network explanation, particularly the use of the power dependence model. The 'gap' in the literature concerns general theories between the type of policy network and the sort of policy output or process path which is most likely. This does not detract from the literature's use in this book. Indeed, the book's findings may help build more general theories concerning policy networks and the policy process.

Nonetheless, the policy networks literature does serve as a good source of hypotheses (Bressers and O'Toole, 1994, p.213). For example, following case studies into water policy networks in five countries, Bressers and O'Toole suggest that if policy formulation takes place in a wide issue network, it is replaced by more stable policy community arrangements at the implementation stage; conversely, for policy formulated by a policy community core, 'the implementation network is likely to be more open and complex as core clusters of actors find they must deal with other interests during execution' (1994, p.213).

Policy network hypotheses explaining IPC's origins and implementation can be enriched by the lessons brought from implementation studies. There are significant similarities between the implementation structures concept developed in the implementation studies literature and policy networks (see Table 2.4). The similarities imply policy network analysis can continue into the implementation stage of the policy process. Hypotheses must consider the scope for policy actors involved in the implementation stage to influence policy output.

Table 2.4
Comparing implementation structures with policy networks

Implementation structures	Policy networks
Analyse the implementation stage of the policy process.	Analyse policy areas, sectors, sub-sectors and issues as well as the whole policy process.
Implementation can be understood as a constellation of interdependent actors.	Policy can be understood from interactions of resource interdependent policy actors.
Use exchange and power dependency theories to explain actor interdependencies.	Use exchange and power dependency theories to explain actor interdependencies.
Unit of analysis is the pattern of interdependencies.	Unit of analysis is the structure of interdependencies.
Implementation structures are embedded in macro-level institutions.	Policy networks must be 'contextualised' within macro-level concepts.
The pattern of the implementation structure is empirically determined.	The patterns of actor interaction in the policy network is empirically determined.
Implementation output is a 'consequence of the structure of the interactions among the actors involved' (Hanf, 1982, p.170).	Policy networks affect policy output.

The IPC policy process research problem

The two research questions framing this book are: why did the IPC regime come about?; and how has IPC been implemented? The justification for using policy networks as an analytical framework was that this study's research problem was concerned with the IPC regulatory process - why and how the new regulatory framework came about, how standards have been set, and so on - and that this was simply one type of policy process. Moreover, policy processes involve policy actors interacting in their attempts to influence decisions and involves further interaction when those decisions have to be delivered. This was recognised by Hancher and Moran (1989) for regulation and is reinforced by studies into the important implementation stage of policy processes (Table 2.4). It was by this path that a policy networks analytical framework was adopted and hypotheses concerning the IPC policy process can now be generated. These hypotheses must offer testable explanations for events along the IPC policy process. This section presents five hypotheses generated from the implementation studies and policy networks literature discussed in the preceding sections.

The research thesis

IPC largely replaced the industrial air pollution control regime. Therefore analysis into IPC's origins must consider the air regime, including the RCEP's integrative recommendations based upon their study of that air regime in 1975-6. Interpreting studies into that regime (Vogel, 1986; Ashby and Anderson, 1981; Hill, 1982; Weait, 1989; Hutter, 1986) with the policy networks analytical framework suggests it fits the policy community model. Membership was limited and exclusive to operators and Inspectors. They shared an appreciative system which viewed pollution control as a non-political, technical issue. Rules of the game existed whereby regulator and regulated would co-operate in confidence in pursuing a consensus on suitable emission controls. Therefore, without yet knowing the precise resource interdependency which bound these two policy actors together, the first hypothesis to be tested is that industrial air pollution was the domain of a policy community.

From existing studies it is apparent that the intellectual case for IPC, that it brings environmental benefits, was made by the RCEP over a decade prior to its formulation into industrial pollution policy (RCEP, 1976). This delay in HMIP's creation suggests motives extend beyond pure environmental rationality. It is also clear that there were a number of 'external' influences on this policy process: the EC; a Cabinet Office Efficiency Scrutiny; public interest groups (O'Riordan and Weale, 1989; Owens, 1989; Frankel, 1974). Given the conservative affect of policy communities generally, the second hypothesis argues that policy change was driven by policy actors external to the industrial air pollution policy community. That there were several interacting forces driving the change (O'Riordan and Weale, 1989; Owens, 1989, pp.184-5) suggests an industrial pollution issue network arose with sufficient gravity to cause the creation of HMIP and formulation of IPC.

48

IPC policy formulation deferred considerable standard-setting discretion to the implementation stage. Two studies have concluded that IPC has come about 'incrementally' (Jordan, 1993; O'Riordan and Weale, 1989). Drawing upon conclusions from the bottom-up literature, the third hypothesis is that it is the implementation stage of IPC that has been the most significant determinant of IPC policy output, and not the initial intentions of IPC formulators at the 'top'. In other words, the IPC policy process fits the bottom-up model presented in the implementation studies literature.

IPC implementation requires knowledge which was not readily available (Owens, 1989), such as dose-response effects or knowledge of the release profile of industrial processes. HMIP needs such information from operators in order to set BATNEEC standards in operators' authorisations. The sequence of this resource interdependency puts industry in a powerful position. Early attempts by HMIP to distance itself from those it regulates, under a more strict and structured arms' length approach, are reported to have failed (Allott, 1994, p.ix). HMIP's attempts to unilaterally impose these preferred rules of the game for IPC implementation had to be modified, with a return to co-operation of mutual benefit to the two key actors involved in regulation: industrial operators; and pollution Inspectors. Empirical studies of IPC implementation point out that transparency is not as clear as anticipated (Lyons, 1992; Allott, 1994).

Thus the fourth hypothesis argues that whilst IPC may have brought top-down changes to the regulatory framework, there have been no corresponding changes in the fundamental resource relationship. The formalities of the public register, authorisations and greater monitoring have still allowed IPC implementation to revert to a policy community exhibiting characteristics similar to its air pollution predecessor, namely: membership is exclusive to operators and Inspectors; similar resource interdependencies exist between those with the regulatory mandate and those with the regulatory information; policy output is negotiated in this policy community through co-operation and consensus; and the negotiations and methods used to set standards remain opaque. There is informality within the formalities of the IPC regulatory framework.

Operators' response to IPC to date suggests implementation has been stalled, and does not fit the pattern anticipated by formulators and observers at the outset. Information is missing from applications (Allott, 1994). An implementation deficit exists. Thus the final hypothesis is that the resource distribution within the policy community places industry in a uniquely influential position which has enabled it to weaken IPC policy output.

Thus the overall thesis drawn here from the literature is that the IPC policy process has been incremental, initiated by the push and pull of a transient issue network of policy actors not usually associated with the industrial pollution policy sector. Consequently, the primary motive for switching to an 'integrated' regulatory regime was not environmental protection. Furthermore, the standards of control have been deferred to the implementation stage in which re-configured policy community arrangements, similar to the earlier industrial air pollution regime, have enabled industry to weaken IPC policy output. It is this implementing policy community which most influences policy output.

IPC was born of top-down disruption, but has grown under a conservative, bottom-up influence. The following chapters will seek to confirm or refute this thesis, with the final chapter drawing some overall conclusions.

Notes

1   The idea that government is simply a *deus ex machina* (Peltzman , 1976) eliminating the unfortunate public consequences of private activities has been rejected by many theorists of regulation (see Mitnick, 1980). It is interesting to note, however, that many environmental economists implicitly assume this when advocating government intervention to 'internalise' the environmental 'externalities' of many market activities.

2   Social regulation is 'designed to enhance health, safety, the environment, equal opportunity, and the quality of life'. This is distinct from the traditional concern of the regulatory literature, the economic regulation of monopolies, trusts and cartels.

3   As Wilson pointed out, 'The [US] Environmental Protection Agency was not born because scores of people were dying from pollution, but because the potential (and possibly large) effects of pollution had become a matter of concern' (1980, p.384).

4   This is the shortfall or divergence between original policy objectives and eventual policy output and/or outcomes. Policy output is the activity or product of government at the point of delivery, such as an emission limit. Policy outcomes are the impact of those activities, such as improved air quality (Hogwood and Gunn, 1984, p.17; Weale, 1992, p.154).

5   Such as the types of processes prescribed, the ability to group some prescribed processes into single 'envelope' authorisations, and amendments to the public register.

6   Pluralism views government as reflecting the outcomes of competing interest groups. No interest group has monopoly representation of an

50

interest, so there is often a multiplicity of groups. All interest groups possess power to access and influence policy decisions, and can do so if they are determined enough. 'Essentially, then, in a pluralist political system power is fragmented and diffused, and the basic picture presented by the pluralists is of a political marketplace where what a group achieves depends on its resources and its "decibel rating"' (Ham and Hill, 1993, p.29).

7   'Corporatism can be defined as a system of interest representation in which the constituent elements are organised into a limited number of singular, compulsory, non-competitive, hierarchically ordered, functionally differentiated categories, recognised or licensed (if not created) by the state and granted a deliberate representational monopoly within their respective categories in exchange for observing certain controls on their selection of leaders and articulation of demands and supporters' (Schmitter, 1974, pp.93-94).

8   Models of interaction such as pluralism are used in distinction from theories of the state, concerned with the distribution of power in society.

9   Consequently 'advantages and disadvantages of policy networks seem to be higher costs in policy formulation (co-ordination costs, decision costs) but significantly lower costs in policy implementation (monitoring costs, control costs)' (Kenis and Schneider, 1991, p.43).

10 Note this application of policy networks to a specific policy process is quite novel, since most empirical studies to date have focused on policy/industrial sectors.

11 The concept of power is a complex subject (see Ham and Hill, 1993, pp.65-79 for a good summary). Power involves influence over which policy solutions are adopted (1st dimension, see Dahl, 1957), which problems are considered worth tackling (2nd dimension, see Bachrach and Baratz, 1970), or even if a problem is perceived as such in the first place (3rd dimension, see Lukes, 1974). See Crenson (1971) for a 2-D approach to air pollution in the US.

12 Independence is characterised as a lack of influence among actors, whereas interdependence involves situations characterised by mutual influence (Baldwin, 1978, p.1235).

13   Note that autonomy and influence are related since autonomy can be used by a policy actor to shield herself from influence or to exert influence. In both cases this ability is contingent upon the resource attributes of the policy actor and of others in combination, and how these functionally relate to the policy issue.

14   For suggested policy network dimensions see: Rhodes (1986); Wilks and Wright (1987); Grant, Patterson and Whitston (1988); Atkinson and Coleman (1989); Kenis and Schneider (1991); Van Waarden (1992); Marsh and Rhodes (1992b); Jordan and Schubert (1992).

15   An example of increased intensity is the shift from consultation to negotiation. The latter is more intense owing to the greater degree to which options are left open for resolving a policy issue before members interact. Consultation involves a decision making policy actor seeking the views on options or a decision before it is finalised. Negotiation is more open and involves shared decision making. The former might be more prevalent in issue networks, the latter in policy communities.

16   These were not new terms nor new patterns of policy actor interaction. Richardson and Jordan (1979) had evoked policy communities and Heclo (1978) issue networks. Placing them on a continuum of possible patterns was the Rhodes and Marsh innovation.

17   This characterisation followed a series of nine case studies into UK policy areas, sectors and sub-sectors edited by Marsh and Rhodes (1992b).

3 A cosy relationship: the industrial air pollution policy community

Introduction

In this chapter, the industrial air pollution regime which preceded IPC is analysed. This part of the analysis relies less on primary data than subsequent chapters, but is essential in terms of the overall thesis design. Empirical material is drawn predominantly from secondary documentary sources (such as pollution Inspectorate Annual Reports), and other examinations of the regime (for example National Audit Office, 1991; Weait, 1989; Hutter, 1986; Hill, 1982; Rhodes, 1981; Frankel, 1974). The regime generated little primary documentation itself (NAO, 1991, p.2). However, two interviews with retired senior Inspectors shed considerable light on past industrial air pollution regulatory practice, as did some operator interviews.

The first objective of the chapter is to demonstrate that a policy community was responsible for industrial air pollution control. It is important to understand the characteristics of this policy community not only for comparison with its IPC successor, but because perceived shortcomings in the air policy community were to prompt the DoE and elements in industry to join calls for its reform in the 1980s. For over a century beforehand emission controls were the outcome of private, informal negotiation between Inspectors and operators.

Responsibility for air pollution control lay with the Alkali Inspectorate[1], who implemented a regulatory framework similar to IPC. The regulatory unit was the industrial process, and the regulatory duty was to operate according to a statutory principle rather than statutory limits. For air pollution control this principle was the 'best practicable means' (BPM) for preventing emissions or rendering them harmless. Moreover, operationalisation of this principle required the mobilisation of similar resources (notably technical and financial information) possessed by similar actors as under IPC.

The chapter goes on to examine how the policy community's dominion over industrial air pollution policy was criticised by a short-lived issue network in the early 1970s. The issue network lacked the resources to impose its desired reforms (greater transparency and consultation over standards, in the public interest), but it was sufficiently vocal to prompt a RCEP investigation into industrial air pollution control. The RCEP's recommendations also failed to change policy community arrangements. Consequently, analysis shifts in the final two sections to examine why this challenge failed.

Nevertheless, those events in the 1970s are important because the RCEP's recommendations included calls for the creation of a unitary regulatory body responsible for the integrated control of industrial process releases. In other words, the RCEP raised the issues associated with IPC, and represented a consensus justification for reform on scientific and public accountability grounds. In this sense their report represents the origin of the IPC policy process by officially raising the issue. The Government finally responded to the RCEP report in 1982, rejecting their recommendations and supporting existing (policy community) arrangements. It is the regulatory framework in which the policy community operated which is the starting point for the chapter.

The industrial air pollution regulatory framework

The history of the Inspectorate is covered by others and not dealt with here (see McLeod, 1965; Ashby and Anderson, 1981). This section simply outlines the long-standing regulatory framework operated by the Inspectorate. Subsequent sections demonstrate how the administration of this framework fitted the policy community model of policy making. That is, industrial air pollution policy was the domain of an exclusive, integrated and co-operative network of policy actors.

The Inspectorate was created in 1863, initially responsible only for the control of hydrochloric acid emissions from alkali works. The 1863 Act appointed a Chief Inspector and four Sub-Inspectors with powers to enter alkali works to ensure that emissions were reduced. Over the years the number of substances and processes[2] scheduled for control by the Inspectorate was expanded.

Early Alkali Acts[3] signalled the dawn of two features in UK environmental policy. Firstly, a substance was singled out for control owing to the unequivocal scientific evidence that it was a serious cause of damage. The reluctance to take precautionary action on other probable pollutants in advance of scientific consensus (Ashby and Anderson, 1981, p.22) became a characteristic of British environmental policy until the 1980s, and arguably longer (Haigh, 1994). The second policy feature was a flexible approach to emission standards. The Inspectorate had a statutory duty to ensure that the 'best practicable means' (BPM) for controlling emissions were being used by process operators. There were few statutory emission limits,[4] only the need for process operators to use the BPM to prevent and render harmless their emissions. By 1906, a legislative framework had been established for years of industrial air pollution control up until the introduction of IPC.

The Inspectorate considered BPM an 'elastic band', providing them with the flexibility to alter their standards to reflect developments in pollution control techniques (Ashby and Anderson, 1981, p.40). It remained the Inspectorate's duty to ensure that the BPM was utilised by operators of scheduled processes[5] right up until the phased introduction of IPC.[6] Thus the subsequent analysis is relevant right up until that introduction - the industrial air pollution policy community was operative whilst moves were being made to formulate IPC policy (the subject of chapter 4).

The legislation for industrial air pollution left the Inspectorate with considerable discretion concerning the operationalisation of BPM. The industrial air pollution policy embodied in the Acts was open to considerable bottom-up influence by its implementers. They were left to formulate and implement physical standards of pollution control. They did this through policy community arrangements with industry, and it is on this basis that it is argued industrial air pollution policy was the domain of a policy community. This will become more apparent as analysis proceeds.

Operationalisation of the BPM principle was described formally by Deputy Chief Inspector Mahler in 1966 (Mahler, 1967) and reiterated nine years later by a successor (Tunnicliffe, 1977, p.55). The Inspectorate used the 'Presumptive Limits' concept to codify BPM for the different types of scheduled process. If a process was operating with emissions at or below the Presumptive Limits for its type, then it was presumed to be meeting the BPM (Mahler, 1967). New processes were expected to be designed to these Presumptive Limit standards. It was a policy the Inspectorate had been following since 1883 (McLeod, 1965, p.108). 'They have the advantage over 'Statutory Limits' in that they can be varied at the discretion of the Chief Inspector' wrote Mahler (1967, p.51).

Presumptive Limits represented the prevention of emissions as far as practicable. The second BPM requirement, that of rendering harmless those emissions which did arise (i.e. impracticable to prevent), was met through choosing a chimney height 'to limit ground level concentrations' (Mahler, 1967, p.52). Suitable ground level concentrations, based on chimney height dispersion calculations,[7] were 'usually of the order' of 1/30th the occupational exposure levels used by the Factory Inspectorate.[8] The apparently arbitrary value of 30 was supposed to account for the 'assumed lesser resistance of the young, elderly and sick among the general population and the difference between occupational and residential exposure times' (Mahler, 1967, pp.152-3).

Formal Presumptive Limits and other pollution control standards, such as chimney heights and emissions monitoring, were published as brief BPM Notes, usually four pages long. There were 26 BPM Notes in existence in 1989 for the 58 types of process regulated. The Inspectorate aimed to update these Notes every five years, but by the late 1980s the Inspectorate (by then HMIP) was having problems and Notes were taking seven to nine years to update (see Table 3.1). Plants which had been operating before a BPM Note was revised with new standards were 'allowed to operate to the older standard for an economic working life in the absence of justified complaint' (Tunnicliffe, 1977).

Table 3.1
Targeted and actual annual production of BPM Notes

Year	Target number of BPM Notes for updating	Actual number of BPM Notes updated.
1987-88	11	8
1988-89	9	1
1989-90	5	2

Source: National Audit Office (1991)

BPM Notes served as guidance for field Inspectors responsible for the site-level implementation of BPM. They were not legally binding standards.

An exclusive membership: the Alkali Inspectorate in partnership with industry

From the outset, industrial air pollution control became a partnership between the Inspectorate and industry (McLeod, 1965, p.93). The responsibility of the process operator for controlling pollution and that of the Inspector for ensuring this was done blurred into the joint task of a policy community - criticism of industry failing to control pollution became, by implication, criticism of the Inspectorate (Rhodes, 1981).

Chief Inspector Damon wrote in the Inspectorate's 91st Annual Report: 'Experience has convinced me that a spirit of mutual confidence and goodwill between inspectors and industrialists is essential to progress'. Bugler (1972, p.11) quotes Frank Ireland, who was Chief Inspector of the Inspectorate from

1964 until 1978 and explained 'we look on our job as educating industry, persuading it, cajoling it. We achieve far more this way. The Americans take a big stick and threaten "solve your problem". We say to industry "Look lads, *we've* got a problem". In this way we've got industry well and truly tamed' (original emphasis).

For much of its history the small Inspectorate operated in relative obscurity. Executive control was never exercised beyond the scheduling of new types of process, often at the Inspectorate's suggestion (Ashby and Anderson, 1981, p.138). In 1972 Secretary of State Peter Walker explained that no 'instructions, directives or guidance' had been given by Ministers concerning the interpretation of BPM (Parliamentary Debates, Written Answers, 24th October 1972, Col. 257). This was the preserve of the industrial air pollution policy community.

For the most part then, industrial air pollution policy was 'an essentially private regulatory strategy' between Inspectorate and industry (Weait, 1989, p.57). The high discretion allowed the Inspectorate put it in the position of solving complex political problems through its operations (Rhodes, 1981, p.154; Hill, 1982, p.170). Policy community membership was exclusive to the Inspectorate and industrial bodies, effectively formulating industrial air pollution policy during the implementation phase - the bottom-up model.

The shared appreciative system: pollution control as a technical issue

Each Inspector had a graduate training in industrial chemistry. Recruitment conditions also required them to have had at least five years industrial experience prior to joining the Inpsectorate (Health and Safety Executive, 1986, p.2). Thus Inspectors and works managers often had shared backgrounds, some Inspectors having been works managers themselves. They had had similar training and spoke the same technical language. This could incline Inspectors toward a sympathetic approach to an operator's pollution problems (Hemenway, 1985). It certainly facilitated integration between policy community members when determining pollution control standards. A shared appreciative system structured their approach to pollution problems.

The shared background also reinforced the policy community rules of the game - that pollution was a technical issue for engineers to solve free of external interference. 'Abating air pollution is a technological problem - a matter for scientists and engineers, operating in an atmosphere of co-operative officialdom. Great care has to be exercised by all to prevent the development of adversary attitudes' (Frank Ireland, Chief Inspector, 104th Annual Report of Alkali Inspectorate, 1967).

These were the shared rules of the game which characterised the policy community. These rules kept membership of the policy community exclusive.

Other policy actors could not offer the Inspectorate much in the way of technical input, but could be critical and disruptive, and so they came to be controlled through limited consultation (see later).

The industrial air pollution policy community

The importance of the Inspectorate-industry policy community with respect to the operationalisation of standards was twofold:

1   The policy community set the (only publicly available) standards which appeared in the BPM Notes, such as Presumptive Limits; and

2   Site-level enforcement of these standards was not automatic. Field Inspectors had considerable discretion themselves - and so the policy community of Inspectors and industrial operators negotiated standards using the relevant BPM Notes for guidance (Downing and Hanf, 1983, p.320), taking account of the plant's economic life and other local circumstances.

The Inspectorate was formally responsible for setting standards and for their subsequent enforcement (Rhodes, 1981). Informally, this was done through the policy community: generally at trade association level for formulation; and at site-level for enforcement. Figure 3.1 illustrates schematically how this occurred.

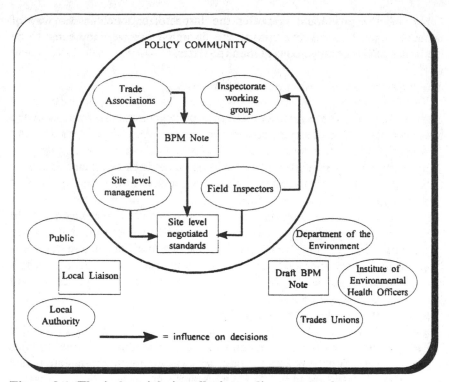

Figure 3.1 The industrial air pollution policy community

BPM Notes and Presumptive Limits: industry's information resource

Presumptive Limits 'are usually arrived at only after close discussion with the interested parties' (Mahler, 1967, p.51). Interested parties did not extend to the public. Discussion took place almost exclusively with industry, upon whom the Inspectorate was dependant for information about pollution control techniques and practice. The Inspectorate were unable to innovate best practice, they could only disseminate advice on best practice as received from industry. It was industry which controlled the generation and supply of the technical knowledge base.

> Our debt to industry is freely acknowledged. Were it not for their work ... on our behalf, our task would be much more onerous than it is, the size of the Inspectorate would need multiplying several times and a department would be needed for specialised techniques of waste gas sampling and analysis as well as for developing air pollution control measures.
> (Annual Report of the Inspectorate, 1964, quoted in Frankel, 1974, p.38)

This resource dependency provided industry with important and influential access to the formulation of the standards by which they were to be regulated. Collaboration was typical, as the Chief Inspector describes in his 111th Annual Report:

> Working parties and discussion groups are set up, consisting of representatives of the industry, its research organisations, if any, and the Inspectorate. Outside specialist bodies are consulted when necessary and when available. The emissions are investigated by the partners, including the routes by which pollutants reach their targets, research being carried out by the industrial side with their own specialists and at their own expense and with Inspectors holding a watching brief. The Inspectorate frequently travels abroad, sometimes in company with industry representatives, to examine foreign technology. Results are reported to both the industry and the Inspectorate. The Chief Inspector makes the final decision on any standards and other requirements, for he is ultimately responsible, but this only follows mutual discussions with industry representatives, where approval is gained if possible.
> (Alkali and Clean Air Inspectorate, 1974, p.12)

The task force established with the Cement Makers Federation in 1981 in order to identify problems and provide input on a revised BPM Note was a typical example (Health and Safety Commission, 1982, p.30).

During one interview with an Inspector, the role of ICI design engineers in drafting a new BPM Note for ammonia works was mentioned. ICI had recently opened a more energy efficient plant with lower emissions. They were thus invited to help draft new BPM Note standards. When the CEGB were upset about a draft BPM Note for large boilers, they were invited by the Inspectorate to draft their own BPM Note.

The Inspectorate used its field experience as a check against complete dependence upon industry for information. The Inspectorate would use the experience of those Inspectors with relevant processes in their Districts. This was possible for updating BPM Notes for scheduled processes but less so for newly scheduled, unfamiliar processes.

A former Inspector explained in interview how experience was used, 'The Inspectors or District Inspectors who had those processes in their Districts would get together in some sort of working group or task force and decide what was the best system that they had got ... they would decide what they thought was best practice throughout the country and we would distil out what we thought industry as a whole was capable of doing'. The small size of the Inspectorate (39 Inspectors in 1987) facilitated such a process of experience sharing. To an extent, this experience of existing industrial practice provided a standard setting floor against complete reliance on industrial research and knowledge - though industry remained the source of the Inspectors' practical experience.

It was on this basis of industry evidence and Inspectorate experience that Presumptive Limits and other conditions were negotiated. Yet as Frankel pointed out (1974, p.11), industry was under no statutory obligation to develop pollution control techniques. The Inspectorate encouraged research through collaboration with industry over issues of mutual concern and by granting access to standard setting. The Inspectorate was following pollution control techniques, not forcing them.

The Inspectorate's weak legal resource and need to seek consensus

Underlying the Inspectorate-industry collaboration was a desire on the part of the Inspectorate to seek consensus. Consensus was important because the Presumptive Limits had no legal standing. An interviewed Inspector explained that the BPM Notes and Presumptive Limits 'had no force in law. You couldn't prosecute someone for offending against the BPM Notes, you could only say this Note is public. You could produce it in evidence to argue that the operator knew what he should do. The industry knew it. It had been agreed with the trade associations and published and sent to all people. But you couldn't go and prosecute for failing a limit, you had to prosecute him for failing to use the best practicable means' (Inspector interview).[9]

In the absence of statutory standards, any transgression of the vague BPM principle proved difficult to demonstrate. For example, 'a certain registered works emitted dark smoke for a considerable period in contravention of the agreed BPM ... But because it could not be demonstrated what had caused the emission of dark smoke and thus that BPM had not been used, the prosecution could not be pursued' (RCEP, 1976, quoted in Reynolds, 1993, p.3). This inability to clearly demonstrate an offence undermined the Inspectorate's legal authority.

Prosecution was further complicated by operators' ability to argue that the Presumptive Limits were not 'practicable' in their circumstances. As Purdue (1991, p.542) noted, 'BPM as a statutory standard has been in operation for many years in the field of air pollution, but it has never been judicially defined by the higher courts in this context'. Moreover, the intrusion of the Courts into the policy community could upset long established, co-operative rules of the game - which the Inspectorate considered to be the most effective way of securing emission improvements, given the balance of resources. Maintaining a good working relationship with operators was important. In his empirical analysis of the Inspectorate's enforcement practice, as recorded in internal correspondence, Matthew Weait found the Inspectorate reluctant to prosecute for three reasons: (1) the difficulty of obtaining strong evidence; (2) the risk to credibility in losing a case; and (3) the harm prosecution could do to the continuing relationship with a firm (1989, pp.67-68).

Seeking consensus on BPM Notes meant the limits would be practicable in a greater number of circumstances: the voluntary compliance sought by the Inspectorate would be more likely. Presumptive Limits had industrial consent, which led to smoother enforcement within Inspectorate realms and not the courts'.

Compounding the lack of a firm and clear legal resource, the Inspectorate also had organisational constraints to overcome. 'Since inspectors cannot be everywhere at all times, they must rely on signs from which they may infer the likelihood of compliance' (Weait, 1989, p.68). Voluntary compliance, through consensus, was organisationally less challenging on the Inspectorate. At the standards formulation stage, the Inspectorate sought to reduce the problems of organisational constraint faced during enforcement by encouraging co-operation - the inclusion of industry in the policy community was vital and beneficial for the Inspectorate.

The combination of industry's information resource, with respect to pollution control research, and the Inspectorate's lack of legal authority owing to the vague BPM ensured industry had an influential place in the policy community. Operators of scheduled processes needed to register their process in order to legally operate it; whilst the Inspectorate needed industrial co-operation to determine BPM and encourage its pursuit. This was the glue which bound the policy community together. The fruits of their labours surfaced in the publication of BPM Notes before submerging again into confidential site-level negotiations.

BPM Notes included qualifications concerning the standards applicable to any particular process. For instance, 'The frequency and time of sampling will depend upon local circumstances and practices, and shall be determined to the satisfaction of the Inspector after discussion with the works management' (HMIP, 1989a, p.2). Mahler suggested in his paper that Inspector experience counted as much after BPM Notes as in their production: 'The final choice of chimney height ... is in practice arrived at by a blend of mathematics and the Inspectorate's experience ... Experience necessarily plays the dominant role in assessing suitable heights in topographical situations to which the mathematics do not apply' (1967, p.152). Divergence from the Notes was allowed (Mahler, 1967, pp.51-58), and site-level implementation re-produced the rules of the game manifest during the negotiation of BPM Notes: confidentiality; co-operation; and consensus.

The high integration of Inspectors and operators in the policy community meant final, site-level agreements were often informal, and any standards for

62

specific processes unrecorded. A National Audit Office investigation into the Inspectorate found 30 out of the 69 regulatory cases it examined had no documentary records. Records were 'insufficient, particularly on air inspections, to enable the NAO to verify operators' performance on pollution control' (NAO, 1991, p.2).[10]

The site-level enforcement of BPM

Inspectors' discretion in their enforcement of BPM was high. The Chief Inspector wrote in his 1973 Annual Report: 'The Chief Inspector, with the help of his deputies, lays down the broad national policies and provided they keep within their broad lines, inspectors in the field have plenty of flexibility to take into account local circumstances and make suitable decisions. They are given plenty of autonomy and are trained as a team of decisions-makers with as much responsibility and authority as possible' (Alkali and Clean Air Inspectorate, 1974).

'Inspectors normally held their post for many years, and were responsible for organising regulatory activity in their districts, on the basis of their knowledge of local plants and operators and with limited central specification of procedures and priorities' (NAO, 1991, pp.7-8). Reports to superiors were on an exceptional basis, such as when an Inspector felt an infraction letter[11] should be issued against an operator.

Facilitated by their shared technical background, Inspectors preferred to advise and encourage operators, rather than routinely administer Presumptive Limits. This was encouraged by superiors. The guidance in BPM Notes was complemented with technical advice to operators from the Inspector on how such limits might be met. Weait (1989) wrote, 'Being "at the sharp end", and having been trained as engineers, inspectors are very aware of the technical difficulties faced by industrial firms in keeping down air pollution levels' (pp.65-66). He concluded his analysis of the Inspectorate's enforcement practice by noting '[i]ts staff have technical, not legal, training and seek technical, not legal, solutions' (1989, p.69).

Solving these technical problems could sometimes involve the Inspector closely with an operator.

One example of how co-operation with industry facilitates the Inspectorate's work is its involvement in a number of extremely large projects, mainly in the organic chemical and iron and steel industries, which have recently been commissioned, or which are being installed in the North East. The Inspector is given the opportunity of taking part in the basic design so far as the airborne environmental effects are concerned.
(Health and Safety Executive, 1980, p.3)

One of the large chemical operators interviewed for this book recalled the Inspector coming and examining designs and checking that calculated emissions were satisfactory. He would also ask for a commissioning report in order to check that the plant met its design performance with respect to emissions. 'That would be virtually it, unless you made a cock up and annoyed your neighbours'.

Inspector visits would involve the Inspector wandering around the plant and having his memory refreshed about operations. Such visits formed an important part of the Inspectorate's proactive enforcement policy (Hutter, 1986, p.115). Table 3.2 records Inspector activity over the period from 1975 up until 1986 (data from annual reports). Over this period the Inspectorate possessed an average of 43 Inspectors. The number of scheduled processes averaged 2, 686 (visits to a works could include inspection of more than one process). Inspectors valued frequent visits, one retired Inspector believed they gave Inspectors a feel for how processes operated throughout the year and provided an important point of contact for advice and negotiation. Monitoring might occasionally be done by an Inspectorate sampling team, more usually the Inspector would check the records of any monitoring done by the operator.

Table 3.2
Inspection activity of the Inspectorate prior to amalgamation into HMIP

Year	Number of registered works	Number of Inspector visits	Average number of visits per works	Number of sampling team visits
1975	2,134	14,526	6.8	674
1976	2,092	14,959	7.2	708
1977	2,075	15,745	7.6	1038
1978	2,033	14,755	7.3	863
1979	1,960	14,099	7.2	952
1980	1,969	14,120	7.2	852
1981	1,915	13,839	7.2	842
1982	1,871	13,399	7.2	905
1983	1,950	11,128	5.7	826
1984	1,975	10,105	5.1	826
1985	1,978	10,847	5.5	649
1986	1,985	9,718	4.9	757

Prosecutions were rare - see Table 3.3 - and often seen as a sign of failure by Inspectors. Angus Smith is quoted in the Alkali Inspectorate's Annual Report for 1963: 'The public can scarcely imagine what a step in advance signifies to the manufacturer, what expenses, what change of apparatus, what teaching of men, what annoyance to foremen, what trouble to chemists, what complicated disturbances to the mind of managers, and what anxiety to owners, but it must be taken occasionally' (Alkali Inspectorate, 1964, p.56).

Table 3.3
Enforcement action of the Inspectorate

Year	Complaints against registered works	Infraction letters	Prosecutions
1975	395	70	2
1976	418	66	8
1977	414	91	8
1978	470	100	13
1979	405	84	7
1980	354	80	10
1981*	343	32	2
1982*	385	41	5
1983*	327	29	2
1984	365	32	1
1985	347	24	1
1986	399	26	1

Source: Annual Reports of the Inspectorate
*: these years do not include an average 28 infractions and 15 prosecutions against small, itinerant cable burners.

One interviewed Inspector expressed similar sentiments 130 years later: 'The general policy was the fact that you yourself were doing an industrial job before you came into this mob - were you a criminal or were the people you worked with criminals? If you thought they were not criminals when you were not criminals, don't treat them as criminals. Treat them as someone who needs instruction and educating; but don't go around smacking their botties as naughty boys'. 'Formally sanctioned, this intuitive empathy often leads to the issue of an infraction letter only after several incidents, or, after infraction, to a recommendation not to prosecute' (Weait, 1989, p.66).

Weait (1989, p.63) found an important determinant in an Inspector's enforcement decision was the attitude of the operator - were they honouring the rules of the game. If the incident had happened a number of times before, or indicated that Inspector advice was being ignored, then action may have been taken. Invariably this action was of an administrative nature: the issuing of an infraction letter explaining the problem and suggesting remedial measures.

Prosecution, assuming a case could be proven, was a threat of last resort when the co-operative relationship had broken down, or if the attitude of the firm toward air pollution control remained consistently cavalier. 'You keep them for the serious cases where you have been unable to convince people to do things by negotiation, by discussion, by shaming them' recalled one Inspector. The concern was that straightforward prosecution of pollution incidents would appear vindictive and harm relationships between themselves and the operator (Weait, 1989, p.63).

This sort of policy community arrangement allowed 'a mutual enhancement in autonomy rather than a loss of autonomy for one actor' (Smith, 1993, p.38): the Inspectorate could meet its requirements without involving the Courts and awkward case histories; industry could quietly negotiate the standards they had to meet with understanding experts. However, it is difficult to evaluate the balance of power within the policy community without access to records of negotiations between them. The confidential and often informal (NAO, 1991) nature of these negotiations makes such an analysis impossible. What evidence there is suggests keeping a process operating was of paramount importance and implies operators possessed an influential economic resource.

Industry's economic resource

A key resource possessed by operators was their economic position. The Inspectorate's legal framework included accounting for the financial implications of the standards which they demanded. The Clean Air Act, 1956, which the Inspectorate used as a reference (Purdue, 1991, p.543), defined 'practicable' to include 'financial implications'. Writing in the 1981 Annual Report, the Chief Inspector explained:

The words 'financial implications' relate to the direct capital and revenue costs borne by the operator of the process. In deciding whether such costs are practicable in any given circumstances, it is the aim to achieve a reasonable balance between the costs of prevention (or dispersion) on the one hand and the benefits on the other. In practice, this is a difficult area in

which to make decisions, not least because the costs and benefits relate to different bodies and because the benefits in particular are seldom quantifiable in monetary terms ... Experience is therefore the usual basis for decisions.
(Health and Safety Executive, 1982, p.15)

Deputy Chief Inspector Mahler (1967, p.42) explained that standards would not be imposed on operators such that they 'were thereby rendered unprofitable or nearly so'. Deputy Chief Inspector Tunnicliffe said the Inspectorate allowed existing scheduled processes to operate below new BPM Note standards until the end of their working lives (1977, p.56). Good maintenance of existing plant would be encouraged rather than pushing for the costly upgrading of plant, 'in order to keep works alive and their staff in employment' (Health and Safety Executive, 1979, p.1).

The approach of the Inspectorate in mitigating upgrading requirements with economic considerations was necessarily pragmatic.[12] As an Inspector explained whilst interviewed, '[Chief Inspectors] Carter and Ireland were tough people, they wanted things quicker. But they would listen to industry and if industry said, we can't afford this, here's the cost data, but we will come forward in three years time with better proposals, they would say, OK, go and do it. It was as pragmatic as that'.

Firms in financial difficulty, the Inspectorate argued, were not allowed relaxed standards, but they were allowed longer periods for reaching standards (Ashby and Anderson, 1981, p.140). One criticism of such pragmatism was that operators were able to secure 'expanding deadlines' for the economic life of their plant (Hill, 1982, p.168).

Limited communication from the policy community

The Inspectorate had been encouraging the creation of Local Liaison Committees in areas where processes were a cause for complaint - there being 72 by 1986. These Committees provided an opportunity for the Inspector, the local authority, a representative of the registered works, and the public to meet twice a year. However, even Sir Eric Ashby (former Chairman of the RCEP), who was sympathetic to the Inspectorate and defended it against critics (see Ashby and Anderson, 1981, pp.135-136), accepted 'their prime purpose is to inform citizens not to consult them, and they are likely to be branded as "tokenism"' (1981, p.139). Frankel considered them a device for diffusing public complaint before it built up sufficient steam to reach Ministerial level (1974, p.25).

Local Liaison Committees provided limited transparency. Local authorities and the public were given information by the policy community: complaints could be aired, and the Inspector and works representative could explain the problems associated with instant solutions. Even then the policy community played a gate-keeper role over the type of explanations given, as comments by A.R. Groom of ICI indicate: 'When meetings were attended by responsible people, industry could and did respond openly' (Health and Safety Executive, 1978, p.3). Key decisions concerning standards and their enforcement remained the preserve of the policy community.

Similarly limited access was allowed to the production of BPM Notes. The Trades Union Congress (represented on the Health and Safety Commission which oversaw the Health and Safety Executive to which the Inspectorate belonged after 1975), DoE and local authorities (through the Institute of Environmental Health Officers) were sent draft copies of proposed BPM Notes for comment. This followed their demands for consultation. Unlike industry, these bodies were not invited to participate in writing the drafts. As a former Inspector put it, 'we didn't mind that [consultation] because it was a technical document, it didn't tell them much'. This peripheral consultation did not alter the substance of BPM Notes, which was the domain of the technical experts in the policy community.

In both instances the policy community was fending off demands for greater participation through limited consultation with selected actors. Consultation involved provision of information and an ability to air views rather than inclusion in the policy community's decision making structures, as illustrated in Figure 3.1. The policy community was practising dynamic conservatism. Modifying its procedures to include limited consultation maintained the exclusive membership of the decision-making core. Michael Hill reported, 'Two of the liaison committees we have encountered have faced problems about inadequate public participation. They have been kept going because the emitters regard them as worthwhile. How much is public involvement limited because people who are dissatisfied with environmental conditions want something done, not information? There is a limit to the appeal of regular meetings to be given reasons why things are not being done' (1982, p.173).

The emergence of a critical issue network

The swell in environmental concern in the late 1960s and early 1970s, following in the wake of events such as Rachel Carson's book 'Silent Spring' (1962) and the 1967 Torrey Canyon disaster (see McCormick, 1991, p.32; Pepper, 1986, p.15), swept the Inspectorate out of relative obscurity and into some public scrutiny (Ashby and Anderson, 1981, p.124).[13] A critical issue network formed around the industrial air pollution policy community.

Jeremy Bugler's book 'Polluting Britain' included an attack on 'industry's ally' (1972). He described the Inspectorate as possessing 'a self-convinced role as an agency to help industry get on with the job, rather than an air-pollution-control agency at all'. Bugler concluded, 'The era of "understandings" reached behind factory gates is over: laws should not only be enacted but seen to be enacted' (1972, p.31).

Other journalists were also critical. Writing in the New Scientist in 1972, Jon Tinker considered the Inspectorate's approach more suited to an Edwardian girls' school than an advanced industrial society, polluters were 'taken quietly on one side by the prefects and ticked off for letting the side down. There is no need for prosecutions: the shame of being found out is reckoned to be punishment enough' (1972, p.530 quoted in McCormick, 1991, p.12). This shame was private too, even prosecuted operators and those receiving infraction letters were not named by the Inspectorate, not even in their Annual Report (Frankel, 1974, p.25; Ashby and Anderson, 1981, p.139).

The secrecy with which the Inspectorate carried on its regulatory activities was a chief cause for criticism and suspicion (Ashby and Anderson, 1981, pp.136-140). The Inspectorate's existence was not generally known - a majority of public complaints against works were received via the local authorities (Frankel, 1974, p.29). The RCEP reported its desire to see public access to pollution information in 1972 (Vogel, 1986, p.96). In the early 1970s the long-standing air pollution policy community was becoming the subject of an emerging and critical issue network unable to penetrate the opaque, non-participatory regulatory process (see Vogel, 1986, pp.96-102).

The Inspectorate argued it did not divulge plant specific details because such action would jeopardise the co-operative relationship it enjoyed with industry. 'An inspector who failed to win the confidence of works managers would fail in his job; if he began to leak information to competitors or to the public he would lose that confidence' (Ashby and Anderson, 1981, p.137). Industry certainly valued confidentiality. ICI reported to the RCEP that, 'Free access to this information by the public leads to pressure for tighter and tighter consents and to the loss of the confidential working relationship with the authorities that we value' (RCEP, 1984, p.25).

More significant criticism, owing to its impact, was Maurice Frankel's 1974 study of the Inspectorate on behalf of the Social Audit pressure group. Frankel acknowledged the Inspectorate's 'highly skilled scientists whose determined efforts have brought significant and long-lasting improvements to the quality of the environment' (Frankel, 1974, p.47). However, Frankel considered the Inspectorate's approach objectionable for the modern age. The confidential and co-operative approach with industry, argued Frankel, meant the public interest in a healthy environment was not being sufficiently served (1974, p.46). His key conclusion was that the Inspectorate be made more accountable to that public; primarily through consultation with local authorities concerning the standards set for local scheduled processes, and that those standards be included in the dissemination of 'complete and honest information to the public' (Frankel, 1974, p.48).

The Social Audit report, along with a series of Parliamentary questions[14] and a failed private members Bill in 1973[15], was acknowledged by Sir Eric Ashby as prompting the Secretary of State to invite the RCEP to investigate industrial air pollution (Ashby and Anderson, 1981, p.133). The issue network had highlighted the blight experienced by communities living around recalcitrant emitters, and it accused the Inspectorate of failing to push through improvements with sufficient force (Bugler, 1972; Frankel, 1974). Consisting of journalists, researchers and Parliamentary politicians, with no material resources other than knowledge of the policy community's operation and the ability to publicly raise awkward questions and accusations, the issue network had caused the policy community to answer to an RCEP investigation.

Conventional wisdom posits the intellectual case for HMIP's creation with the findings of this RCEP investigation. The investigation is given some space in the next section since it raised issues highly relevant to IPC. Yet policy formulation along the lines suggested by the RCEP did not really occur until 1987 (chapter 4).

Defining the issues: the Royal Commission on Environmental Pollution

In June 1974 the RCEP was invited by Anthony Crossland, the Secretary of State for the Environment, 'To review the efficacy of the methods of control of air pollution from domestic and industrial sources, to consider the relationship between the relevant authorities and to make recommendations' (RCEP, 1976, p.1).

Bulmer wrote of Royal Commissions in general standing apart from the political process, 'It is not expected that they will necessarily have much direct impact compared with all the other influences. In fact their importance is often symbolic rather than substantive: they provide a signpost or beacon to an area of policy which will affect its future course, without necessarily shaping it directly in the short term' (1983, p.16). Such a characterisation accurately portrays the RCEP's role in the IPC policy process. The RCEP stood outside of the policy community and endowed the issues they identified with respect and credibility (O'Riordan, 1988, p.9). This issue definition is the first stage of the IPC policy process:

1   An integrated approach to controlling pollution from industrial processes.

2   Administrative reorganisation.

3   Uniform or discretionary emission standards.

4   Confidential regulation or transparent controls.

5   Wider participation in regulatory decision making.

The RCEP is a standing commission created by the Wilson government in 1970. Though independent of government its administrative expenses are met by the DoE. RCEP members do not receive a salary, tending to be drawn from the 'Good and the Great' (Bulmer, 1983, p.5). Members are well established in their respective fields, which are generally 'technocratic': natural science; engineering; law; social sciences and business.[16] Usually the RCEP chooses its own topics of investigation, requiring 'detailed and rigorous analysis' before policy decisions and action can be taken in the medium term (RCEP, 1993, p.2). RCEP investigations utilise several methods: receiving written evidence; hearing oral evidence; visits; and informal discussion. Different interests are provided with the opportunity to present their views. After consideration the RCEP's conclusions are reported along with recommendations for government.

The Fifth Report elaborates a rational reform to industrial pollution policy

Investigation into industrial air pollution control formed the RCEP's Fifth Report. The key conclusion from their investigation was that solving air pollution problems in isolation would not provide optimum environmental solutions (RCEP, 1976, pp.73-76). They pointed out that single media controls (as practised by the Inspectorate) can merely shunt the pollution to other environmental media, for example heavy metal dust removed from air emissions by filter bags is disposed to landfill instead. Their notion that controlling releases to air, water and land should be integrated was not new[17] (Irwin, 1989, p.3-5); the RCEP simply confirmed favourable opinion upon integration and raised its respectability.

The RCEP believed an integrated approach was required which considered releases to air, water and land together, and which sought the 'best practicable environmental option' (BPEO), 'taking account of the total pollution from a process and the technical possibilities for dealing with it' (1976, p.3). From this scientific insight the RCEP made recommendations which included changing the organisation of industrial pollution control.

They recommended the creation of a new, unified Inspectorate to administer integrated pollution control. The industrial process as the regulatory unit would be maintained, with the RCEP envisaging the air Inspectorate forming the basis for the new regulatory body. The RCEP considered the flexibility of

71

the BPM approach superior to nationally-fixed, uniform emission standards.[18] The BPM approach should be maintained, they suggested, but should be integrated across media so that the BPEO would be sought. Thus their recommendations remained within the discretionary,[19] flexible tradition of UK industrial pollution control.

However, whilst the RCEP were content with the BPM approach, they were 'unhappy about some ways in which the system has worked in practice' (1976, p.4). Identifying the BPEO would need changes to the existing system, which the RCEP considered defective.

First, the system needed greater transparency. The RCEP believed there had 'been much unnecessary secrecy about air pollution' (1976, p.5) which exacerbated public distrust in the relationship between Inspectorate and industry (1976, p.34). Transparency would be brought to the system by introducing a consent based approach to regulation. Regulatory conditions would be included in a consent issued by the Inspectorate to operators, making specific and transparent the interpretation of BPM.[20] Breach of the consent would be an offence. The consents would be held on a public register by the local authority, as would monitoring results.

Second, changes in the determination of BPM were needed. The RCEP wanted to see more participation than the narrow Inspectorate-industry policy community. Selecting both industry-wide and site-specific BPM 'involve similar and complex considerations' (1976, p.56). The RCEP recognised the Inspectorate's expertise on pollution control technologies, but pointed out that Inspectors did not possess the accounting expertise to assess a company's local financial circumstance, nor the economic expertise to consider costs and benefits to the nation. 'And although they do take into account the employment effects of their decisions they have no formal qualifications to do so. Moreover, there is no formal machinery through which the views of local people, amenity associations and the scientific community about pollution from industry can influence the Inspectorate's negotiations. We consider these are significant weaknesses in the present system' (1976, p.56).

Missing expertise and appropriate professional competencies should be recruited into the new regulatory body. In addition, the RCEP wanted to see mechanisms for the inclusion of local authorities and other interested parties in the determination of abatement programmes and BPM. 'It is no longer acceptable that decisions on emissions which directly affect the lives of many people should be taken by a small, specialist body consulting only with industry; greater participation is needed, not least so that the assumptions and problems on which decisions depend are more widely understood' (1976, p.56). The RCEP proposed wide consultation procedures which could be understood by 'non-experts' for both national BPM guidance and registered works' consent conditions.

The Fifth Report brought together the seeds of debate surrounding industrial pollution control and crystallised them into an agenda for change. The Inspectorate's flexible BPM approach to controlling air emissions from an industrial process should be extended to the control of other environmental releases. The RCEP did not question the dominant appreciative system, that pollution control was a technical issue, but they did propose some changes to the rules of the game. Formality needed to be introduced both to participation in regulatory decision making, and in transparently recording those decisions in a legally binding consent. This procedural change required organisational change too. A new unitary Inspectorate should be located within the DoE.

Yet the RCEP lacked the authoritative resource to influence the policy community and instigate changes. Instead the RCEP report was to become a knowledge resource for others who sought environmental and public interest justifications for reform.

The RCEP was to return to some of these issues in later investigations. In 1984 they reviewed the country's track record on tackling pollution. They again called for greater transparency and expressed their desire to see greater co-ordination between regulatory agencies responsible for pollution to different media (RCEP, 1984). They noted a nascent change in attitude amongst practitioners[21] toward more disclosure of environmental information, which the RCEP believed should extend to all information regulatory authorities are entitled to receive by statute (RCEP, 1984, p.38).[22]

In 1988, following the eventual creation of a unified Inspectorate a year earlier, the RCEP elaborated upon their BPEO concept in a report dedicated to the topic (RCEP, 1988). This report was an attempt to operationalise their regulatory principle. The BPEO for a process should be the outcome of a systematic, consultative, and transparent decision making process. An 'audit trail' should be traceable, distinguishing between scientific issues and value judgements, and highlighting all assumptions made in arriving at a BPEO.

The RCEP's recommendations provide a knowledge resource for others

Secretary of State Anthony Crossland made no commitments in his press release greeting the Fifth Report (DoE, 1976) and it was not until 1982 that the government made a formal, but negative response (DoE, 1982). The independent prestige contained in their Royal Commission status meant the RCEP reports provided useful and credible 'off the shelf' justifications for other policy actors with reason to pursue changes to the industrial air pollution policy community. Their report conveyed a scientifically based consensus. However, there were other motives for HMIP's creation beyond the RCEP's environmental science and public accountability arguments (chapter 4). The

73

RCEP's influence was limited to a legitimating intellectual case for a unified pollution Inspectorate and the pursuit of integrated pollution control.

A new policy actor: the Health and Safety Commission and Executive

By the second half of the 1970s mass environmental concern had diminished (Pepper, 1986, p.15). The vocal issue network which had prompted the RCEP investigation lacked the resources to force changes to industrial air pollution policy and faded away. Another policy actor had joined the industrial air pollution policy network: the Health and Safety Commission and Executive. Their influence in other policy areas effectively made any government action upon RCEP recommendations a non-decision.

During the RCEP's investigations in 1975, the air pollution Inspectorate had been transferred from the DoE into the newly created Health and Safety Commission and Executive (HSC/E). The creation of this new regulatory body effectively prevented the reforms the RCEP wanted (O'Riordan and Weale, 1989). The RCEP were firmly against the air Inspectorate's inclusion in the HSC/E and wished to see it returned to the DoE (RCEP, 1976, pp.68-72).

The HSC/E were created on 1st January 1975 to implement the Health and Safety at Work etc. Act, 1974. This reform arose from the investigation of the Committee on Safety and Health at Work, chaired by Lord Robens and established in 1970. Control of industrial air pollution was very much a marginal issue for the Committee, yet they recommended the air Inspectorate be included in the HSE (Committee on Safety and Health at Work, 1972, p.34).

The logic behind this recommendation rested upon the regulatory focus common to the HSE: the industrial process. The RCEP pointed out in their Fifth Report that the HSC/E was predominantly concerned with industrial matters and not the whole environment. This wider environmental concern meant, in their opinion, that the air Inspectorate should be returned to the DoE. But changes had already taken place of sufficient magnitude to prevent Government from moving the Inspectorate from the new HSC/E.

O'Riordan and Weale (1989), in their study of HMIP's creation, attribute the long period of government inaction[23] on the RCEP's report to the institutional significance of the new HSC/E. The Health and Safety Commission[24] was a corporatist institution responsible for policies which the Health and Safety Executive enforced. Representatives of the trades unions, the Confederation of British Industry (CBI), and government made up the HSC. The Labour government was reluctant to disrupt a potentially successful tripartite organisation, particularly at a time when the trades unions' political support was important for Labour's maintenance in government (O'Riordan and Weale,

74

1989, pp.284-285). Workplace health and safety issues were important concerns for the unions. Consequently, the importance of the HSC/E for the government in politically more significant policy networks effectively allowed the HSC/E to exercise non-decision making power with respect to reforming industrial air pollution control.

Reasons for the Conservative government's inaction are more diffuse (O'Riordan and Weale, 1989, p.285). First, the CBI wished to see the Inspectorate continuing as a technically competent, chemical engineering organisation linked with the Factory Inspectorate in the HSE. This was confirmed by an interviewed Inspector who explained that the CBI later switched to lobbying for the Inspectorate's return to the DoE, 'Industry initially condemned the Fifth Report. I talked with one or two people who were on the CBI Committee and they later said to me, we made a mistake there, we misread it, we imagined we were going to get lots and lots of extra regulation, being industry we don't want more regulation but in fact we can now see that it could mean more streamlined and simplified legislation'. This change prompted pro-DoE lobbying activities by the CBI in 1984 (see chapter 4). Weale and O'Riordan (1989, p.285) add that the Conservatives were reluctant to meddle with the HSC/E at a time when they were 'taking on' both the unions and the Civil Service elsewhere.

Research for this book has not sought to confirm or refute these explanations - the objective for the analysis is to discover why IPC was introduced rather than the reasons for its delay. However, the Inspector's interview confirms part of O'Riordan and Weale's case. Moreover, their contention that 'to try to complicate a very delicate piece of reformism that had no currency in the regulatory world was regarded as unnecessarily provocative' (1989, p.285) points out the rarefied atmosphere of the politics of pollution during this period.

The issue network of the early 1970s had disappeared in the second half of the decade (Boehmer-Christiansen and Skea, 1991, p.177). Writing in 1986, Vogel concluded 'There is in Britain today no significant domestic pressure to change the way British pollution-control policy is either made or enforced. Complaints about pollution tend to focus on particular sources, not on the system of regulation itself'. Environmentalists were more concerned with more transparent land use planning and countryside policy issues (Vogel, 1986, p.101; McCormick, 1991, p.13; Rose, 1990). Public concern for the system of industrial pollution control during the period up to the mid-1980s just did not warrant sufficient government attention to precipitate action.

The government rebuffs the RCEP recommendations

The government finally responded to the RCEP's Fifth Report in a DoE Pollution Paper in 1982 (DoE, 1982). It was the government who had the authority needed to create a unified Inspectorate and provide legislation changing pollution control procedures. They chose not to.

Michael Hesletine, the Secretary of State for the Environment, welcomed the RCEP's endorsement of the BPM principle. The government accepted the RCEP had recognised a real environmental problem - the cross-media transfer of pollutants - and believed 'the BPEO concept is one of considerable power and utility' (DoE, 1982, p.3). But their response went on to reject the RCEP's recommendations. In this respect, the 1982 response presents a statement of the government's policy on industrial pollution at the start of a decade which eventually saw IPC reform. Table 3.4 compares the government's position with the RCEP's and also with eventual government policy in 1990.

Table 3.4
Comparison of RCEP recommendations with government policy in 1982 and 1996

Policy Issue	RCEP	Government in 1982	Government in 1996
Regulatory body	A unified regulator in the DoE.	Existing, fragmented system is sufficient.	A unified regulator in the DoE.
Integration	Regulation of all releases should be considered together, and the BPEO sought for the industrial process.	BPEO concept is 'of considerable power and utility' (DoE, 1982: 3), but organisational change is thought unnecessary.	All releases regulated together according to the BPEO.
Pollution control standards	Prefer the flexibility of the UK's BPM approach over uniform emission standards.	Prefer the flexibility of the UK's BPM approach over uniform emission standards.	Prefer the flexibility of the UK's approach over uniform emission standards.

Standard setting procedure	Would like to see more formal and wider consultation on standard setting.	Believes existing standard setting procedures are adequate.	Procedures require consultation with other bodies and allow for public consultation.
'The regulation'	Wish to see regulatory standards written into a formal consent. Breach of consent conditions is an offence.	Maintain the existing approach. Believe consents would 'entail employment of more staff in government and industry' (DoE, 1982: 9).	Regulatory standards are written into a legally binding consent.
Transparency	The public should have access to information which the regulators receive by statute. Consents should be placed on a public register.	No change in access to information. Industrial provision of publicly available environmental information should be voluntary.	The public has access to information which the regulators receive by statute. Consents are placed on the public register.
Enforcement	The co-operative approach is preferable to an aggressive enforcement policy.	The co-operative approach is preferable to an aggressive enforcement policy.	The co-operative approach is preferable to an aggressive enforcement policy.

The government's overall response in 1982 was to preserve the status quo. It felt the few cases where an integrated approach would benefit could be achieved by encouraging existing regulators to co-operate with other pollution control authorities (DoE, 1982, pp.2-3). Yet research by the Inspectorate and DoE shortly after the RCEP's Fifth Report estimated that over half the air pollution Inspectorate's scheduled processes might be suitable for 'cross-media' control (Efficiency Scrutiny, 1986, p.11; DoE, 1988a, p.7). This work was not mentioned in the government's 1982 response.

Ironically, the research done in 1976 was cited a decade later by a Cabinet Office Efficiency Scrutiny into industrial pollution and safety as a reason for unification (as was the RCEP's Fifth Report) (Efficiency Scrutiny, 1986, p.11); and a DoE consultation paper of 1988 cited both as reasons for providing the

Inspectorate with IPC (1988a, p.7). Conditions had changed between 1982 and 1988.

A unified Inspectorate, HMIP, was created in 1987 and was part of the DoE. In 1982 government argued such change would introduce complexity, add another layer of regulation and increase bureaucracy (DoE, 1982). In 1986 they argued it would provide the opposite: reducing complexity, and improving the efficiency of pollution control without expanding the bureaucracy (Efficiency Scrutiny, 1986). These changes are the topic of the next chapter.

Summary and conclusions

This chapter has demonstrated how a policy community effectively controlled industrial air pollution policy. Membership of this industrial air pollution policy community was exclusive to the Inspectorate and industry (the regulator and regulated). There was a large degree of integration amongst members. Operators and Inspectors shared an appreciative system which viewed pollution control as a non-political, technical issue. They followed agreed rules of the game in determining the BPM for controlling emissions from a process: negotiation would be confidential; the relationship would be co-operative; and a consensus solution should be sought. Members exchanged their resources in the pursuit of mutually beneficial outcomes.

Operators needed to register their process in order to operate it legally. The Inspectorate had to ensure those operations used the BPM for controlling emissions. Industry was the source of technical information necessary for defining BPM. They also had an economic significance appreciated by the Inspectorate. The Inspectorate could register the process and enforce standards. However, its legal resource was weak. Nor did it have the organisational resource to police all scheduled processes closely. Thus the Inspectorate was happy to practice rules of the game which sought consensus with operators, allowing them access to decision-making procedures in return for the information this would uncover. With this Inspectors could advise, educate and encourage operators generally to voluntarily pursue good practice. But this gentlemanly approach did not satisfy all parties.

An issue network of policy actors arose in the early 1970s, critical about the way the public interest appeared to be excluded from the policy community. The issue network wanted greater transparency and participation in industrial air pollution policy. Though the issue network was vocal enough to prompt an official investigation into policy, it did not have the resources to force the changes it desired and soon fizzled out.

The RCEP, which conducted the investigation, brought together all the issues which were to concern reform of industrial air pollution policy. As such, the origin of the IPC policy process can be traced to their Fifth Report. However, events had moved on and the government was reluctant to interfere with the industrial air pollution policy community. Executive responsibility for industrial air pollution was now the domain of the HSC/E, whose members the government needed for support or were taking on in other policy areas. Moreover, with environmental issues falling back down the public agenda there were no politically significant constituencies calling for reform.

Thus the industrial air pollution policy community withstood the criticism of the issue network and maintained its hold over policy. The government eventually published a rejection of the RCEP's investigations in 1982, satisfied with the existing arrangements. However, over the decade another, more significant issue network built up and the government reversed its position to one close to that of the RCEP, as the next chapter demonstrates.

Notes

1   The Alkali Inspectorate underwent several name changes in its last decades. By 1969 there were only five registered works using the original alkali process. In 1971 Peter Walker, Secretary of State for the Environment, wished to update the Inspectorate by re-naming it; but the Inspectorate wished to retain links with a tradition of which it was proud. Consequently the compromise re-title was the Alkali and Clean Air Inspectorate (Bugler, 1972, p.9). In 1982 there was a final re-naming to the Industrial Air Pollution Inspectorate; and in 1987 the Inspectorate formed the largest constituent of Her Majesty's Inspectorate of Pollution. For convenience the term Inspectorate will be used in this chapter.

2   There were 58 types of scheduled process in 1982.

3   Alkali Acts built up the legal framework in 1863, 1868, 1881 and 1906.

4   Hydrochloric acid; sulphuric acid; and nitric acid (McLeod, 1965, p.107; Bugler, 1972, p.24). Experience in the field meant that by the turn of the century the emphasis had shifted from uniform limits to the more flexible 'best practicable means' (McLeod, 1965, p.109).

5   Scheduled processes are equivalent to IPC prescribed processes, i.e. included for regulation by statute.

6   Prior to IPC the Inspectorate (and HMIP after it) was administering Section 5(1) of the Health and Safety at Work Act, 1974. This required

operators at registered works to 'use the best practicable means for preventing the emission into the atmosphere from the premises of noxious or offensive substances and for rendering harmless and inoffensive such substances as may be so emitted'.

7   The equation used was based upon a simple wind and topographical model: chimney height squared = (9*mass rate of emission)/(4*permitted ground level concentration).   'The actual height so obtained is not necessarily the one finally chosen except in very straight forward circumstances and it may be appreciably modified by the Inspector's assessment' (Mahler, 1966, p.53).

8   For IPC, many applicants used a 1/40th quotient to demonstrate their emissions were not causing harm for precisely the same reasons as the 1/30th.

9   The closest one gets to a statutory definition of BPM is found in the Clean Air Act, 1956 (S.34): 'reasonably practicable, having regard amongst other things, to the local conditions and circumstances, to the financial implications and to the current state of technical knowledge'.

10   An interviewed Inspector confirmed the informal nature of many pollution control agreements between Inspector and operator. When promulgation of the EC Air Framework Directive finally forced the provision of a record of such agreements, to be placed upon a public register, the Inspectorate (then in HMIP) found the workload distracting them from preparations for IPC.

11   Infraction letters were an administrative device for notifying operators of their failure to meet BPM. If an infraction letter was persistently not met with corrective action by the operator then the Inspectorate might consider prosecution.

12   The Inspectorate did not possess any economists.

13   See Hogwood and Gunn (1984, p.68) on the 'particularity' of policy issues from general concerns.

14   See, for example, the following in Parliamentary Debates, Oral Answers: Michael McNair Wilson MP, 8/12/1971 Col. 1281; Mr Meacher MP, 14/6/1972, Col. 1479. And in Written Answers: Mr Orme MP, 25/5/1972, Col 476; Harold Walker MP, 26/5/1972, Col. 519; Mr Skeet

MP, 14/11/1972, Col. 98; Mr McBride MP, 28/2/1973, Col. 359; and Michael Shaw MP, 26/6/1973, Col. 313.

15 Neil McBride MP failed to get his 'Alkali Inspectorate Bill' enacted. It would have required consultation with local authorities concerning standard setting, and the publication of all relevant information about a process except genuine trade secrets.

16 RCEP membership for the 1974-75 investigation contained seven natural scientists, two social science academics, five heads of public institutions, two businessmen, and a trades unionist.

17 Sweden, for example, established a single permitting process for releases from major installations to land, air and water in 1969.

18 This position put the RCEP at odds with the EC, which favoured uniform emission standards.

19 In terms of taking local conditions into account.

20 Or BPEO if an integrated system of control was adopted.

21 Both Inspectors and operators.

22 Trade secrets and information of national security significance would be exempt from disclosure. The RCEP believed such instances were rare.

23 The Labour government (1976-79) and the first Thatcher government (1979-1983).

24 Accountable to the Department of Employment.

4 Defensive reform: IPC policy formulation

Introduction

Industrial air pollution policy was the domain of a policy community of Inspectors and operators traditionally. This was one conclusion from the previous chapter. That chapter also demonstrated how an agenda for integrated reform was proposed by the RCEP but not taken forward by government. This chapter analyses why reforms eventually took place by analysing the formulation stage of the IPC policy process. Why did the IPC reforms happen?

Policy formulation involved the creation of a unified pollution Inspectorate (HMIP) and introduction of new IPC legislation. IPC legislation introduced more formal and transparent procedures to industrial pollution control. Furthermore, HMIP decided to adopt a more formal regulatory relationship with operators when implementing IPC. Thus the outcome of the IPC policy formulation stage appeared to present significant changes to regulatory practice.

This change did not derive from the policy community responsible for industrial air pollution. Policy communities are conservative entities. HMIP's creation and the introduction of IPC were dramatic departures, hence the hypothesis tested in this chapter is that this change was driven by policy actors external to the policy community, becoming the concern of an issue network which shaped the policy formulation that took place.

Thus it is necessary to identify the policy actors involved in events over this period, assess their resource attributes, and to analyse how resource interdependencies between the policy actors influenced the policy process. This has been done through the use of primary and secondary documents (for example, DoE consultation papers and contemporary journalism respectively) and with interview evidence from participants.

IPC policy formulation was a complex and disjointed process. Discussion begins by identifying the two issues which drove the process - the EC, and a dispute about executive control over the Inspectorate - and describing how these created an issue network in the industrial air pollution policy sub-sector. The aim of this following section is to provide a familiarising overview of policy formulation events, before the detailed analysis proceeds in the main bulk of the chapter. That detailed analysis begins by focusing upon the EC, a major exogenous force on the policy process.

After discussion of the EC, the analytical focus turns to the issue network members responsible for HMIP's creation: industrial leaders concerned that pollution controls remain flexible; the HSE wishing to bring the Inspectorate further into its organisational structure; a Cabinet Office Efficiency Scrutiny seeking bureaucratic rationalisation in the industrial pollution policy sector; and the DoE attempting to meet EC requirements. The discussion seeks to demonstrate that the decision to establish integrated pollution control was not based upon the sort of rational environmental considerations provided by the RCEP. Instead this shift in policy was because it was believed economies could be gained from a unified Inspectorate. This arose because the issue network could not resolve the problem of Inspectorate control without the intervention of a deregulatory government.[1]

Government intervention was also needed to provide HMIP with an IPC legislative framework. The chapter finishes by pointing out that like the air regime, much of the substance of IPC, such as pollution control standards, was deferred to the implementation stage. However, the legal framework provided more formal regulatory procedures for IPC than its air predecessor, and HMIP appeared to be adopting a tougher approach to its implementation - to the concern of industry.

An industrial air pollution issue network

Interest in industrial air pollution policy grew again in the 1980s. An issue network emerged which influenced policy. This section aims to summarise the issues which drove the process and to introduce the key policy actors.

Just like the early 1970s, a new campaign began in the 1980s to allow public access to environmental information, forming part of a wider Campaign for Freedom of Information launched in 1984. Public interest in environmental issues was growing again; and the acid rain issue had rekindled environmental NGOs' interest in pollution issues (Rose, 1990).

However, such public interest actors did not play a direct role in the air pollution issue network of the 1980s.

European pressure

There were two issues concerning the industrial air pollution issue network. The first was a tension between the formality of a growing body of EC environmental legislation and the flexible British tradition (which was falling into public disrepute). Issue network members agreed the latter needed some sort of defence against the former. This was their shared appreciative system. Non-members, such as environmental NGOs, were more inclined to EC formality. The second issue was a wrangle between the DoE and HSE for executive control of the air Inspectorate, precisely at a time when reforms were felt necessary.

The first issue effectively prised open the industrial air pollution policy community. The EC was drafting industrial air pollution legislation which needed incorporating into UK law. The DoE had to arrange this, which prompted their interest in the industrial air pollution policy community. More EC law was possible, particularly uniform emission standards challenging the British tradition of site-specific flexibility. This concerned both members of the industrial air pollution policy community. In his 1982 Annual Report, Chief Inspector Reed criticised the uniform emission standards approach the EC was taking. He said the plans lacked the 'flexibility in granting approvals, which is an important factor in gaining the confidence and support of industry' (HSE, 1984). An interviewed Inspector said the Inspectorate was pointing out to the DoE its concerns about the significance of the EC's proposals.

Industry, the other policy community member, disliked moves toward European formalism too. It began lobbying for defensive reform of the UK system of industrial pollution control. Thus the industrial air pollution policy community membership became involved in the issue network, whilst continuing its day to day regulatory activities.

Whitehall wrangling

It was the second issue, concerning executive control of the Inspectorate, which eventually triggered reform. During the 1980s the Inspectorate was increasingly being absorbed into the organisational structure of the HSE. It appeared industrial air pollution control was becoming an offshoot of health and safety policy rather than a distinct regulatory activity. This concerned the Inspectorate and industry for similar reasons to the EC's intervention: loss of control over pollution standards. The

DoE was also concerned because losing the Inspectorate within the HSE would weaken further its executive control over industrial air pollution policy, precisely at a time when the EC was requiring its intervention. Thus a concerted effort was made to return the Inspectorate to the DoE.

Prompted by the dispute for control of the Inspectorate, a Cabinet Office Efficiency Scrutiny was launched to examine the scope for efficiencies in the industrial pollution policy sector. Their conclusions finally triggered reform of industrial air pollution policy and set it upon an 'integrated' trajectory. They argued that a bureaucratic rationalisation creating a new unified Inspectorate, practising multi-media pollution control, would bring public sector savings and reduce the regulatory burden upon industry. The Scrutiny's Cabinet status and deregulatory conclusions convinced the government to intervene with reform. HMIP was created as part of the DoE. As a new regulator it had credibility restoring potential.

HMIP's creation solved one of the issue networks' concerns: control of the Inspectorate. However, it did not resolve EC requirements. Yet proposed air reforms put forward by the DoE in December 1986, satisfying EC requirements whilst maintaining traditional flexibility, were not carried through into legislation. The government chose not to intervene with legislation. The issue was eventually resolved through DoE proposed IPC legislation which accorded with EC requirement, but maintained flexibility and discretion over standards. Securing the legislation required the government to intervene and provide Parliamentary space for a Bill. Obtaining this legislative resource for the industrial pollution issue network was made easier thanks to the high political profile of environmental issues in the late 1980s.

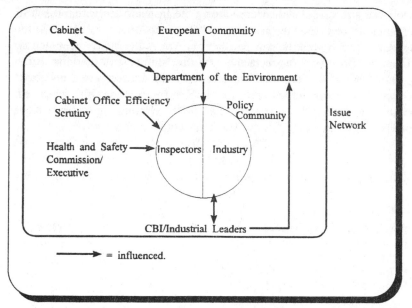

Figure 4.1   Schematic of the issue network which disrupted the industrial air pollution policy community in the 1980s

Policy formulation - the creation of HMIP and introduction of IPC - was completed in November 1990. Figure 4.1 is a schematic of the issue network involved over the policy formulation stage. Table 4.1 lists the policy actors affecting industrial pollution policy in the 1980s, and for each characterises their objectives, their resources, and whether they were members of the issue network.

Throughout the formulation stage the issue network had a fluid membership. The Efficiency Scrutiny was only briefly concerned with the industrial pollution issue. Their involvement had been prompted in part by the HSE's increased involvement, which itself ceased with the Scrutiny's recommendations for HMIP. The Scrutiny was also an example of the issue network having to look outward, to the resources of others (government authority), in order to resolve policy problems. It had to do this again to secure IPC legislation.

Finally, HMIP's creation from an amalgam of existing Inspectorates introduced a new policy actor to the industrial pollution control policy network: the Radiochemical Inspectorate (RCI). The RCI were one of the constituent Inspectorate's going into HMIP. They did so in a position of leadership over the air Inspectorate concerning control of HMIP. This leadership enabled the RCI to introduce their rules of the game

87

concerning the regulation of operators. Their arms' length approach to regulation, and the formality of IPC procedures provided in the legislation, suggested the new regulatory regime would differ from the air policy community it was replacing. By this late stage of the formulation process the issue network's membership was dissolving. Only those policy actors concerned with the implementation of IPC remained: industry and HMIP. The remainder of this chapter provides a more thorough analysis of the IPC policy formulation stage.

Table 4.1
Policy actors, objectives, resources and influence over the IPC policy process

Policy Actor	Objectives	Resources	Network member
European Community.	European formalism. Harmonisation of Member State regulations on basis of Precautionary Principle.	Constitutional authority to pass Directives.	No.
Department of the Environment.	Balancing necessity of EC law with British tradition.	Formal authority over industrial pollution policy.	Yes.
Industry.	Avoid imposition of uniform emission standards. Restore credibility for British approach to pollution control.	Technical information necessary for process based controls. Money and ultimate agent (organisation) for controlling pollution. Wealth and job creation (economic resource).	Yes.
Inspectorate.	Maintain control over flexible standards. Return to the DoE.	Political legitimacy to set standards. Technical competence (knowledge resource).	Yes.

Environmental NGOs.	Greater access to information. Tougher standards. EC viewed favourably for these reasons.	Some ability to mobilise public support.	No.
Health and Safety Executive.	Bring Inspectorate closer into new HSE structure.	Organisational ability to re-organise Inspectorate.	Yes.
Cabinet Office Efficiency Scrutiny.	Seek efficiencies through bureaucratic rationalisation.	Political legitimacy to influence decisions within Cabinet.	Yes.
Government.	Deregulation. Re-election.	Authority to introduce legislation to Parliament and to re-organise the bureaucracy.	No.

EC intervention in industrial air pollution policy

The body of EC environmental policy and legislation expanded in the 1980s. This growth became a major pressure forcing a domestic review of British industrial air pollution policy. The EC approach to pollution control was perceived by policy actors in stark contrast to the British tradition. Where UK practice sought consensus and collaboration on technical solutions for each specific case, its practitioners feared the EC would impose a formal and legalistic style of regulation, based upon uniform emission standards and lacking flexibility.

EC Directives were being passed containing more formal regulatory procedures, and there was a real potential for EC regulatory standards to be set external to the UK policy community and imposed upon it. EC intervention threatened to disrupt the industrial air pollution policy community and impose contrasting rules of the game.

EC authority over environmental policy

Prior to 1987 EC environmental legislation had to seek legitimacy by arguing that it removed barriers to the operation of the common market. The 1957 Treaty of Rome made no reference to the environment (Haigh, 1989, p.11). Following the Single European Act, 1987 environmental protection became a Community duty under the revised Treaty. This strengthened EC authority over domestic environmental policy.

In some instances the Single European Act, 1987 made it easier to pass environmental legislation. Before the Act, all Directives concerning environmental protection had to be unanimously agreed amongst the Community's Member States. After the Act, environmental legislation which was concerned with the single market harmonisation of Member State legislation needed only a qualified majority vote. Measures more concerned with protecting the environment than with harmonisation still required unanimous agreement but now had firm legal standing (Haigh, 1989). The significance of this is that the basis for EC environmental policy and legislation became assured and procedures for its adoption made slightly easier. An exogenous institutional change had occurred in the sense that the EC's authoritative resource had increased and with this its ability to intervene in domestic regimes.[2]

EC Directives on air pollution

In 1980 a Directive was passed requiring the adoption of mandatory air quality standards for smoke and sulphur dioxide.[3] Such air quality standards presented a departure for British pollution control policy (Haigh, 1989). Two years later, standards were passed for lead;[4] and then for nitrogen dioxide[5] in 1985. These gave the DoE an impetus for systematically reviewing its framework for air emission controls (DoE, 1982, p.7; Haigh, 1989, p.191).

Another significant piece of EC legislation was the June 1984 air framework Directive for combating air pollution from industrial plant.[6] The Directive provided a framework whereby Member States had to give prior approval to new industrial plant and to substantial changes to existing plant listed in the Directive. In order for operators to secure authorisation, the regulator had to be satisfied the operator's plant design or change had:

1   Taken all preventive measures against air emissions, including use of the Best Available Technology Not Entailing Excessive Cost (BATNEEC).

2   That no significant air pollution will occur.

3   No emission limits will be breached.

4   Air quality standards will be taken into account.

Applications for authorisation and the decision of the regulator would be placed on a public register. A DoE civil servant said in interview that this Directive introduced the 'big conceptual change': industry would have to publicly demonstrate compliance and the Inspector would authorise on this basis. He contrasted this with the traditional British approach of, 'I'm going to build a new plant and I'll go and ask the Alkali Inspector what I've got to do and he'll tell me what I do and I'll do it'. The industrial pollution policy community would have to operate new rules of the game.

The Directive's origins can be traced to the emerging acid rain issue of the early 1980s, particularly in Germany[7] (Haigh, 1989, pp.224-226). The framework Directive was dwarfed by wrangling over a subsequent 'daughter' Directive intended to tackle sulphur emissions from Large Combustion Plants. Other daughter Directives were intended which could establish fixed emission limits for other substances,[8] and there was provision for the EC to stipulate suitable measurement and assessment techniques. The air framework Directive and any daughter Directives would require incorporation into British law and practice, including a degree of regulatory transparency only recently rejected by the Government (DoE, 1982). EC legislation was forcing British pollution policy development.[9]

The British tradition and the EC: different rules of the game

The Directive's provision for creating fixed emission limits, the public register of applications, and initial attempts to seek the 'state of the art' control technology (replaced with BATNEEC in the final Directive) clashed with Britain's flexible, co-operative, and consensual approach to industrial air pollution. The Directive changed the rules of the game for controlling pollution.

Though pollution control was still viewed as a technical problem, the different rules of the game did reflect a difference in the EC's appreciative system concerning pollution itself. The British system of pollution control understood pollution as an 'effect' caused by a substance. A substance became a pollutant only when scientifically linked to a detrimental effect, as elaborated by the then DoE Chief Scientist (Holdgate, 1979).

In contrast, the EC viewed 'pollution as the simple presence of undesirable substances' (Skea and Boehmer-Christiansen, 1991, p.15). The EC interpretation followed the 'Precautionary Principle' (von Moltke, 1988, p.58; Boehmer-Christiansen, 1994), which suggests preventive pollution control measures in anticipation of probable environmental damage, and often in advance of certain knowledge of cause and effect (see O'Riordan and Cameron, 1994). Such a precautionary stance implied a more interventionist approach to pollution than the 'scientific' philosophy traditional to the British system (O'Riordan, 1992, p.306). Britain practised flexibility over standards to limit effects, based in part on the local receiving environment; in Europe the tendency was more toward uniform emission standards for precautionary reasons, but also because this does not upset trading barriers (Haigh, 1989, p.20-22).

In the Third of its five yearly Action Programmes on the Environment, the EC committed itself to stabilise and gradually reduce emissions of pollutants (EC, 1983). Britain's domestic industrial air pollution policy community was faced with intervention by a policy actor (EC) possessing authoritative resources sufficient to do so, and operating by different rules of the game (formally fixed emission limits) based upon a contrasting appreciative system. By the mid-1980s such a prospect was becoming a concern for British industry.

Industry becomes an issue network member

Industry's concern for some reform of industrial air pollution was threefold. Firstly, more enlightened firms and associations were accepting the need for some sort of environmental management, and were prepared to see legislative change to underscore this effort. Second was recognition of a fall in public faith in the regulator and industry's environmental performance: the policy community was being challenged. Compounding this was the third source of concern, the 'Europeanisation' of UK regulatory practice. Industry did not wish to lose the participation in industrial air pollution policy it had enjoyed in the policy community. It became an issue network member, seeking defensive reform of policy which maintained its involvement, restored credibility for UK pollution control and made its case more effectively in Brussels.

The industrial appreciative system: from issue resistance to issue management

The 1980s witnessed an increase in the sophistication of industrial organisations toward pollution problems. A former UK Director of the International Chamber of Commerce characterised this as a transition from dismissing problems and resisting pollution controls, to a desire to ensure controls were flexible and to manage environmentally driven

92

changes on terms suitable to business (Wyburd, 1992; see also Fischer and Schot, 1993).

At its 1984 Annual Conference the CBI debated the environment for the first time.[10] They passed a resolution acknowledging the 'considerable' investment industry made in abating pollution, but it 'must recognise the weight of current environmental pressures and do far more to ensure that its case is better known and understood by the general public' (CBI, 1984, p.56). Some business leaders[11] argued that overcoming environmental problems was becoming, at worst, essential to business survival and, at best, presented new business opportunities (Wyburd, 1992, p.206).

The chemicals sector was particularly vulnerable to environmental pressure. The 1980s saw some high profile events which harmed public trust in the industry. There was the methyl isocyanate leak from Union Carbide's Bhopal plant which killed as many as 10,000 people (Morehouse, 1994), pollution of the Rhine in 1986 following a fire at the Sandoz chemical plant, and the discovery that CFCs were causing the huge ozone hole above Antarctica (Nilsson and Pitt, 1994, p.13). In a 1986 opinion poll[12] the chemical industry ranked eighteenth out of twenty two in terms of public favourability. The same poll found 65 per cent of the public 'very concerned' about chemical pollution (Liardet, 1991).

In response, larger chemical firms were beginning to establish environmental policies and produce environmental reports. In 1989 the Chemical Industries Association (CIA) launched its 'Responsible Care' programme aimed at demonstrating the industry's green credentials.[13] To what extent these limited changes signalled effective environmental management is not the issue here.[14] Their significance for this analysis is that industrial leaders were conscious of environmental pressures and the importance of being able to respond and manage the issue. 'Bad practice has made controls inevitable and given ammunition to those who want to create more' (CBI, 1986, p.9). They were building up organisational resources in order to maintain political legitimacy and pre-empt pressure on the pollution control policy community.

The CBI policy shift on the release of environmental information was indicative of industrial leaders adapting their 'rules of the game' to the new context. In 1979 it believed environmental information to be the property of the firm, who had a legitimate right to limit its dissemination- since such technical information was open to 'misinterpretation' by 'non-experts' (CBI, 1979). By 1986, it was advising firms to proactively release information 'on the side of as full disclosure as possible', since misleading and inadequate information given under pressure engenders distrust from others (CBI, 1986).

The CBI had also shifted policy toward the Inspectorate and the HSC/E. Industrial leaders were increasingly calling for credibility restoring investment in the Inspectorate and its return to the DoE, where its technical expertise could be more effectively used as a resource to defend UK pollution policy from European encroachment.

Defending the British industrial air pollution policy community

Industrial leaders were becoming concerned about growth in EC environmental legislation. Industry generally preferred the flexible, client-regulator relationship characteristic of domestic industrial air pollution policy (ENDS, 1986a). They were, after all, partners in an exclusive industrial air pollution policy community.

In 1980 the CBI had issued a policy statement in support of contemporary practice, including close consultation, limiting statutory constraints to those which were absolutely necessary and which did not inhibit industrial development, and all based upon good scientific knowledge and practice (CBI, 1980). In 1986 industry provided a number of reasons why it supported the Inspectorate. Amongst the benefits of policy community membership were: guiding management through complex legislation; disseminating pollution control practices; providing an impartial source of advice for reassuring the workforce, trade unions and local communities about risks; influencing local authorities on planning issues; and as a defence against the encroachment of EC standards (Efficiency Scrutiny, 1986, pp.94-95).

Intervention from outside authorities such as the EC could detrimentally disrupt the policy community with unsympathetic, uniform pollution control requirements. The CBI were encouraging members to 'be aware of local, domestic and international pressures, particularly those originating from the EC' (CBI, 1986). The EC was a new policy actor with the authority to intervene in the industrial air pollution policy community. Industry felt the autonomy and tradition of this policy community needed defending.

The CIA were moved to report, 'Our industry is particularly vulnerable to any loss of public confidence in the management of environmental issues ... We have therefore told the DoE forcibly that we are becoming increasingly concerned that the present fragmented system of controls is not sufficiently responsive to current needs' (quoted in ENDS, 1986b, pp.4-5). An article in an earlier 'ENDS Report' quoted a spokesman from a 'leading' chemical operator arguing, 'there is a very urgent need to get the enforcement of our air pollution laws on a more effective basis. If we fail to do so the legislation itself will fall into disrepute, and the UK will be totally incapable of defending itself against pressures from Brussels' (ENDS, 1986a, p.4).

Concern involved events external and internal to the policy community: the British system of flexible pollution control based upon 'scientifically justified' criteria[15] appeared under threat from EC legislation; and the policy community upholding the British tradition was facing a crisis of public confidence.

Criticism of the industrial air pollution policy community

The 1980s saw the Inspectorate suffering falling inspection rates, a lack of resources, low morale and recruitment problems (Skea and Boehmer-Christiansen, 1991, p.177). Industry feared this was undermining the Inspectorate and the credibility of the British system of industrial air pollution control.

The Inspectorate was finding it increasingly difficult to recruit staff up to its full complement of Inspectors. There would 'have to be a re-assessment of the level of surveillance of the scheduled processes and of the depth of response to complaints, incidents, and requests' (HSE, 1986). The number of Inspectors in 1986 had dropped by 20 per cent compared to 1979, and Inspection visits were 40 per cent lower than their peak in 1977 (see Table 3.2). The time taken to update BPM Notes (important evidence of UK standards) was lengthening (see Table 3.1).

This was at a time when the public credibility of the Inspectorate was low.[16] In an interview with a DoE civil servant it was acknowledged that the approach practised by the Inspectorate had fallen into disrepute. 'The educative approach slipped into the Alkali Inspector almost being taken onto the Board as it were; which then prevented the Inspector standing back and taking the public view ... It was clearly identified as something we needed to do something about. We needed a system that was more open, it had all got to look too cosy to the public'. A consensus was building that change was needed. The question was whether this would be imposed by the EC or done domestically, and what form should it take?

Dynamic conservatism: industry lobbies for defensive reforms

These events were concerning industrial leaders. Managers from two UK based, multi-national chemical operators explained in interview that their firms had lobbied Ministers about the future of industrial pollution policy. Informal talks had taken place both with the firms themselves and through committees of the CBI and CIA (confirmed in DoE, 1988a, p.23). The DoE had also held consultative meetings with industry in November 1987 to consider air pollution control laws (ENDS, 1987a, p.19).

One interviewed operator explained changes were being sought because they were 'hoping for better public acceptability of the chemical industry, and assessing how much better we had to be to earn that acceptance ... We wanted a change in legislation that would boost public confidence in the chemical industry'. Such a view had been mooted at the CIA's 1987 annual dinner. Their President, Allen Rae, Chairman of Ciba-Geigy, told members, 'Any incident at any plant, while obviously felt most by those whose factory it is or those who are directly affected by or suffer from it, is without doubt today a problem for the whole industry, and none of us can afford to sit back and think it is someone else's problem. Ecology and safety must be the first charge on profitability' (ENDS, 1987b, p.8).

Several of the large firms interviewed welcomed some legislative change because they were investing in improved environmental management, and didn't want it undermined by the poor performance of other operators.[17] Nor did they want their activities undermined by either a regulatory system lacking credibility or one which imposed unsympathetic standards that were discordant with their efforts.

In the 1980s industrial leaders came to realise the significance of environmental issues. This altered their appreciative system to the extent that they realised positive measures were necessary to maintain a regulatory regime with perhaps some transparency, but otherwise practising preferred rules of the game. Some industrial leaders became involved in the issue network, seeking to restore the acceptability of industrial activity through more credible regulations in keeping with the 'scientific' and flexible British tradition. This included returning the technically expert Inspectorate to the DoE, where it could provide advice on policy developments, particularly those in Brussels. Their membership of the industrial air pollution policy community and economic position secured industry access to the DoE and membership of the issue network, where they could press this case for reform.

Dispute over control of the inspectorate

The Inspectorate had never been happy with its inclusion in the HSE in 1975; it felt it belonged in the DoE (Efficiency Scrutiny, 1986, p.21). 'Recognising the anxiety that exists on this question of organisation' (DoE, 1982), the government produced a Memorandum of Understanding. This Memorandum between the DoE and the HSC/E formalised the responsibilities each had with respect to industrial air pollution control. The HSC/E would remain responsible for implementing air pollution control legislation and be responsible to Environment Ministers in this respect, who in turn were responsible for general air pollution policy.

Significantly, the Inspectorate was to remain distinct within the HSE and its Chief Inspector was to sit on the HSE's management board. Until the 1980s the Inspectorate continued to enjoy considerable autonomy within this arrangement.

The HSE interferes in the industrial air pollution issue network

Contrary to the Memorandum, some incorporation of the Inspectorate within HSE did take place. At first this was simply to review the Inspectorate's district boundaries with a view to harmonising them with the HSE's Factory Inspectorate[18] (HSE, 1984, p.1). The review was followed by a programme of co-locating the Inspectorate in HSE buildings. By 1986 eleven of the Inspectorate's twelve offices were co-located (DoE, 1986a). But further incorporation was taking place which caused anxiety amongst the Inspectorate and the DoE regarding the former's distinct identity.

In 1984 the Inspectorate's sampling teams were transferred to the HSE's general Field Scientific Support Unit, supporting all HSE Inspectorates (ENDS, 1985a, p.). In February 1985 the retiring Chief Inspector, Dr Lesley Reed, was replaced by Rod Perriman. However, as an Inspector recalled in interview, there were disputes over grading which seemed to imply the new Chief Inspector was to be more junior than was traditional, which in turn had implications for his position on the HSE management board.

Earlier, in October 1984, John Rimmington, the HSE's Director General, had proposed the Inspectorate be incorporated with elements of the Factory Inspectorate, the Nuclear Installations Inspectorate, and the Major Hazards Assessment Unit in a specialist Division of HSE (ENDS, 1985a, p.3; HSC, 1987, p.26). This new Technology and Air Pollution Division was created in September 1985 under the HSE's Technical, Medical and Scientific Group, to the concern of the DoE, the Inspectorate and others.

This organisational integration threatened the autonomy of the Inspectorate. The HSC/E wanted more control over industrial pollution (ENDS, 1985b). Industrial safety and pollution policy networks were becoming enmeshed precisely at a time when the DoE clearly needed to exercise domain over industrial air pollution policy owing to authoritative intervention from the EC. The HSE's moves threatened to complicate air

97

pollution reforms being considered by the DoE (see later) and were degrading access to the technical resource embodied in the Inspectorate - which concerned industrial lobbyists too. As a DoE civil servant pointed out in interview, 'the DoE, needless to say, firmly believed it [the Inspectorate] should be in DoE'.

The issue network manoeuvres for DoE control of the Inspectorate

In mid-1984 the National Society for Clean Air (NSCA) and the CBI had both lobbied Ministers to see the Inspectorate back at the DoE (ENDS, 1986c, p.3). Environment Minister Patrick Jenkin wrote to Employment Minister Tom King in September 1984 to express his concern over events. William Waldegrave, also an Environment Minister, had taken the CBI's cue and used it as a platform for his ideas for an environmental protection agency (ENDS, 1986c, p.3; O'Riordan and Weale, 1989, p.287). An Inspector explained in his interview: 'This came at a time when environmental issues were beginning to rise more to the surface (1985/86) in Europe. The CBI and industry was aware of what was happening in other countries. Together it stiffened DoE's resolve to get the Inspectorate back'.

The DoE was facing EC driven change to industrial pollution policy at a time when the Inspectorate faced greater incorporation into an HSE out of direct DoE control. Industry and the DoE wished to see the Inspectorate's technical expertise returned to the DoE, but they lacked the authority to reclaim the Inspectorate.

Amidst this Whitehall dispute over Inspectorate control a policy actor intervened in the issue network in December 1985 with sufficient authority resources to determine the outcome of the wrangle and prompt the creation of HMIP. This was a Cabinet Office Efficiency Scrutiny team established specifically to investigate industrial pollution and safety. After the build up of various pressures for reform (European and domestic), it was this Efficiency Scrutiny which finally triggered a switch to integrated pollution controls.

The Cabinet Office Efficiency Scrutiny enters the issue network

Smith (1993, p.98) suggests the membership and integration dimensions of a policy network are influential in its ability to withstand external pressures for policy change, such as that coming from the EC in this study. Small memberships with a strong consensus, he argues, can withstand a great deal of pressure - such as the air policy community in the 1970s. The likelihood of external pressure creating internal tension increases with membership and/or as consensus weakens. There may be conflicting prescriptions for managing pressure and the policy network can break down. Resilience is further reduced if membership includes more than one policy actor with political authority, owing to conflict between the different decision-making institutions of those authoritative members. Each may draw in other groups for support, and the network loosens as it shifts from a de-politicising entity to a politicising mode in the face of external pressure.

This latter instance occurred during IPC formulation as the HSE increasingly became involved in the air pollution issue network. Conflict between the DoE and the HSE (under the Department of Employment) emerged concerning their respective authority over the Inspectorate. This complicated issue network attempts to manage EC pressure. Other members in the network wished to see the Inspectorate returned to the DoE. Members had to turn to the more senior authority of the government to resolve the issue. The government's Cabinet Office Efficiency Scrutiny intervention clearly affected policy output by recommending integrated reforms to industrial pollution policy - the DoE had hitherto considered air reform alone (see later).

Cabinet Office Efficiency Scrutinies into Whitehall departments were introduced by Mrs Thatcher in 1979. She appointed first Lord Rayner of Marks and Spencer and later Sir Robin Ibbs of ICI to bring efficiencies and a private sector management ethos to the civil service (Hennessey, 1987; Collins, 1987).

Efficiency Scrutinies had two objectives: first, to conduct small scale scrutinies into specific activities in order to remove administrative overlap and duplication, and to demonstrate to staff (who were included on the scrutiny team) that efficiency improvements could be made; and second, to build upon these small improvements to make wider reforms credible within the civil service (Metcalfe and Richards, 1987, p.7). Being in the Cabinet Office with Prime Ministerial backing gave an Efficiency Scrutiny authority within Whitehall and ensured its recommendations were listened to by a sympathetic, de-regulatory[19] government (Metcalfe and Richards, 1987, p.9).

Metcalfe and Richards (1987, p.11) suggest Ministerial and departmental support was won for these inquisitorial scrutinies by presenting them as an opportunity for departments to get to grips with long-standing problems, such as the future of the industrial air pollution Inspectorate. The solution of inter-departmental conflicts are an official function of Cabinet (Hennesey, 1986, p.5). DoE pressure on the Prime Minister for organisational reform was greeted as an opportunity for an Efficiency Scrutiny and 'rationalisation' (Owens, 1989, p.185). An interviewed Inspector felt, 'I think somewhere a decision to push for a return of the Inspectorate and the formation of an integrated Inspectorate had been taken in principle, and that the Cabinet Office inquiry was the means to getting it going'. Formally, it was a joint initiative between Employment and Environment Ministers, but had been 'launched by the Cabinet Office' (O'Riordan and Weale, 1989, p.288).

The Efficiency Scrutiny was to review the working arrangements between inspection bodies responsible for industrial pollution and safety. These bodies were: the Industrial Air Pollution Inspectorate (IAPI - in HSE); the Hazardous Waste Inspectorate (HWI - in DoE, monitoring local authority controls on landfill disposal); the new water pollution staff (in DoE, controlling Water Authority discharges and Appeals against Water Authority imposed controls on other dischargers); the Radiochemical Inspectorate (RCI - in DoE, controlling the holding and disposal of radioactive substances); and the Nuclear Installations Inspectorate (NII - in HSE, handling employee and public safety at nuclear sites). The Scrutiny's objective was to seek improvements yielding a better service for Ministers and industry.

The Efficiency Scrutiny recommended that a unified pollution Inspectorate be created by amalgamating the first four of the above Inspectorates (Efficiency Scrutiny, 1986). Such an Inspectorate could, they argued, bring regulatory and policy improvements.

Some of these improvements accorded with the RCEP's observations ten years earlier: a unified Inspectorate would facilitate the development of the BPEO principle, with all its benefits to the overall control of pollution. Despite assurances from the government in 1982, the Efficiency Scrutiny found little evidence of co-operation between the Inspectorates to ensure optimum multi-media control of releases (1986, p.13).

The Efficiency Scrutiny also believed a unified Inspectorate would provide better technical advice on policy. This would 'increase the effectiveness of the UK input to the development of new pollution policy and standards within the EC' (1986, p.12).

The Efficiency Scrutiny did not specify which Department should be responsible for the new Inspectorate. Their recommendation that it should provide technical advice to environmental policy makers implied it should be in the DoE. One Inspector explained that 'the way the [Efficiency Scrutiny's] questionnaire[20] came out, it was so obviously going to lead to the conclusion that the Inspectorate's relationships within HSE were minor compared with its relationships externally'. The tenor of the report clearly favoured the DoE (O'Riordan and Weale, 1987, p.288).

However, the environmental benefits of unified pollution control were eclipsed by the Scrutiny's cost-effectiveness arguments. The aforementioned improvements were nothing new, having been raised by the RCEP in 1976. The Efficiency Scrutiny added more compelling reasons for change and were in the authoritative position to get them heard by Cabinet level decision makers.

The Efficiency Scrutiny believed there were several areas where value for money could be increased. First, by comparing the air Inspectorate's work with its smaller Scottish counterpart, the Scrutiny thought the air Inspectorate could meet its functions with three-quarters the resources it currently deployed. Inspection visit frequency (already falling) could be reduced without detriment to control standards, argued the Efficiency Scrutiny. In a unified Inspectorate the quarter saving on existing resources could be diverted to controlling water and land pollution - fields to which the air Inspectorate's industrial process knowledge could soon be contributing (1986, pp.23-25). Regulation through a single, unified Inspectorate would also ease the regulatory burden on industry by providing a one-stop-shop for pollution controls (Efficiency Scrutiny, 1986).

Further efficiencies were proposed by suggesting emissions monitoring be contracted out under competitive tendering (1986, p.25). Finally, the Efficiency Scrutiny considered the Inspectorates well placed to identify opportunities for reducing the regulatory burden on industry. 'We recommend that the Chief Inspectors be given a responsibility for reviewing the need to continue existing regulation and reporting the results to senior management at regular intervals, with a view to eliminating any unnecessary burdens on industry and to avoid any unproductive use of Inspectorate resources' (Efficiency Scrutiny, 1986). The Efficiency Scrutiny finally secured government commitment to integrated reforms.

The creation of HMIP

Recommendations for the introduction of competitive tendering[21] and scope for deregulation came straight from the Thatcherite lexicon.[22] The Efficiency Scrutiny recommendations identified an opportunity for administrative rationalisation rather than the creation of a new administrative system (McCormick, 1991, p.59).

The recommendations were in step with the government's deregulatory appreciative system, following rules of the game which the Conservatives were trying to establish throughout the networks of Whitehall. Thus one type of exogenous factor behind HMIP's creation was a deregulatory ideology. Moreover, with a general election approaching, in which opposition parties were favouring new environmental agencies, unification provided an easy opportunity for the government to build 'green' political capital (O'Riordan and Weale, 1989, p.288).[23]

So it was a combination of exogenous factors - ideology and knowledge (Efficiency Scrutiny, 1986) - which succeeded in changing the industrial air pollution policy community where knowledge alone had previously failed (RCEP, 1976). The environmental justifications given by the Efficiency Scrutiny were nothing new. They echoed the recommendations of the RCEP ten years earlier, yet the Efficiency Scrutiny was acted upon.

The deregulatory arguments and Cabinet Office authority of the Efficiency Scrutiny meant the DoE gained stewardship of policy in a way it was itself unable to with its planned Clean Air Bill (see later). On 7th August 1986, with the agreement of the Prime Minister, Nicholas Ridley the Secretary of State for the Environment, announced the government's intention to create a unified pollution Inspectorate: HMIP, formed on 1st April 1987 (DoE, 1986b).

HMIP was an amalgamation of the HWI, the IAPI, the RCI and a newly formed water pollution staff. The immediate task for HMIP was to alloy itself into a single, unified Inspectorate. This was to take over two years, with a unified structure emerging in October 1989. Up to and beyond this date HMIP pursued its separate, inherited regulatory functions - until the phased introduction of IPC beginning in 1991. Following the statement about HMIP's creation, the DoE announced plans to give HMIP a legislative basis for an integrated approach to pollution control (DoE, 1986a).

Creating HMIP did not dissipate all external pressures upon the issue network. EC legislation still needed implementing. The DoE had been formulating procedural reforms to industrial air pollution policy and released a proposed Clean Air Bill for consultation in December 1986. These proposals were not taken up by government, as the next section illustrates. This suggests the government was influenced by the deregulatory potential of 'integration' as much as any desire to improve the transparency or environmental effectiveness of industrial air pollution policy. Nevertheless, some of the procedural reforms proposed by the DoE were eventually carried forward into IPC legislation, hence discussion of them is necessary.

Policy formulation at the Department of the Environment

Alongside the dispute over executive control of the Inspectorate, EC legislation was forcing the DoE to review industrial air pollution policy. Like some industrial leaders, the DoE also perceived a decline in public confidence in existing arrangements. Their responsibility for policy meant the DoE became a focal issue network member. They enjoyed industrial support for reform. However, as analysis in this section and the next demonstrates, they were dependent upon government authority when it came to carrying through policy reform. The DoE failed to win government support for its initial air pollution reforms.

The environment had been a minor concern for the Department of the Environment ever since its creation[24] by the Heath Government in 1970. In February 1989, only 10 per cent of the DoE's staff were dealing with environmental protection issues (Friends of the Earth, 1989). Housing and local government have been the Department's dominant functions.

In 1984 the RCEP reported their worries that environmental policy within the DoE lacked sufficiently 'distinctive status and stature', operating 'on too slender a basis' (RCEP, 1984, pp.61-62). With 330 staff at the DoE's Environmental Protection Group in April 1995 (ENDS, 1995b, p.15), levels remain similar to those in 1980. Thus environmental protection has historically resided in the backwaters of government.[25]

EC driven policy development: a proposed Clean Air Bill

In 1982 the DoE, whilst stating on behalf of government its satisfaction with the contemporary regulatory regime, did begin reviewing elements of its pollution control policy. The air quality Directives and negotiations concerning the air framework Directive had made apparent to the DoE the need to review its air pollution policy (DoE, 1982, p.7).

That review culminated in the issue of a consultation paper in December 1986 (DoE, 1986c). In it were proposals for rationalising and updating air pollution legislation through a new Clean Air Bill.[26] A large part of the proposed Bill related to introducing a prior approval system for control by local authorities of less complex and less polluting industrial processes - who until then had had to rely on post-facto nuisance measures under the Public Health Acts (DoE, 1986c). These industrial processes formed a 'middle tier' owing to the inadequacy of existing powers or because the current list of scheduled processes[27] was 'inconsistent with emerging EC legislation' (DoE, 1986c, para. 10).

Other proposals were included in the Clean Air Bill for harmonising Inspectorate procedures with EC requirement (DoE, 1986c, para. 11).

The DoE had 'sought to identify ways in which, without abandoning the fundamental principles of the UK system, the law might be adapted to take account of existing and prospective Community legislation' (DoE, 1986c, para. 11).

The proposed legislative changes were fivefold. First, it was necessary to enact primary legislation to allow the Secretary of State to set statutory air quality standards. Second, similar powers would be needed for creating statutory emission limits. Both were possibilities under EC legislation. However, it was the three remaining changes that would have more immediate impact upon Inspectorate procedures.

The DoE wished to maintain the BPM principle, but the third change proposed to clarify its breadth of application and make more explicit its meaning such that it accorded with the EC terminology of Best Available Technology Not Entailing Excessive Cost (BATNEEC).

Fourthly, a consent procedure would replace the existing registration system. These consents would record the main elements of BPM agreed between operator and Inspector. The DoE argued items in the consent, such as emission limits, should not be legally binding since this would entail unnecessary rigidity of control. Flexibility and consideration for local circumstances should be maintained - rules favoured by both policy community members.

Finally, the consents should be available for public inspection, though the precise nature of information which should be included was left open by the DoE for comment from respondents to the consultation paper.

Some transparency over pollution controls was beginning to be accepted into the DoE's appreciative system. Like industry, they now believed that too much confidentiality was a source of criticism and could undermine public confidence (DoE, 1984, p.5; 1986d, p.2). Regulations had finally been passed in July 1985 enabling provision in the Control of Pollution Act, 1974 for the creation of public registers of water discharge consents. The EC Air Framework Directive made greater transparency inevitable for air pollution control. However, the government still wished to limit public disclosure in order not to 'undermine the proper relationship between the pollution control authorities and industry' (DoE, 1984, p.7).[28] The issue network's appreciative system was willing to concede some transparency if it meant the maintenance of its core value of flexible standards.

The DoE lacks the resources to get its Clean Air Bill

The DoE's 1986 consultation paper was issued during a period of growing industrial receptivity to some reform of the British system of industrial pollution control. EC legislation was requiring changes to British industrial air pollution practice. It was recognised by the DoE (1984), the RCEP (1984) and industrial leaders that air pollution policy needed defensive reform which would maintain its traditional flexibility.

Over 400 organisations responded to the consultation paper and 'there was widespread approval for the main proposals' (DoE, 1988b, p.2). To carry through its reforms the DoE had to persuade government that industrial air pollution policy was a sector worth allotting Parliamentary time.

However, the DoE's environmental protection team lacked the authority to win the intended Parliamentary time in the 1988/89 session (DoE, 1988b, p.2). Issues of higher political priority crowded out the Parliamentary timetable with legislation for the Poll Tax, the National Curriculum for schools, a paving Bill for water privatisation, and so on. Failure to secure the Clean Air Bill meant the Secretary of State for the Environment had to issue several stop-gap Regulations[29] in March 1989 in order to satisfy EC pressure for their Directives to be more clearly implemented in UK law (ENDS, 1989, p.26).

So there was a lack of political support from government for procedural reform of industrial air pollution policy. An issue network existed in support of reforms - policy community members and the DoE - driven by EC pressure and to a lesser extent by public opinion (fanned by NGO campaigning). That is, the issue network was responding to challenges external to the issue network. But the issue network membership lacked the political and authority resources to secure the legislative reforms it needed. Reform would have to wait until the government could be influenced into providing Parliamentary time for legislation. Moreover, the creation of HMIP meant the reforms would now have to be for an integrated pollution control system.

Incremental IPC policy formulation

The formulation stage of the IPC policy process was incremental, following no overall strategy and deferring many substantive issues to the implementation stage. The decisive factor in adopting an integrated policy for industrial pollution control was one of bureaucratic efficiency rather than environmental effectiveness. Once this decision had been made, the DoE had to formulate a framework for IPC. It was an opportunity for them to carry through policy formulation work done earlier. A DoE civil servant said in interview that a large proportion of the groundwork for IPC had been done in their 1986 consultation on air pollution control, which had itself respected the air framework Directive.

Domestically, the government had decided upon an 'integrative' reform to the pollution control system in creating HMIP. Andrew Campbell, a civil servant who worked on the subsequent IPC legislation, pointed out that:

> Once that decision was made, the detail of the legislation had to be fully compatible with existing European law. Two pieces of legislation were of particular importance - the Air Framework Directive of 1984 and the Water Framework Directive for dangerous substances 1976. The important point here is that the detail of the British IPC system had to respect European law and became in consequence and in large part an amalgamation of those two Directives.
> (Campbell, 1991)

The structure of IPC legislation is presented in Table 4.2 alongside the two framework Directives.

So the EC was an important policy actor in that it had to be accommodated in policy formulation. Indeed, the 'integrative' BPEO element of IPC legislation is contained in a single sub-section of the Environmental Protection Act, 1990.[30] BPEO has received scant treatment during IPC implementation (see chapter 6; ENDS, 1995a, pp.22-25).

In their 1988 IPC consultation paper, the DoE acknowledged three origins to IPC (DoE, 1988, pp.22-23). Analysis in this chapter has enabled an identification of the roles played by these acknowledged origins:

1   The Efficiency Scrutiny (deregulatory ideology influenced the shift to 'integration').

2   The European Community (new institutional authority shaped IPC regulations).

3   The Royal Commission on Environmental Pollution (provided legitimating justification).

However, the DoE lacked the authority to put IPC onto a legal footing. They still needed the authority resource of the government in order to legislate the necessary procedural changes.

Table 4.2
Comparison of IPC legislative features with component EC
Directives

IPC regulatory feature (1990)	Air Framework Directive (1984)	Water Framework Directive (1976)
Prescribes processes and substances for regulation.	Processes and substances.	Substances.
Public register.	Yes.	No.
Industrial operators must use BATNEEC.	Best Available Technology Not Entailing Excessive Cost.	Best Technical Means Available.
Existing processes must conform to an upgrading timetable.	Yes.	Yes.
Authorisation conditions binding.	Yes.	Yes.
Authorisations to be subject to periodic review.	No.	Yes.
Operators must apply for Authorisation prior to operating their process.	Operators to apply for process Authorisation (including process description).	Authorisation needed to discharge substances.

Parliamentary time is secured

The DoE needed to win government support for their proposed IPC legislation. It had not been long since they had failed to secure Parliamentary time for the Clean Air Bill. Since then the government's general appreciative system had become more favourable to environmental issues and Parliamentary time was found eventually.

The year 1988 saw the Prime Minister's 'conversion'[31] to concern for environmental issues. In September and October 1988 she made two speeches, one to the Royal Society and the other to her Party's conference, in which a commitment to sustainable development and environmental protection was revealed. In her enthusiasm Mrs Thatcher called an international ozone conference in London for the following July. July 1989 also saw the appointment of Chris Patten as Secretary of State for the Environment. John McCormick, who worked for environmental groups[32] in the 1980s, wrote how Patten 'was generally accepted by the environmental lobby as having strong sympathies with the objectives of the lobby' (1991, pp.60-61).

Not unrelated, the late 1980s also saw another episode[33] of sufficiently widespread public concern for the environment to capture corresponding media and political attention. The environment ascended the political agenda to the extent that the Green Party won 15 per cent of the national vote in the June 1989 European elections.

In this context, the DoE was able to secure government support where it had earlier failed. As a DoE civil servant recalled in interview, 'Margaret Thatcher's famous speech was one thing. That had a quite extraordinary affect on projecting the environment. Our then Secretary of State was Chris Patten who was a strong personality and rode the political wave for all it was worth and got us a big slot'. The government agreed to allot Parliamentary space for the 1989/90 session to an Environmental Protection Bill.

The importance of the government's authority resource to the IPC policy process

McCormick divided government environmental policy into two phases - before and after the Prime Ministers' speeches of 1988 - 'little was done during her first two administrations to reform or amend the administration of environmental management' (1991, p.58). The second phase provided the DoE with an opportunity to draw up legislation for its reform of industrial pollution control.

It is clear from this episode, and the one which created HMIP, that government is an important policy actor. In the IPC instance, government controlled an important authority resource (legislation-making) which the issue network needed in order to proceed toward IPC implementation. 'Although the legislative process may not have policy-making significance, it remains of considerable political significance as a means of legitimation'[34] (Kingdom, 1991, p.292). In this case the DoE needed the legislative process to grant HMIP with the authority to implement IPC. The Parliamentary legislative process acted as a conduit between formulation and implementation stages of the policy process.

108

Government's intervention in a policy network must, by definition, rest upon a resource interdependency. Its enabling legislative resource is secured if the policy network is perceived by them as providing a political resource: the solution to an issue of political significance to government.

The DoE were unable to secure Parliamentary time in 1986/87 for their air pollution reforms because the government, under strong leadership, had no interest in the matter. Yet HMIP was still created. This was because the Cabinet Office Efficiency Scrutiny recommendations resonated with government ideology, as manifest in general policies of bureaucratic efficiency and reducing regulatory burdens. Once agreed, creating HMIP proved a measure which was relatively easy to carry through since it did not require Parliamentary time.

Circumstances changed over the following few years. The political saliency of environmental issues grew. A populist Prime Minister declared a green conversion. Industrial leaders were sympathetic to reform. The need to promulgate EC legislation was more pressing A mixture of network characteristics - a consensus for reform amongst a membership of key industrial pollution policy actors - along with a buoyant context - mass environmental concern - meant the DoE were able to draw government intervention in the environmental protection issue network generally, not just industrial pollution control. Parliamentary time was secured for environmental legislation.

The importance of the government's legislative resource is reflected in the contents of the Environmental Protection Bill itself. The Parliamentary slot, explained a civil servant, provided the DoE's environmental policy directorates with an opportunity to legislate many policies which they had been formulating.

Alongside the IPC reform of industrial pollution was a new system for controlling disposal of solid waste, enhanced nuisance provisions against noise, stiffer sanctions for litter louts and duties to sweep the streets, reform of countryside institutions, provision for the control of genetically modified organisms, the identification and control of dogs, controls for straw burning, and even measures to tackle the abandoned supermarket trolley problem! The Shadow Environment Minister, Brian Gould, used this character of the Bill to partisan effect when debating it in Parliament:

The Bill is disappointing because it is little more than a rag-bag of measures drawn from disparate sources, many of which have been dusted down and brought to life again simply to be cobbled together to give [the government] a lick of green paint and the impression of action and cohesion.

(Official Journal, Parliamentary Debates, Column 50, 15/1/1990)

IPC formed the first Part of the Bill, which was enacted on 1st November 1990. The DoE had formally consulted on IPC in July 1988, informal consultation with industry having preceded this (reflecting their important policy community status). The legislative framework for IPC dusted off some earlier proposals from the DoE, but was mostly influenced by EC imperative. Cost recovery charging was included (whereby the costs of administering the regulations would be recovered through financial charges on the operators being regulated), in line with government policy.

Government also influenced the pace of implementation. Several of the civil servants interviewed attributed the tight timetable for starting IPC to the desire of Ministers. Implementation was to begin on 1st April 1991, allowing only a few months for enabling Regulations to be passed prescribing processes and adding detail to regulatory procedures (what information is required in an Application, for example).

The stated objectives of IPC were as follows (DoE, 1988a, p.1; DoE, 1993, pp.3-4):

1   To develop an approach to pollution control that considers releases from industrial processes to all media in the context of the effect on the environment as a whole.

2   To improve the efficiency and effectiveness of pollution controls on industry.

3   To streamline and strengthen the regulatory system, clarify the roles and responsibilities of HMIP, other regulatory authorities, and the firms they regulate.

4   To contain the burden on industry, particularly by providing for a 'one stop shop' on pollution control for the potentially most seriously polluting processes.

5   To maintain public confidence in the regulatory system through a clear and transparent system that is accessible and easy to understand and is clear and simple in operation.

6   To provide a flexible framework that is capable of responding both to changing pollution abatement technology and to new knowledge on the effects of pollutants.

7   To provide a means to fulfil certain international obligations relating to environmental protection.

IPC and formal rules of the game

IPC introduced formality to regulation in several respects. There was greater formality concerning procedures and accompanying documentation. Operators would have to submit applications, HMIP would need an invoicing system to recover administrative costs from operators, applications had to be sent to statutory consultees for comment, authorisations would need issuing and so on. The division of regulatory responsibility between regulator and regulated was more formally defined. Finally, IPC was far more transparent, opening up regulatory standards to public scrutiny. All of these features implied IPC implementation would be more formal than its air pollution predecessor. The contrast is made in Table 4.3 overleaf.

Legally binding authorisations make pollution control standards more central

It was the provision of legally binding authorisation conditions which altered the regulatory rules of the game. In their 1986 consultation the DoE had wished to preserve the flexibility of the pollution control system by denying any legal force to conditions in a consent. These consent conditions, such as emission limits, were intended to make explicit and transparent the BPM for specific processes, whilst prosecution would still require proof that the general duty of using the BPM had been breached. Breaching an emission limit in the consent was not an automatic offence; the DoE wished to maintain a 'duty based approach' (DoE, 1986c). This contrasted with the RCEP's opinion that breach of consent conditions should leave operators open to prosecution: their's was a 'consent based approach'. Consultation responses showed equal support for the RCEP and DoE approaches (DoE, 1988b).

111

Table 4.3
Comparison of industrial air pollution control with IPC

Regulatory Feature	Industrial Air Pollution Control	Integrated Pollution Control
Legislation	Alkali Act, 1906; Health and Safety at Work Act, 1974.	Environmental Protection Act, 1990.
Processes under control.	2,000 to 3,000 (approx.).	5,000 (approx.).
Releases controlled.	Air.	Air, water, solid waste.
Prior notification.	Once off registration.	Authorisation, reviewed every four years.
Focus of control.	Process techniques.	Process techniques.
Enforcement principle.	Best practicable means	Best available techniques not entailing excessive costs; and best practicable environmental option.
Regulator.	Industrial Air Pollution Inspectorate.	Her Majesty's Inspectorate of Pollution.
Consultation.	None.	Up to six statutory consultees.
Burden of proof.	IAPI: need to show operator failed to use BPM.	Operator: need to demonstrate in an Application document that they are pursuing BATNEEC and BPEO. Must meet all subsequent Authorisation conditions, issued by HMIP.
Maximum fine.	£2,000	£20,000 or imprisonment.

Upgrading of existing plant to new standards.	No explicit deadline.	Upgrading timetable required demonstrating process will achieve new plant standards.
Administrative costs.	No registration fee.	Met through cost recovery charging of operators.
Public register.	No.	Contains operator Application (demonstrating BATNEEC etc.), Authorisation conditions (including emission limits), and monitoring results.

Wishing to bring clarity of responsibility and transparency to the control of industrial pollution, whilst maintaining the tradition of flexibility, the DoE decided to combine both approaches for IPC (1988b). Moreover, EC legislation held consent conditions to be binding. The consent conditions, now called an authorisation in keeping with EC terminology, would be legally binding. But there would also be a general, residual duty on the operator to pursue the BPM, now called BATNEEC, again in keeping with EC terminology. 'This option combines the legal and administrative clarity of the consent system with the adaptability, economy and comprehensiveness of the duty based model' (DoE, 1988a, p.16).

The DoE argued a residual BATNEEC duty would encourage adoption of cleaner technologies and operational practices since it would 'automatically adjust to the latest developments' (1988a, p.16).

As regulatory principles, BATNEEC and BPM are not very different: neither of them prescribe a level of standard (such as, say, performing at 75 per cent of the 'best'); both suggest a method for arriving at a standard (balance the 'best' performance against the cost of achieving it). The DoE suggested the BATNEEC 'formulation spells out more explicitly the considerations in applying BPM', that is 'using the best commercially available technology at a reasonable cost with maintenance and supervision of the process according to best practice' (DoE, 1988a, p.11).

Moreover, as the air framework Directive stipulates and the DoE explained in guidance on IPC, mitigating costs were to be assessed on the basis of the economic performance of the industrial sector, and not the financial performance of individual operators (DoE, 1993, pp.12-13). This suggested IPC's central regulatory principle had more formality to it (BATNEEC cf. BPM).

More formal or not, it was the framework which IPC legislation built upon the regulatory principle which was significant. The inclusion of a consent based authorisation into IPC procedures had implications for the implementing policy network: it introduced formality. Once specific regulatory standards were agreed for a process, they were to be written as legally binding authorisation conditions. The terms of an offence became clearer: if an operator transgresses a condition then they are vulnerable to HMIP prosecution.

The authority of HMIP had been enhanced through providing it with the means to clearly demarcate legal and illegal activity. However, that demarcation (legally binding standards) is still dependent upon knowledge of the environmental performance of the 'best' techniques and economic knowledge of the industrial sector. The source of this knowledge resource continued to be the operators. Thus the resource interdependency through which standards were set remained unchanged. It was the subsequent enforcement of these standards where the authorisation's formality had enhanced the authoritative resource of HMIP.

The new consent based approach did not fundamentally alter the resource interdependency between regulator and regulated. It actually raised the standard setting stakes by enhancing the regulator's ability to demonstrate failure to meet negotiated regulatory standards. Thus the new formality meant that standards would become a more central regulatory activity.

Explicit regulatory standards also meant that setting them would be keenly contested. In this way the rules of the game were altered from informal agreement over process design to formal standard setting procedures. Yet IPC legislation deferred the creation of these pollution control standards to the implementation stage.

IPC standards deferred to the implementation stage

The IPC legislative framework introduced formality to regulatory procedures, and altered the rules of the game as a result: the duty was on operators to demonstrate compliance; and authorisation conditions were now legally binding. But the determination of actual pollution control standards were deferred to the implementation stage: the derivation of guidance on BATNEEC for specific classes of prescribed process; the receipt of operator applications; and the setting of authorisation conditions. IPC legislation introduced the BATNEEC and BPEO regulatory principles, but left interpretation to the discretion of HMIP.

In common with its air predecessor, the IPC legal framework deferred potentially contentious technical policy decisions to the implementer, such as process specific pollution control conditions, monitoring regimes or upgrading requirements. Like its air pollution predecessor, IPC policy output would be heavily influenced by the aggregate decisions made during implementation. In other words, determining precisely where IPC standards lay on the regulatory continuum (see Figure 2.1) was deferred to implementation.

DoE guidance explains how the regulator is responsible for pollution control standards:

> The inspector determining the case must decide what is BATNEEC in relation to each application, and translate that decision into conditions to be included in the authorisation. There must, however, be broad consistency in these decisions, especially between processes of the same kind. It is important for process operators and the public that BATNEEC is determined and applied in a transparent, rational and consistent way.
> (DoE, 1993, p.13)

Having created the legislative framework for IPC, the DoE deliberately took a hands-off approach during the implementation phase. The legal framework established the DoE as the Appeal authority, requiring them to stay out of the standard setting and enforcement activities deferred to HMIP - since they would have to pass judgement upon such decisions in Appeal cases. Another element to HMIP's discretion was the way it approached its relationship with operators during implementation and enforcement. New leadership at HMIP felt the formality of IPC procedures required more formal relations with operators too.

HMIP adopts an arms' length approach to implementation

HMIP decided IPC implementation should be conducted at arms' length from operators. The formality of IPC procedures raised the importance of explicit pollution control standards. HMIP's preparation for IPC and early implementation saw it attempt to alter unilaterally the rules of the game by which those standards would be set and enforced, much to the chagrin of industry.

The traditional approach to regulation in Britain has been one of informal working together between operators and enforcing authorities ... However, the Environmental Protection Bill marks a shift to a more formal approach to regulation. In line with this, HMIP feels that its is appropriate to develop a more "arms' length relationship" with the individual operators whom it is charged with regulating ... HMIP will in future not expect to provide detailed advice or assistance to individual operators on the design or operation of particular installations, on the basis that this type of involvement is inappropriate in terms of the "arms' length" relationship and enforcement role.
(HMIP, 1990, p.17)

New rules of the game

IPC implementation would not be along the lines of close collaboration characteristic of the air pollution policy community. HMIP was determined to require industry to deliver IPC through a more structured and hierarchic relationship (HMIP, 1991b, p.6) - they intended to judge industry on IPC rather than advise it on IPC.

Industry would no longer be intimately involved in standard setting. Nor would there be any site-level discussion prior to an operator submitting an application. Operators would have to make their case independently and would be assessed on this basis. Only after this assessment would inspectors and operators come together for consultation (ENDS, 1989b, p.12; interview with Inspector).

The emphasis for enforcement would shift from Inspectors paying visits, looking around plant and checking the results of any ad hoc monitoring, to requiring operators to install rigorous monitoring regimes and record keeping in order to demonstrate compliance with HMIP limits (ENDS, 1989b; interview with Inspector).

The arms' length approach rested upon an operator requirement to show they made the grade rather than the local inspector offering friendly advice and free consultation. The relationship was hierarchical in the sense that standards would be set by HMIP centrally, and field inspectors would judge the evidence of industrial operators against these standards. Implementation of IPC would follow new rules of the game: transparency replacing secrecy; clear regulatory standards rather than autonomous Inspector judgement; formality in decision making procedures instead of informal consensus seeking; and Inspectors as distant regulators not close advisors. Behind this switch in regulatory rules of the game was a new policy actor which won leadership of HMIP: the Radiochemical Inspectorate.

116

The component Inspectorates from which HMIP had been fashioned had different traditions. The IAPI formed the largest element of HMIP bringing 39 Inspectors with it from the HSE. The IAPI's regulatory tradition was the topic of chapter 3. Second largest was the RCI, with 18 inspectors under DoE responsibility. Both the water pollution staff and the HWI were very small and swamped by the larger IAPI and RCI.

The RCI's approach to regulation stood in stark contrast to the air Inspectorate. It's duty was to regulate the discharge of radioactive substances to all three environmental media - an approach which, it argued, made it highly suited for implementing IPC.

The RCI operated 'a centralised planning framework and uniform and more formally defined regulatory procedures' (NAO, 1991, p.8). Work plans were formulated by the Chief Inspector and his Deputy. These were translated into tasks, objectives and targets for individual Inspectors. Regulatory procedures were formalised in Manuals and formal desk instructions for Inspectors. Operating from within the DoE in London, and with a single regional office in Lancaster, the RCI had a highly centralised structure. Administrative standards, set centrally, would be enforced with less scope for Inspector discretion. Thus the RCI's approach to regulating operators was arms' length.

Terry Coleman of HMIP's Technical Policy Unit believes HMIP's arms' length approach arose because the former IAPI had been perceived as too close to industry, and because the RCI attained a position of leadership in HMIP with their contrasting approach (Coleman, 1992, p.6). These two factors were not unrelated.

One air Inspector recalled moving into HMIP: 'The Alkali Inspectorate had run through severe public criticism at several times, what with Jeremy Bugler's book and Social Audit reports and things like that. There was this kind of feeling that "they're tarred a bit those people, we've got to show everyone that we're different to them". That kind of attitude came out several times'.

An RCI Inspector agreed in his interview, 'The air Inspectorate had always worked very closely with industry on an intimate basis to find solutions to problems. They acted often as the research arm of industry, the professional arm of industry that had no professional staff of their own'. The greater transparency associated with IPC regulation meant HMIP would need to become more publicly accountable for their regulatory decisions. Public registers opened HMIP's enforcement up to scrutiny. In an interview with 'ENDS Report' at the time, Chief Inspector

Feates foresaw a greater emphasis on emission limits. This would provide the greater clarity required for enforcement (ENDS, 1989b, p.13).

The creation of HMIP had effectively introduced a significant new policy actor to the policy process in the guise of the RCI.[35] It brought to HMIP, and consequently to industrial pollution control, an approach to regulation different to that of air inspectors'. Given the air Inspectorate's somewhat tarnished image of working too close with those it was supposed to police, the RCI approach became the HMIP approach. These developments drew sympathy from a DoE 'greened' by the pro-environment climate of the late 1980s. According to interviews with two civil servants, the DoE thought that 'a cultural change was needed' and European and domestic public opinion emboldened the DoE in its pursuit of this change.

Industry dislikes the new rules of the game

The new stance caused some alarm amongst industry. One Inspector believed this was partly because many operators lacked the environmental science and monitoring capability the arms' length approach necessitated. He recalled even larger operators such as ICI, who had the organisational resources, did not like the arms' length approach because it meant more work for them. Moreover, the withdrawal of close inspector involvement in design decisions, and greater reliance upon emission limits and authorisation condition, provided the distance between regulator and regulated which could make prosecutions easier to secure.

The rules of the game in a policy network regulate the process of interaction (Rhodes, 1988, p.42) and guide behaviour between members (Wilks and Wright, 1987, p.305). HMIP's arms' length approach would limit the benefits industry received from participation in the policy community (see Efficiency Scrutiny, 1986, p.94-95). There would be no individual guidance through the legislation, no participation in setting site-specific standards, inspectors would not come in as an independent pacifier of the workforce or local community about risks, and it appeared HMIP, like Europe, were becoming more reliant upon emission standards.

Operators feared HMIP was becoming inflexible. The CIA kept complaining publicly that it was not being consulted over standards or procedures. The consensus amongst implementing policy actors - HMIP and industry - was beginning to break down.

With the mutual benefits which members accept and expect from participation in the network (Wilks and Wright, 1987, p.305) being withdrawn, so operators behaviour toward HMIP altered. Industrial leaders such as the CIA became very critical of HMIP and the IPC regime. They threatened to swamp HMIP with applications during the first chemicals tranche and to use this as a lever for changes to the regulatory framework. The organic chemicals sector contained by far the most number of prescribed processes, presenting HMIP with its biggest regulatory challenge owing to the number and complexity of processes. The CIA argued a stalled IPC system[36] would come into disrepute. 'Chemical industry lobbyists plan to use the collapse to twist Ministers' arms into weakening the legislation' (Wheal, 1993, p.12). Dr Ken Speakman, head of HMIP's Northern Region, was reported to have told industry representatives at an HMIP seminar that 'we are very aware that the industry could frustrate and delay the authorisation process' (ENDS, 1993c, p.20). This disruptive potential proved to be an influential organisational resource for the chemical industry (see chapter 5).

Industry believed closer consultation and less application information,[37] along lines more like the old rules of the game, would prevent any implementation problems. Industrial leaders recognised the legitimating benefit of statutory controls, but they were nervous about the shape the reforms were taking (CBI, 1993).

However, industry need not have been too concerned. HMIP's unilateral imposition of arms' length rules of the game not only upset industry by denying them the benefits of close participation, but it also ignored the resource interdependency which had bound the air policy community together. Like the air regime, IPC still relied upon a statutory principle rather than statutory standards.

Determining BATNEEC would still require the information resources of industry. Moreover, HMIP was still a relatively small Inspectorate. Its organisational resources were constrained and consequently its ability to impose and enforce its BATNEEC standards remained limited. HMIP's attempt at an arms' length approach only served to highlight its resource interdependency with industry. The following two chapters demonstrate how the realities of this resource dependency forced a return to policy community arrangements. In other words, an artificial change in a policy network's integration dimension cannot be sustained without an accompanying change in the resource dimension.

Environmental NGOs and the IPC policy process

Environmental NGOs were not directly involved in IPC formulation, and their absence carried through to implementation of IPC. But they represented a legitimate concern for environmental protection, so it is perhaps surprising that they did not join the issue network. Instead they played only a contextual role, in the revived environment movement that grew during the late 1980s, 'politically active but only sporadically influential' (O'Riordan, 1988, p.7).

The air policy community's appreciative system, that pollution control was a technical matter for expert regulators and operators, excluded environmental groups from industrial air pollution policy. Equally, the appreciative system of NGOs, which was more in step with the EC (public access to tough, uniform standards), clashed with that of the issue network. So contrasting appreciation of the problem and solutions encouraged exclusion. Greenpeace wrote off IPC from the outset. It considered the 'control' of pollution insufficiently radical for their clean production (zero emission) campaign objectives.

So the issue network was occupied primarily with managing external pressure. Its membership consisted of policy actors involved or close to the air policy community. The agenda was not about an environmentally rational reform of pollution controls. It was about maintaining influence, for which NGO membership was inappropriate. NGOs had no contact with the DoE over specific reforms.

In addition, environmental NGOs simply lacked the organisational resource and technical information to become involved in the IPC policy process, particularly at the implementation stage. It was the implementation stage when the important pollution standards would be set. Though consulted by HMIP about standards, NGOs generally[38] lacked the time, personnel and the technical and economic knowledge to respond with comments on specific process-based standards. It was too detailed and specific a policy level for close NGO involvement.

Instead, most environmental NGOs have used IPC as appropriate for other campaigns. Friends of the Earth (FoE), for example, have used it in recent campaigns on greater access to environmental information and against the use of chemical wastes as fuel in cement kilns. NGOs recognise their inability to participate in formal consultation exercises on the minutiae of IPC implementation, and they question whether policing the regulators in this way is an appropriate role for them. Some NGOs are keeping an eye on IPC developments. Recognising that it is only now reaching maturity, they have hitherto been giving it the benefit of the doubt (campaigner interview). But NGOs are not members of the IPC policy network. They remain in the wider issue network associated with the broader environmental policy area.

Summary and conclusions

This chapter has sought to demonstrate that the forces driving IPC policy formulation lay outside the industrial air pollution policy community. Contrary to the initial hypothesis, it would seem that the issue network which arose in the policy sector during the 1980s was not responsible for the changes. Indeed, the issue network appears to have sought conservative management of externally driven change.

An issue network did not arise having a variety of members with diverse views, in which a wide-ranging debate concerning industrial pollution policy could take place. The changes were not the outcome of such wide participation or issue network debate. Environmental NGOs, for example, were not members of the issue network and have played a very minor, contextual role in the IPC policy process, even though they represent a legitimate concern about industrial pollution.

Instead, the industrial air pollution policy community opened up into an issue network defending some of the community's regulatory practices. EC pollution legislation prompted DoE involvement in the industrial air pollution policy sector. They began preparing reforms of policy which included EC requirements whilst maintaining elements of the British tradition. Further EC legislation in the form of uniform pollution standards was a possibility concerning both industry and the Inspectorate.

Core policy community members joined the DoE in an issue network. The consensus amongst this issue network membership was that the British tradition of site specific flexibility on pollution standards needed preserving, based upon scientific proof of pollutants' harm. They believed a redistribution of resources was required in the sense that the Inspectorate's technical expertise needed returning to the DoE so that it could more effectively restore credibility and defend British policy, particularly in Brussels. In this respect, the issue network maintained a shared appreciative system.

However, the HSE was becoming more interested in industrial air pollution control (ENDS, 1985b). Inspectorate absorption into the HSE structure threatened the former's autonomy. Such HSE issue network membership was unwelcome, and other members sought to deny it influence over the Inspectorate and industrial pollution policy. However, to secure a transfer of the Inspectorate from the HSE (under Department of Employment authority) to the DoE needed the agreement of government, who possessed the authority to make such arrangements between Departments.

Appeal to government resulted in it taking the opportunity to launch an Efficiency Scrutiny into this policy sector. It was the deregulatory

121

recommendations of this Scrutiny which convinced government that HMIP should be created in the DoE, and which launched an integrated approach to industrial pollution control. DoE proposals for a Clean Air Bill at that time had been turned down by government.

So policy change arose outside of the industrial air pollution policy network. EC pressure meant regulation of processes would become more transparent and follow more formal procedures. It required policy reforms. HSE interest in the policy sector threatened DoE control over those reforms. The DoE, supported by other issue network members, had to appeal to yet another external policy actor (government) in order to secure control over policy. In both cases the issue network was reacting to external intervention. So IPC was the result of two exogenous change agents: the first was new institutional arrangements (enhanced EC environmental policy); and the second was ideological (deregulation). Knowledge (the RCEP's environmental arguments for an integrated approach) played only a small, legitimating role.

However, as with all issue networks the consensus was not monolithic. The creation of HMIP introduced the RCI to the policy sector. They practised different rules of the game with respect to regulation. Moreover, the political ascent of environmental issues secured the DoE a Parliamentary slot for IPC legislation (based upon EC requirement), and emboldened it to the extent that they supported the RCI in recognising the relationship between HMIP and industry had to appear less cosy than in the air pollution policy community - though their appreciative system maintained pollution control was a technical issue for experts.

HMIP's creation removed the HSE from the issue network. The Efficiency Scrutiny's attention was transitory. Having put the legislative framework in place, the DoE distanced itself from any further close involvement in IPC. EC requirements appeared satisfied. Thus the issue network that had built up began to dissolve. Only those policy actors who would be involved in IPC's implementation retained an interest in influencing developments.

The policy formulation stage certainly left considerable scope for influencing policy output during implementation. There remained discretion over the actual standards of pollution control to be applied under IPC. HMIP appeared to be moving toward centrally set pollution standards, but it was far from inevitable that site specific flexibility had been lost - particularly with the same resource interdependencies remaining from the air pollution regime.

So on the eve of its introduction, it appeared a policy network would be responsible for IPC implementation. Its membership consisted of HMIP and industry. Integration was not as tight as under the air regime. The technocratic appreciative system with regard to pollution control remained, but the membership wanted to pursue contrasting rules of the game (formal procedures cf. close negotiation).

Interestingly, the same resource interdependencies existed. HMIP's legal authority had been boosted thanks to the introduction of a consent based approach, but the basis on which standards would be set still needed industrial information. The following two chapters analyse how this distribution of resources was fundamental in reversing some of the formalism HMIP hoped to introduce to pollution control implementation.

Notes

1   Taken to mean the Prime Minister and the Cabinet (Dearlove and Saunders, 1984, p.29).

2   Note that the Maastricht Treaty has made legislation easier by providing qualified majority voting (QMV) for virtually all types of environmental legislation. So, for instance, the Integrated Pollution Prevention and Control Directive needs only QMV.

3   EC Directive 80/779/EEC.

4   EC Directive 82/884/EEC.

5   EC Directive 85/203/EEC.

6   EC Directive 84/360/EEC.

7   Germans voted their first Greens into the Bundestag in 1983. German air pollution controls have traditionally imposed uniform standards upon sources (Weale, 1992, p.164).

8   These would need unanimous voting by Member States. Qualified majority voting had been proposed in the initial draft of the Directive (Haigh, 1989).

9   The deadline for incorporating the air framework Directive was 30 June 1987.

10   As did the main political parties.

11   Note that the majority of British industry, medium and small sized firms, are less enlightened and continue to react against regulation even today (Fischer and Schot, 1993, p.6-7). The larger firms and trade organisations, though less numerous, are significant because they have the organisational resource to lobby and participate in the policy process, the outcomes of which can affect all firms (Grant, 1984; Coleman and Grant, 1984).

12   Conducted annually by MORI for the Chemical Industries Association. 4,056 people over the age of 15 were interviewed from 255 random constituencies.

13   Though critics suggest its lack of independent scrutiny render it little more than an 'educational' exercise for gaining public credibility rather than demonstrating public accountability (Simmons and Wynne, 1993).

14   Although industry's response to IPC suggests that environmental management was poor (Smith, 1996).

15   Dr. A Barbour, Environmental Scientist for RTZ quoted in ENDS (1986a, p.4).

16   The Inspectorate refused to require Flue Gas Desulphurisation as the BPM for power stations (contributing to acid deposition). Instead they stuck to a dilute and disperse policy of tall chimney stacks which was transferring acid deposition problems to Northern Europe. This provoked the scorn of environmentalists (Rose, 1990).

17   Incidents do continue to tarnish the industry, such as the fire at Allied Colloids in 1992 whose fumes hospitalised 30 people, or the explosion at Hicksons the same year which killed five people.

18   By June 1983 Inspectorate districts had been reduced from 15 to 12.

19   The Cabinet Office had produced a de-regulatory White Paper in 1985 called 'Lifting the Burden' which was about 'reducing burdens imposed on business by administrative and legislative regulation' (Cabinet Office, 1985, p.1).

20 The Efficiency Scrutiny's research method involved sending questionnaires and discussions with practitioners, including industrial operators.

21 A policy of compulsory competitive tendering was announced at the Conservative Party conference in 1986.

22 Taken to include the twin aims of reducing the size and cost of public bureaucracy, and minimising the regulatory burden upon industry.

23 Painter (1989, p.466) argues that re-organisations, such as amalgamating Inspectorates into HMIP, have a symbolic value for Government through appearing to be doing something whilst actually distracting attention away from awkward policy choices, such as reducing industrial releases.

24 Ministries for housing and local government, public building and works, and transport were forged together in the new Department.

25 Departments such as the DTi are more influential in government. For example, it was the DTi who chose to delay the introduction of VOC controls by two years, with the DoE's agreement (Brown, 1996).

26 The last major air pollution legislation had been the Clean Air Acts 30 years earlier.

27 Controlled by the air Inspectorate and listed in S.I. 1983/943 'Health and Safety (Emissions Into the Atmosphere) Regulations, 1983'.

28 The disclosure of environmental information remains an issue amongst some members of the general environmental issue network. The Chemical Release Inventory compiled by HMIP and listing emissions of prescribed substances from prescribed processes has been criticised by environment NGOs for being far less comprehensive than its US counterpart: the Toxic Release Inventory. Friends of the Earth launched a Right to Know campaign in October 1995.

29   S.I. 1989/317, 'The Air Quality Regulation, 1989'; S.I. 1989/318, 'The Control of Industrial Air Pollution (Registration of Works) Regulations, 1989; and S.I. 1989/319, 'The Health and Safety (Emissions into the Atmosphere) Regulations, 1989'.

30   Part 1, Section 7(7) Environmental Protection Act, 1990.

31   This contrasted with her 1982 speech to the Scottish Conservative Party, during the Falklands war, in which she said: 'When you've spent half your political life dealing with humdrum issues like the environment, it's exciting to have a real crisis on your hands' (quoted in McCormick, 1991, p.58).

32   The World Wide Fund for Nature and the International Institute for Environment and Development.

33   Lowe and Goyder (1983, pp.16-17) date previous episodes, based upon growth in numbers of environmental groups, as: the mid-1880s to the turn of the century; the middle inter-war years; the late 1950s to early 1960s; and the early 1970s.

34   Predominantly by exposing government policy to Parliamentary political debate under media scrutiny, for the benefit of the electorate.

35   The first two Directors were from the RCI: Brian Ponsford (April 1987- December 1989); and then Frank Feates (December 1989 - April 1991).

36   The CIA pointed to the fact that some of the first large combustion plants had not been authorised two years after their application deadline owing to disputes between HMIP and the generators.

37   For instance, the CIA argue the public register need not contain process information and that the public was just interested in release data.

38   Some technically expert members of the National Society for Clean Air (NSCA), and from the field of industrial pollution control, commented on the standards for a few processes on behalf of the NSCA.

5 Driving down standards: implementing the IPC framework

Introduction

The following two chapters are concerned with the implementation of IPC, using the organic chemicals industrial sector as a case study (the largest sector to come under IPC). The discussion in this chapter focuses upon the production of Chief Inspector's Guidance Notes (CIGN). These occupy a similar position under IPC as BPM Notes did under the air regime: they specify the BATNEEC pollution standards HMIP expects for specific types of prescribed process.

Together, this chapter and the next seek to demonstrate how a policy community reformed for IPC implementation, sharing characteristics similar to that which implemented industrial air pollution policy. Such an argument implies implementation did not follow the pattern anticipated by HMIP and the DoE at the outset: HMIP intended to pursue an arms' length approach to implementation, in which a hierarchical and structured relationship would exist between regulator and regulated. CIGNs would occupy an important role in the arms' length scheme owing to their BATNEEC standard setting status - which is why they merit special attention in this chapter.

Kenis and Schneider (1991, pp.42-43) argue that an absence of explicit information makes top-down, command-and-control relations difficult to sustain. Policy network arrangements are more likely (see chapter 2). The point made in this chapter is that HMIP's dependency upon industry for process information provided industry with the opportunity to influence CIGN content. The outcome was that the authority and prescriptiveness of standards in CIGNs was undermined. Thus CIGNs no longer provided centrally set standards. Standard setting was deferred down to the site-level, paving the way for a re-created policy community of operators and Inspectors - the subject of chapter 6.

So the hypotheses being tested here are that IPC implementation fits the bottom-up model in the sense that policy output was deeply influenced by policy actors at the site-level. Moreover, IPC became the domain of a policy community. The distribution of resources amongst its membership was such that industry was the most influential policy actor. In this chapter, evidence of industry influence rests upon their ability to weaken the authority of CIGNs, frustrating HMIP's arms' length approach, and regaining deep industry participation in standard setting: a reversal in HMIP's intended rules of the game.

Since the organic chemicals sector provides case study material for this element of the book, discussion begins in this chapter with a brief description of the industry. An assessment is also made of the resources possessed by the industry, and of how it wished to influence IPC. Attention then turns to HMIP. The resources it needed to implement IPC along arms' length lines are contrasted with the resource problems HMIP was actually experiencing.

The chapter then considers the central role CIGNs were intended to play in IPC implementation, before analysing their production. Access to copies of draft CIGNs for prescribed organic chemical processes, comments from operators arising during formal consultation, and the final CIGNs themselves allow their development to be tracked. This evidence is complemented by interviews with participants in this element of the policy process. After demonstrating that the weakening of CIGNs was not unique to the organic chemicals sector, the chapter finishes by considering the demise of HMIP's arms' length approach.

The organic chemical industry

The organic chemicals sector is a complex and pervasive element of the chemical industry. Its core activity is using chemistry to manufacture marketable organic chemicals from simple, building block chemicals supplied by the petrochemical industry. There is tremendous trade in manufactured chemicals between chemical firms and with firms in other industrial sectors. The array of production activities carried on by the sector is vast. The industry is very organised too, as this section seeks to demonstrate.

The complexity of the organic chemicals sector

Processes in the organic chemicals sector are not as homogenous as in other industrial sectors. A distinction has to be drawn between the chemistry of the process and the technology of the process. The latter can consist of standard pieces of kit, for example reactors, distillation units, condensers, and so forth. Ensembles of this hardware are used to carry out a huge array of chemical processes. Companies can have more efficient or innovative pieces of kit, but competitive advantage is often won through the research and development of better chemical routes to marketable chemicals or the manufacture of new chemicals. The computer industry may be considered somewhat analogous, with its hardware and software components.

Like some software houses, contract chemical manufacturers develop or manufacture chemical processes on a bespoke basis, often for other chemical companies.[1] Their contracts may specify a short lead time for such manufacture: an ability to quickly produce the desired chemicals for a contractor being another competitive factor. Speciality and fine chemical manufacturers produce relatively small quantities of complex chemicals or chemicals of high (fine) purity. All three types of manufacture - contract, speciality and fine - tend to be operated on a batch-wise basis.

A company may make a different chemical product using the same equipment (with a batch reactor as the building block) on a week by week basis. Often the same company can have its 'speciality' or 'fine' line of chemical products which it markets, whilst also marketing its chemistry and chemical engineering services as a contract chemical company. Thus speciality, fine, and contract are descriptions which tend to be used inter-changeably. Their regulatory significance is that these manufacturers use the same pieces of equipment for a variety of chemical processes over time.

At the other end of the organic chemicals sector are the bulk chemical manufacturers. They use continuous or semi-continuous processes to manufacture large quantities of the same chemical. Big ensembles of equipment can be used in this manufacture, using highly integrated collections of chemical processes in the manufacture of chemical products. Dedicated side processes manufacture chemicals which become feed-stocks for the main reaction; or which might be sold, depending upon market demand. This flexibility and variety is a defining characteristic of the sector.

There is a great deal of trade within the sector, between bulk producers and speciality firms,[2] between speciality firms and speciality firms, and so on; whilst companies such as ICI manufacture both chemical intermediates and final consumer products, such as paints.

The products of the organic chemicals sector feed into all sectors of industrial economies. This pervasiveness gives the chemical industry a strategic significance for industrial economies (Grant, Paterson and Whitston, 1988, pp.48-49). It is one of the UK's most successful sectors (Bird, 1993, p.1), and so enjoys an influential economic resource. It is the country's fourth biggest manufacturing industry (in terms of value added), accounting for 2.3 per cent of GDP, and is the country's biggest export earner (£18.7 billion in 1994) (CIA, 1995).

The chemical industry is a very 'clubable' industry. Grant, Paterson and Whitston contrasted its large physical scale with its relatively small managerial scale: 'the number of key decision makers, even at a global level, is relatively small; and there are recognised channels through which a debate about the industry's future can be conducted' (1988, p.7). Nationally, the Chemical Industries Association (CIA) is a key trade organisation with a membership of 200 companies (CIA, 1995). It organises committees made up of staff from member companies to tackle industry issues. Committees were formed for IPC, including some to respond to CIGN consultation (see later).

There are other domestic business groupings too, such as the Specialised Organics Manufacturers Eastern Region (SOMER) made up of 22 firms. SOMER holds 'quarterly meetings on members premises and discuss matters of mutual interest. Presentations by members and external speakers cover a wide range of topics such as pollution and the environment ... SOMER ... is particularly useful as a channel for information flow between companies, the CIA and from there to governmental and pan European institutions' (SOMER, 1994, p.2). Forums such as this, and the CIA's local Responsible Care cells,[3] provided operators with opportunities to exchange impressions, experiences and lessons regarding IPC. Interviewed operators were all able to cite examples of other operators' treatment under IPC.

This ability to transmit information meant the sector could exploit favourable precedents granted by HMIP and challenge inconsistent decisions. Inspectors interviewed for this drafting knew their decisions were being monitored in this way.[4] Equally, the CIA was able to gather examples of the burden it believed IPC was placing upon its members for presentation to the Ministers it was lobbying (CIA, 1994). One operator said the CIA had used his wrangle with HMIP over an authorisation as such a case study. A Department of Trade and Industry (DTi) report recognised the CIA 'as a well informed mouthpiece for the chemicals industry' (Bird, 1993, p.33).

The CIA was also able to build up guidance based upon early authorisations (of new or substantially changed processes) for dissemination amongst members: 'The advice in this document has been prepared following discussions with representatives of member companies who have gained practical experience in dealing with HMIP and in obtaining authorisations' (CIA, 1992b, p.1). For example, an application for a new process submitted by speciality firm Hickson and Welch in July 1991 innovated a way of circumventing IPC confidentiality procedures. Commercial confidentiality was a source of dispute between Hicksons and HMIP; the former claimed it was necessary under the contract rules with its customer, the latter said it was already publicly available on the patents register. The compromise reached was for IPC application details to use generic terms for the process chemistry (ENDS, 1992b, p.6). Guidance issued in August 1992 by the CIA to members suggested that confidentiality claims could be avoided through such presentation of information (CIA, 1992b, p.6).

CIA guidance on IPC encouraged operators to contact HMIP and to make sure Inspectors understood the process, whilst pointing out that Inspectors had a heavy workload, so 'an open and understanding attitude is likely to generate a helpful response from HMIP' (CIA, 1992b, p.2).

Moreover, the CIA circulated a 'model' application amongst members. This was for a new process operated by speciality firm Fine Organics. The application did not have HMIP's endorsement as a model. Annual releases were not quantified. Nor did it have an assessment of likely environmental consequences or the BPEO. Justification that the process was BATNEEC got a superficial treatment that was to become familiar in the IPC public register: 'Fine Organics has experience in operating this type of plant, over a number of years, in a way which affords adequate levels of safety and environmental protection ... The levels of containment afforded by the plant together with the control mechanisms which are in place ensure that high standards are achieved and maintained. For the type of process we carry out this represents the best available techniques not entailing excessive cost' (Fine Organics, IPC Application No. AA5533, p.11).

This may not have been an application of the calibre HMIP had hoped. However, this was an application for a process which was authorised by HMIP. Thus it was a valid application, and it suited the CIA's objective of reducing the task it believed applications presented to members. As an operator explained, 'The CIA saw IPC as a significant cost overhead for firms. Therefore they wanted to put together a minimum cost application for firms, so that companies could do similar cheap ones.'

Unofficial guidance for operators also came from the Specialised Organics Sector Group of the National Economic Development Council (NEDC - SOSG). This corporatist body comprised chemical industry representatives, the unions, academia and central government (DoE and DTi). Their advice was based on consultation with companies and HMIP staff in London and covered many implementation issues. Operators were told IPC charges and fees could be minimised if one was 'to apply for as many processes as possible under one authorisation' (NEDC - SOSG, 1992, p.3). They suggested:

that by keeping problems high profile, not only with the Inspectors, but also with trade organisations and government bodies, we should then see a softer approach in the interpretation of the legislation by the HMIP.
(NEDC - SOSG, 1992, p.2)

One final example of the sector's organisational resource was their ability to help one another with application and authorisation problems. Help which took place between sites occasionally extended beyond those operated by the same company. One multinational operator explained how their knowledge concerning the scientific uncertainty about some alleged carcinogens was used to help a customer chemical operator successfully challenge an HMIP emission limit. More generally, operators looked at one anothers' applications on the public register to see how each had approached the presentation and detail of information for IPC applications.

All this amounted to a considerable organisational resource for the chemical industry. Operators possessed the ability to become well informed about HMIP's regulatory decisions. They could obtain guidance on how to negotiate IPC with an Inspector. Operators could make co-ordinated responses to HMIP proposals, such as the pollution standards put forward in draft CIGNs. Material could be gathered together[5] for use as evidence when lobbying Ministers. And operators had the capacity to seriously disrupt the IPC programme (see chapter 4).

Industry's objectives for IPC implementation

Industry did not like HMIP's arms' length approach. The chemical industry was threatening to disrupt IPC implementation. HMIP appeared to be excluding industry from the close regulatory participation with which it was familiar. Industry was not integrated into the preparation of standards, being excluded from draft CIGN production - a departure from BPM Note production (chapter 3). Instead, operators were invited to respond, along with others, during formal HMIP consultation on the drafts. They were to be provided with no preferential treatment.

Operators wished to discover how IPC would affect their individual activities (interviews). New regulatory principles such as BATNEEC and BPEO did not indicate the standards to which individual processes would be expected to perform. CIGNs provided the first indication of what BATNEEC standards would be for specific processes, in terms of release limits, upgrading requirements, and so on. Thus operators had a keen interest in CIGN production, but annoyingly found themselves excluded from setting the standards built into them. Moreover, arms' length announcements from HMIP suggested the standards in CIGNs would not be as flexible as their BPM Note predecessors. Industry feared HMIP would adopt and enforce uniform standards for pollution control. Under IPC it appeared the pollution control reforms called for in the 1980s were not going industry's way.

Ironically, release limits are attractive to industry owing to the certainty they contain. Principles such as BATNEEC appear ambiguous regarding the physical pollution control requirements for practical application. What does BATNEEC allow me to emit exactly? Limits are preferable because operators can modify the process to meet them, certain of what is required of them.

However, industry did not wish to meet centrally set limits, applied uniformly across all processes of a specific type - the line HMIP appeared to be taking with CIGNs. Industry wanted to be able to negotiate limits with Inspectors. They wanted them tailored to their individual circumstances. This was an important objective for operators.

So whilst operators were very interested in CIGNs, because they provided the first indication of the level of pollution standards expected for specific types of process, they were also concerned that these CIGN standards would be prescriptive and uniformly applied. Fortunately for industry, they were the source of information necessary for setting BATNEEC standards. This information resource, coupled with their organisational and economic resources, enabled industry to steer IPC implementation in a preferred direction.

HMIP's resource problems

HMIP's introduction of an arms' length approach did not meet the approval of everyone in HMIP. Former air inspectors in particular had grave doubts about the efficacy of the arms' length approach (interview with Inspector; ENDS, 1989b, p.3).

The Radiochemical Inspectorate had been the driving force within HMIP for an arms' length approach. Yet radiochemical processes were managed by operators such as the CEGB or BNFL, arguably possessing technically competent personnel trained to control radioactive releases. They had the resources to respond to the RCI's arms' length approach. One RCI Inspector admitted as much when contrasting the air Inspectorate's approach with that of the RCI. For the latter he recalled, 'industry had plenty of technical expertise, they didn't need to be led by us, and we could act much more like regulators'. HMIP's leadership wanted to see industry in general adopt or buy in such expertise and not to rely upon the Inspectorate for advice.

The variety of processes was less diverse in the radiochemical field and it was easier, argued critics, for distant regulators to keep pace with technical developments than would be the case for wider industry. Air inspectors defended their frequent and close contact with operators in the field as a valuable way of following the latest developments across a wide variety of processes (interview with former air Inspector). IPC contains 33 classes of prescribed process and scores of different process types. Moreover, the staff and time provided to HMIP for IPC implementation was limited.

More independent, arms' length standard setting would require a capacity to maintain an up-to-date information base on the best available technologies across a large array of processes. If decision making was to become more structured then inspectors would need to be at ease with economic cost-benefit arguments (Pearce and Brisson, 1993, p.39). They would have to determine what does or does not entail excessive cost, based upon their own database of an industrial sector's economic performance. In turn, evaluating the benefits likely from any process upgrade would require environmental assessment techniques and expertise.

Two case studies were conducted by HMIP between October 1987 and February 1988 into the regulatory implications of IPC. Both had the co-operation of the operators. In each case the task was to attempt to quantify the releases from the process, assess the environmental effects of this release profile, and to consider the scope for reducing releases along BPEO lines (HMIP, 1989b, pp.59-60).

The studies identified knowledge gaps at HMIP. They lacked the skills to assess and quantify the environmental effects of releases. Comprehensive information about the receiving environment was also lacking. And 'HMIP will need to establish a more comprehensive information base of technologies that are currently available or soon to become available, with associated characteristics in terms of waste generation, fitness for function and costs' (HMIP, 1989b, p.60). The intention was to carry out further studies in preparation for IPC (DoE, 1988a, p.16). Staff shortages at HMIP prevented these taking place.

A senior Inspector said in his interview that he believed inspectors needed to spend as much as half their time over the first five years of HMIP in training for the multi-disciplinary challenge of IPC. HMIP knowledge was particularly weak in the area of effluent treatment and discharge control technologies (ENDS, 1989b, p.14). There wasn't the manpower or time for such extensive training. Instead, Inspectors attended one of four residential training courses held by HMIP between January and March 1991 (HMIP, 1991d, p.12).

HMIP did establish Industry Groups to assist Inspectors in the field. Industry Groups consisted of Inspectors from each region who had useful experience in a particular industrial sector. There are Industry Groups for energy and fuel, chemicals, metals, minerals, and waste industries. The Groups meet periodically to compare and build experience for the resolution of recurring problems pertinent to the regulation of that sector. Thus the knowledge and information resource of the Groups is built up during and after site-level implementation, not in advance of it. Evidence, and subsequent events, suggest that HMIP's information and knowledge resources were insufficiently formidable for its arms' length approach to succeed. Site-level implementation saw Inspectors reverting to informal standard setting approaches reminiscent of their air predecessors (chapter 6).

Staffing problems

In its 1994-95 Annual Report HMIP was able to announce its full complement of staff for the first time (HMIP, 1995, p.61). Prior to this it had always suffered staff shortages.

The DoE grossly underestimated the number of staff HMIP would require to implement IPC. In its IPC consultation paper, and in keeping with the tone of the Cabinet Office Efficiency Scrutiny, the DoE anticipated IPC requiring three Inspectors and two support staff in addition to the complement of 202 staff which existed on HMIP's creation (DoE, 1988a, p.28). This belief was confirmed in May the following year by Environment Minister Virginia Bottomley (Parliamentary Written Answers, 22nd May 1989, Column 380). But the pressure of preparing for IPC meant the Treasury were eventually forced to allow the DoE a series of increases in HMIP staff complement and salary in order for it to recruit sufficient staff and prevent the collapse of IPC (NAO, 1991, p.35).

HMIP's staffing history is presented in Table 5.1. The last column contains a staff forecast made by HMIP in a 'Forward Look' project (HMIP, 1990). This projection of staff need was based upon the anticipated future demand of IPC: authorising processes; managing public registers; running the charging system; reviewing authorisations; and inspectors prosecuting in the magistrates court (DoE, 1990, pp.16-17).

The persistent staff shortage meant inspection visits, which had been declining under the air regime, fell further after HMIP's creation - see Table 5.2 (cf. Table 3.2). The preparatory demands of IPC was of such magnitude that field inspectors were having to be pulled in to help. The proportion of planned, routine visits declined from 50 per cent in 1977 to 11 per cent in 1989-90. Other visits were in reaction to incidents or complaint. For the year 1990-91 HMIP's new Director and Chief Inspector, David Slater, reported to the Secretary of State for the Environment that, 'The priority given to the preparation of guidance material, and the extensive consultation which resulted, has involved a considerable amount of effort by field inspectors ... as a result inspection levels have fallen short of the targets in MINIS 11' (DoE, 1991, p.5). He went on to inform his superiors that no routine inspections were planned for the following year (DoE, 1991, p.7).

Table 5.1
Staffing at HMIP

| Date | Pollution Inspectors | | Total Staff (Inspectors & Admin.) | | HMIP's |
	In Post	Complement	In Post	Complement	Forecast of Need
1987	75	-	133	199	-
1988	96	120	158	183	-
1989	105	130	165	194	-
1990	105	130	172	212	-
1991	115	131	232	248	416
1992	148	176	287	313	434
1993	170	185	349	377	442
1994	192	192	435	435	458
1995	-	-	435	435	-

Source: HMIP Annual Reports; National Audit Office; Parliamentary Official Journal; Parliamentary Question

Table 5.2
Decline in air inspections prior to IPC

Year	Scheduled Processes	Target No. Visits	Actual No. Visits
1986-87	2,915	10,000	9,718
1987-88	2,839	9,000	9,134
1988-89	2,806	7,500	8,671
1989-90	3,092	6,000	7,065
1990-91	3,079	4,400	3,310

The decline in inspections, staffing problems, disputes about HMIP's organisation and concerns about resource shortages fuelled rumours about low morale within HMIP and raised concern about its ability to fulfil its functions. 'Confidence in the Pollution Inspectorate dropped so low in 1989 that the National Audit Office was asked by the Public Accounts Committee to launch an inquiry into the organisation' (Rose, 1990, p.319). This was barely two years after the creation of this 'new' pollution regulator.

The National Audit Office (NAO) reported that, 'nearly all the industry groups consulted by the National Audit Office were concerned that the level of the Inspectorate's resources was too low for effective regulation of air pollution' (NAO, 1991, p.22).   Criticism of historically poor regulatory performance (by the regulator) was avoided thanks to HMIP's plans regarding its implementation of IPC (Committee of Public Accounts, 1992, pp.xiii-xiv; NAO, 1992, p.ix).   But 'there is still some way to go and continued vigorous effort by the Inspectorate will be required to secure the full benefit from these initiatives and the successful implementation of integrated pollution control' (NAO, 1991, p.6). The House of Commons Committee supported 'the need to have more standardised and formal procedures and documentation and that these are now being introduced' (1992, p.ix). HMIP appeared to be growing in the opposite direction to Bernstein's (1955) theoretical regulatory body: starting as a declining and devitalised body but seeking to become more vigorous (see chapter 2).

However, in order to cope with the anticipated 650 organic chemical processes requiring authorisation (DoE, 1994, p.5), HMIP had to second all non-field Inspectors into the field.   Thus the initial development of its implementation policy and research into regulatory tools for IPC came to a halt.   As HMIP's Director, David Slater, explained in his 1993/94 MINIS report to the DoE: 'Given the current estimates of time taken to determine an authorisation it was clear that the existing number of Inspectors in the field was insufficient to deliver authorisations within the statutory targets. Accordingly the Senior Executive took the decision to transfer 17 staff from headquarters divisions (Business Strategy Division, Regulatory Systems Division and Pollution Policy Division) to assist Operations Division.   This meant that for the period from the 1st November 1993 to 1st March 1994 all business and strategy work ceased as did work on regulatory procedures ... Input to the development of Inspectorate of Pollution Corporate Information System was reduced, Chief Inspector's Guidance Notes were less polished and the production of Technical Guidance Notes put off until 1994/95' (DoE, 1994, p.5). HMIP was struggling to find the organisational resource necessary to implement IPC, including gathering sufficient information to assist with standard setting.

A tight implementation timetable

The time-scale over which IPC was to be implemented was very tight in comparison to previous pollution control Acts (see for example Levitt, 1980 on the years of delay to implementing elements of the Control of Pollution Act, 1974). Several interviewees confirmed that a political decision was made by Ministers not to repeat such delay with IPC.

With the Environmental Protection Act passed in November 1990, enabling Regulations for IPC's implementation were laid before Parliament early in March 1991. Phased implementation of IPC was to start the following month with a tight rolling programme for industrial sectors (Table 5.3).

Table 5.3
CIGN production demand and publication dates

Industrial Sector	IPC Implementation Period	No. of CIGNs	Date Published
Fuel and Power Industry	April 1991 - June 1992	17	February 1992[1] (revised Nov 1995)
Waste Disposal Industry	August 1992 - October 1992	11	May 1992
Mineral Industry	December 1992 - February 1993	6	August 1992
Chemical Industry	May 1993 - July 1994	25	January/August/December 1993
Metal Industry	January 1995 - October 1995	12	October/November 1994
Other Industry	November 1995 - January 1996	9	March/May 1995

[1] Except IPR 1/1 for large boilers and furnaces, published July 1991.

Source: HMIP (1995b) and DoE (1993)

HMIP had to prepare guidance for all the types of process coming into IPC between 1991 and 1996. This amounted to 80 CIGNs, and was in addition to HMIP providing over 200 guidance notes for use by local authorities implementing new air pollution regulations.[6] Ministers wished to see CIGNs publicly available three months ahead of the IPC application window for the relevant processes. A breakdown of this task is given in Table 5.3. Unification and re-organisation of HMIP was still taking place. For instance, staff moved into the Bedford regional office in February 1991, only eight weeks before the start of IPC.

The authorisation of actual processes had to be carried out alongside this programme of work on guidance. HMIP could not afford to allow its determination of IPC authorisations to become too delayed since it would interfere with the implementation timetable and affect the credibility of IPC. Inspectors spent an average 6.14 man-days per authorisation for the organic chemicals sector (written correspondence with Environment and Countryside Minister David Atkins, via Sir Derek Spencer MP). The IPC timetable has been maintained, but HMIP has struggled to authorise processes within the statutory four month period[7] (Table 5.4).

Table 5.4
HMIP's ability to authorise processes within four months

Year	Percentage authorisations determined within four months of receipt of application
1991-92	22%
1992-93	19%
1993-94	52%
1994-95	55%

Source: HMIP (1995e, p.3)

Six CIGNs had to be prepared for the organic chemicals sector, with an additional CIGN for pharmaceutical processes and one for pesticide processes. Work began on these CIGNs early in 1992 with the CIGNs published in January 1993. A new Inspector who had joined HMIP from a chemical company in December 1991 was put in charge of the work.

The regulatory role of Chief Inspectors Guidance Notes

The previous two sections introduced the two key policy actors regarding CIGN development and site-level implementation of IPC. The organic chemical industry was introduced, its resources were examined (particularly its organisational capability), and its concerns over IPC implementation sketched out. HMIP's intention to pursue an arms' length approach was covered in the last chapter. In this chapter it is the resource problems HMIP faced in relation to this stance which is the topic of analysis. The purpose of this section is to point out the regulatory role CIGNs were intended to hold with respect to setting standards, before turning to an analysis of their development in subsequent sections.

Top-down regulatory standards

HMIP's arms' length approach, coupled with the legal status of authorisation conditions, suggested IPC would place particular emphasis upon release limits. There was the prospect of centrally set limits being uniformly applied:

139

In deciding BATNEEC for preventing and minimising the releases of prescribed substances, no account should be taken of the absolute environmental effects of the releases. For new processes the same standards should apply whatever their location.
(HMIP, 1991c, p.5)

Existing processes would have to upgrade to these new process standards (DoE, 1993, p.13). Defining those standards for specific types of process were the CIGNs. 'The release limits given in the Notes are presumptive, and are based on what is generally considered achievable for a plant employing the BATNEEC for process control and abatement' (HMIP, 1993, p.30).

The CIGNs guide Inspectors on the standards expected from specific types of process pursuing the BATNEEC (HMIP, 1995, pp.19-20), and against which individual processes should be judged (DoE, 1993, p.15). CIGNs define the type of process they cover, set out general IPC regulatory requirements, and provide release limits for air, water and land which HMIP believes can be achieved by the application of BATNEEC (DoE, 1993, p.13). Annexes include abatement techniques available to that process, and the monitoring required to demonstrate compliance with release limits. CIGNs are revised every four years.

HMIP was aware, however, that CIGNs would be of interest to industry too. One of the Inspectors managing the production of CIGNs said in interview, 'obviously we had a mind to the fact that these were public documents that were going to be used by industry'. CIGNs carry no statutory authority and their administrative standards were open to challenge. Being technology based standards, industry was the key source of information. This information resource, or rather the poor state of this resource (very few industrial processes had data concerning their environmental release levels), put industry in an influential position with regard to the operationalisation of BATNEEC.

The standard setting task

HMIP's initial task was to organise research to discover the best available techniques (BAT) for organic chemical processes. 'The results of the BAT reviews assist HMIP in identifying what constitutes BAT and, to some extent what constitutes BATNEEC (though the 'excessive cost' component is dependent on a wide range of industrial investment and market factors in each sector and can be considered by HMIP only in generic terms). These conclusions are published in formal Guidance Notes (Chief Inspector's Guidance to Inspectors) in line with the Ministerial undertaking that HMIP's thinking on BAT be made available to industry in advance of each process coming under IPC' (HMIP, 1993b, p.16).

The articulation of BATNEEC was to be administered by HMIP along the following lines:

1   Review the Best Available Techniques for specific types of prescribed process.

2   Use the findings of this review to produce CIGNs containing performance standards which HMIP considers BATNEEC for new processes.

This then was the standard setting task.   Though the following analysis focuses upon CIGNs for organic chemical processes, many of the features presented are not particular to those processes.   The approach adopted by HMIP for organic chemical CIGNs followed that for earlier industrial sectors and was repeated for subsequent sectors (HMIP, 1993b; 1993c).

Resource shortages and BAT reviews

An 'independent' approach was adopted by HMIP in its review of BAT.   BPM Notes emerged through the collaborative effort of the air policy community. Industrial involvement was sufficiently deep for them to be involved prior to the issue of any draft BPM Notes for more formal consultation.   This was to change with CIGN production.   HMIP regarded industry as one type of consultee following the formal issue of internally drafted CIGNs, albeit an important consultee.

Contracting in resources

The 'RCI' leadership at HMIP had been used to receiving technical advice independent of industry (from the Radioactive Waste Management Advisory Committee).   In keeping with this, HMIP contracted consultants to conduct the BAT reviews for IPC.   It was consistent with their new rules of the game.

There were also more pragmatic reasons for using consultants.   As one Inspector recalled:

The reason we used consultants was resources.   It was a huge, huge task, there was no way we could do it ourselves ... We also liked the idea of an independent look, so that we didn't go in with preconceived ideas about what could or could not be achieved.   That was part of the reason for

141

consultants. The other was, clearly, we just didn't have the time anyway - so we had to use consultants.

The undermanned and technically ill-prepared HMIP had to boost its resource base by contracting consultants. But it wasn't a reluctant decision; using independent advice on BAT satisfied senior HMIP and DoE intentions that IPC would be a break from the past. Any perception and criticism of regulatory capture coming from the broader environmental issue network could thus be forestalled.

Consultants were selected through competitive tendering. Four different consultants were chosen for organic chemical BAT reviews: Ashact Ltd; Cremer and Warner; Radian; and W S Atkins. Their objective was 'To assess the range of technology options available for the design and operation of all stages of the scheduled organic chemical processes from the receipt of raw materials onward, together with the associated equipment for the abatement and treatment of all gaseous, liquid and solid waste streams, thereby enabling the Inspectorate to judge whether the Best Available Technique (BAT) to minimise pollution is being proposed for any particular circumstance' (HMIP, 1993f). Groups of process were allotted to each, such that some of the resulting BAT reviews fed into more than one CIGN. The BAT reviews and related CIGNs are listed alongside one another in Table 5.5.

Having six months to report on BAT, most consultants relied upon an examination of UK practice. For this they visited some UK chemical operators. Several of the operators interviewed had been visited by consultants. Some of the comments on draft CIGNs sent to me by other operators also mentioned the consultants. Consultants were not policy actors, they had no agenda and did not seek influence. However, they did alter the mechanism for setting regulatory standards.

Lack of knowledge and authority and the effect on resource interdependency

Operators used to participation in the formulation of BPM Notes were unhappy with their exclusion from the production of CIGNs. Some of the air Inspectors within HMIP also criticised the use of consultants (Inspector interview).

HMIP Inspectors worked from consultants' BAT reports in drafting CIGNs. The process 'didn't have that element of sitting down and thrashing it out with industry. It was worked off a consultant's report straight through, and all the weaknesses were there to be seen ... I think what it means is that the Chief Inspector has said they are not prescriptive. In other words you have to make your own mind up' (Inspector interview). Operators had been involved in

142

producing draft BPM Notes and formulating the standards to be applied. The BPM Note process actively sought consensus.

Table 5.5
BAT reports and CIGNs for the organic chemicals sector

BAT Review and Published Report	Chief Inspector's Guidance Note
Evaluation of processes for the manufacture of organic chemicals containing oxygen or sulphur, with particular reference to pollution control.	Processes for the production or use of organic sulphur compounds, use or recovery of carbon disulphide (IPR 4/4).
A review of the available techniques for pollution control in the manufacture and use of nitrogen containing organic compounds.	Processes for the production or use of acetylene, aldehydes, etc (IPR 4/3). Processes for the production and use of amines, nitriles, isocyanates and pyridines (IPR 4/2).
Pollution control for organic monomer processes.	Production and polymerisation of organic chemicals in multi-purpose plant (IPR 4/6).
Pollution control for organic fine chemicals.	Batch manufacture of organic chemicals in multi-purpose plant (IPR 4/5).
Pollution control for metal carbonyl processes and the manufacture of compounds of chromium, magnesium, manganese, nickel and zinc.	Processes for the manufacture of organo-metallic compounds (IPR 4/7).

One criticism raised by air Inspectors and operators for CIGNs was a perceived lack of knowledge from consultants. Air Inspectors in particular, who took a pride in their technical professionalism, didn't like the consultants' involvement. 'We said, we don't want this. We don't want consultants wandering into works. In fact the consultants who were signed up were appalling. I had one of the major cement manufacturers 'phone me up and say, what on Earth's this man doing here? He happens to be a surveyor, we've had to show him the front end of the cement kiln. They got so stroppy' (Inspector interview). This is anecdotal and may not be generalisable. However, studying the consultancy entries in KOMPASS and Kelly's Directories, none of them profess an expertise in chemical engineering. Their knowledge resource was more in environmental engineering and pollution control, that is, general end-of-pipe activities.

One of the operators interviewed recalled the consultants who visited him as not appearing particularly knowledgeable about chemical industry operations, tending to ask uncritically about processes and abatement techniques, and recording what his company said 'which obviously suited operators I suppose'.

Another firm commented 'The process descriptions for polystyrene manufacture are rather poor and even inaccurate in certain areas. The information for preparing the draft guidance (for styrene polymerisation) was collected from [the consultant] under a consulting contract from HMIP. In my view this was not good procedure. Two people from [the consultant] spent about two hours with me during which time I described the processes, they took notes, and finally had a plant tour. They worked their notes into a draft and submitted it to me. I had to re-write about 80 per cent of it, but had no feedback from them when I submitted my re-draft. I suspect this may explain some of the discrepancies in the actual guidance note'. A specialities manufacturer said, 'our impression was that they didn't really know what they were talking about'.

The CIA were particularly angered by the lack of industrial involvement in the BAT review. One of their environment experts wrote that 'despite the amount of work put into the Guidance Notes, they are not of a consistently high quality and are in some respects misleading. This stems in our view from the HMIP use of consultants of variable qualities rather than asking industry directly for input'. The CIA argued that BATNEEC for individual operations needed to be applied. Similarly, a CBI submission to the government's Deregulation Unit (see chapter 6) noted concerns amongst its membership about 'the lack of consultation' over IPC implementation (CBI, 1993).

Technically competent or not, the consultants like the Inspectors were dependent upon operators for the technical information necessary to determine BAT. But this dependency was even more acute with consultants. They lacked any legal authority with which to prise information from reluctant operators. Some operators were reticent about providing consultants with lots of technical information which they could commercially exploit after their HMIP contracts. Thus the inevitable resource interdependency between operator and regulator weighed more heavily against the consultants. 'One of the headaches was that they had no powers of entry, and so the only information they could get was what companies were prepared to tell them. And if companies refused to tell them anything, there was nothing they could do about it' (Inspector interview). Their provision to HMIP of an independent source of technical advice was compromised, their dependency upon operators more acute.

The BAT reports produced by the consultants were a disappointment to HMIP. They lacked important information necessary to draft CIGNs with confidence. One Inspector involved with CIGNs explained:

> Obviously, we had preconceived ideas as to what we would hope would come back. We'd like them to come back and say, "well these are the options that are available, this is how much it costs for this option, and this is the performance of this plant". That would have been great. Unfortunately we didn't get that. Part of the reason we didn't get it was there was a very limited amount of monitoring data available. Companies didn't know how well this equipment was performing because they hadn't been monitoring; and they hadn't been monitoring because they hadn't been required to monitor. So the first snag was how do you assess one method against another when you don't know how its performing ... So [consultants] would say, these range of abatement options are being used, this is the range of processing options, and look qualitatively at what is generally used in industry. And that was really as much as they could do.

HMIP did not receive as high a quality information resource as it had hoped. A historical lack of necessity with regard to industrial environmental management meant many operators did not know the environmental performance of their processes. Even those processes registered under the air regulatory regime had limited emissions data. Consequently, the BAT review became a more qualitative study of the range of processes and abatement techniques used in the organic chemicals sector. Environmental data to distinguish between techniques was lacking. Examination of the published BAT reports confirms this (for example, HMIP, 1993f).

Compounding HMIP's problems was a lack of economic information such that 'NEEC' could be systematically determined. HMIP was unable to modify this resource imbalance in order to achieve the authoritative, standard setting autonomy it desired. HMIP could draw upon Inspector experience in coming up with emission limits, but it did not have the economic armoury to defend them as being efficient for an industrial sector. Inspectors were chemists and engineers not economists. HMIP had no database of abatement technology or process costs (Inspector interview). Dependency upon operators for regulatory information passed, by default, to the site-level.

Draft Chief Inspector's Guidance Notes and a return to bottom-up standard setting

So BAT reports provided drafting Inspectors with qualitative descriptions of process operations and abatement techniques. The environmental performance of the BAT were, in many cases, simply unknown to operators, consultants and now Inspectors. Ideally, the Inspectors responsible for working BAT reports into CIGNs would have experience with the relevant processes, either from working in industry or regulating them under air regulations. But at the time it was a question of seconding whoever was available in the field, 'again because of resources it wasn't always possible to get "the expert". They could be wrapped up in something equally important elsewhere' (interview with Inspector). Consequently, many of the drafting Inspectors were new recruits to HMIP.

The consultants' BAT reports helped provide descriptions of the types of processes, likely prescribed substances released, and abatement techniques used by operators. However, the drafting Inspectors had to fall back upon more traditional techniques in determining emission limits and other BATNEEC standards for their draft CIGNs. Quantification was introduced to the CIGNs by a variety of methods familiar to BPM Note production: limits being met under previous regulations; knowledge about emissions based upon individual Inspector experience; discussions with a few operators; and drawing upon 'reasonable' limits used overseas (such as the German TA Luft) (interview with Inspector).

It was important to HMIP that limits included in the draft CIGNs should appear 'reasonable' . The basis for those limits was not robust. HMIP's authority could have been damaged had it revealed to operators its lack of knowledge concerning industrial operations. Operator perception became an influential factor in the production of CIGNs.

A key audience was obviously going to be the industry that was going to be regulated by [the Notes]. So we had to listen to them. They made some fair points about the prescriptiveness of them. They said what they didn't want was for expectations to be unfairly raised in either the media, the general public, pressure groups, or indeed for Inspectors. That, you know, here are these Notes telling you what industry will be able to achieve. So I think it was a good point made by industry that we had to make sure the Notes didn't come over as being prescriptive.
(Inspector involved in CIGN production)

Note that HMIP did not consider using favourable public expectation[8] to boost its political legitimacy to set tough standards. Indeed, from the

146

production of the first draft onwards, any notion of the CIGNs being prescriptive was dispelled by HMIP. HMIP decided to dilute its intentions rather than mobilise diffuse public support. Distribution of (knowledge) resources was not in HMIP's favour, and they accepted industry's appreciative system concerning expectations about IPC's stringency.

Changes made to the draft CIGNs which appear in the published CIGNs are catalogued in the following section. Some consultee responses provided HMIP with new information to be included in a second draft CIGN before final publication - such as better emissions performance than expected (fed into tighter limits[9]). Comparing the original draft CIGNs with those finally published provides snapshots of an important element of the policy process. Pressure from industry shifted standard setting from centrally produced CIGNs to site-level negotiation with operators. The arms' length approach received its coup de grâce and allowed a return to policy community relations.

Industrial criticism and changes to the draft CIGNs

Consultation responses from industry and discussion with some operators prompted several revisions to organic chemical CIGNs. By comparing the original draft CIGNs issued for consultation (in April 1992) with the final CIGNs it has been possible to identify these changes. A list of the consultation respondents was obtained from HMIP, and by writing to those on the list it was possible to obtain a number of industrial responses. Examination of these consultation responses has enabled analysis of industrial influence upon the CIGNs. Out of a total of 32 organic chemical consultee responses, 14 were thus obtained for analysis.

Formal consultation on CIGNs was a HMIP-industry affair predominantly. Some operator comments were particular to their process, such as noting CIGN emission limits were laxer than their experience, or that the wording of the draft didn't make sense. Others commented upon the limited consultation.

A general criticism from operators was that the process descriptions included in Annex I of the CIGNs were too superficial to be of use. One operator said HMIP had failed to capture all the techniques used with processes relating to specific CIGNs. 'The various introductions to Annex I are of mixed quality. We would recommend that you review these with a view to emphasising that Annex I is not an exhaustive description of all processes covered by that Guidance Note'. One multi-national failed to see how the descriptions could serve any practical regulatory purpose. 'We find it difficult to see the point of these process descriptions. The level of detail is mostly that which could be obtained from standard texts on chemical engineering technology.[10] No guidance is apparent on which aspects of the technology described are

147

considered to be BAT nor is guidance given on how to assess in the particular circumstances on a site, the BPEO in relation to each process'.

Indeed, interviewed operators found the CIGNs of little use for their understanding of BATNEEC. One of the operators interviewed said the relevant CIGN process descriptions 'bear no resemblance to what we do on site'. He criticised the CIGNs, 'I don't know why they print them 48 pages long, because people pick them up and think, yep, it applies to my industry. So that's the cover that matters. What are the emissions to air? Page eight, read those. Stick it in the corner. Very little else'. Judging from operator criticisms of the CIGNs, Inspectors unfamiliar with organic chemical processes can only have gained an introductory knowledge of the types of operation being carried on by operators. The authority of any centrally set guidance had been undermined, as illustrated below.

It is the more general and repeated points made by industrial respondents, reflected in CIGN changes, which are of interest here. The first two industrial influences are of general importance and became relevant to all CIGNs under IPC, the remainder tend to be more specific to organic chemicals. The changes made to CIGNs are listed below in order of significance with respect to their impact upon making IPC implementation site-specific, and all are elaborated in the following sub-sections:

1   A softening of the prescriptiveness of emission limits and other guidance.

2   A loosening of the requirements for a process upgrading timetable from operators.

3   Introduction of flexibility concerning the definition of the 'process' to be regulated (envelope authorisations).

4   Removing practical examples of what might be deemed a 'substantial change' to a process, as termed in the legislation.

5   Less comprehensive guidance for Inspectors on elements that might constitute a waste audit, which should be asked of operators.

6   Modification of Volatile Organic Chemical (VOC) substance classification, with a relaxation of limits for some classes of VOC.

Emphasising the non-prescriptiveness of the guidance

Faced with challenges from industry, HMIP emphasised the non-prescriptive nature of the CIGNs. Most release limits were for air, with none for land and only two set for water (cadmium and mercury). This reflected HMIP's inherited strength in air pollution, and an acknowledged gap in knowledge concerning the effects and control of prescribed substances in the aquatic environment (ENDS, 1992, p.19). It also indicates the extent to which the quantification in CIGNs was dependent upon experience within HMIP compared to data collected by consultants.

The limits set were the same across all the organic CIGNs, based as it was on Inspector experience of the sort of emissions achievable from standard end-of-pipe abatement equipment (interview with Inspector involved in CIGN production). 'At one point we were considering whether it was appropriate to actually put any limits in at all, because of the diversity of processes being carried on. But we felt that that would be even less helpful, and what we wanted to do was to give as much advice as we could about what we were expecting. Even if it ended up as being fairly consistent advice across a wide range of processes, that was better than saying nothing', explained the Inspector.

One of the speciality operators interviewed was involved in a team of operators who responded to the draft CIGNs through a CIA committee. He said, 'we almost certainly challenged most of them [the limits]. The main thrust of our challenge was not the $5mg/m^3$ when we wanted it to be $50mg/m^3$; but our main sort of thrust was, well why is it $5mg/m^3$? Where had that come from? What is the logic behind that? Let us comment on that to see where you've come from. But we never really got any response. That was our main complaint ... I think this was the compromise in the end. In the end they decided they were going to go their own way, they were going to set their own limits even tighter than in the first draft, as they'd had a chance to think about them. Then they clearly kept coming out with the fact that, well why are you so upset, this is guidance, this is just guidance for interpretation. In other words it doesn't mean to say that that's going to be slapped on you and you've got to meet that law by day one'.

Consequently, appearing in the published CIGNs and absent from the initial drafts is a boldly typed caveat making plain the CIGN's non-prescriptory nature:

Potential operators and other interested parties should appreciate that whether an authorisation is granted, and on what conditions, will depend on all the circumstances of an individual application, including this Guidance. Although this Guidance is intended to assist, it should not be misunderstood as binding Inspectors and the Chief Inspector to grant (or refuse) an application, or to impose particular conditions. What follows should be understood as Guidance, and not a binding commitment.
(HMIP, 1993, p.1)

149

This meant the CIGNs sat uncomfortably with DoE guidance on IPC. The latter 'expected that [new] plant will be designed to meet the standards in the appropriate guidance note' (DoE, 1993, p.14); and 'the lack of profitability of a particular business should not affect the determination' (DoE, 1993, p.12). The CIGNs themselves now appeared to say it all depended on the individual circumstances for each application. The DoE was maintaining the formality of sector-wide economic considerations and standards to which new plant are expected to conform. HMIP, under industry pressure, was moving back toward the site specificities of the old air regime. The DoE received draft CIGNs, but was concerned only with their compatibility with the Environmental Protection Act (interview with DoE civil servant); that is, with the law not policy. The DoE's role was consequently very limited. The detail of CIGNs was a matter for it's technical experts at HMIP. Indeed, this lack of interference, and their policy of encouraging Appellants back into negotiation with HMIP, places the DoE outside the IPC policy community.

Loosening the upgrading timetable requirements

Draft CIGNs included specific instructions concerning the operator's inclusion of upgrading timetables in applications. Existing process applicants were to 'provide the Inspector with a detailed programme for upgrading or closing the plant as part of the first application' (HMIP, 1992, p.13). The published guidance was less exacting: 'those areas that require upgrading should be identified, and the possible techniques to be employed to bring them up to new plant standards indicated. A provisional timetable of upgrading should be submitted with the application. A detailed programme should be submitted within six months of the date of the issue of an authorisation and should take into account any provisions of the authorisation' (HMIP, 1993, p.9).

The guidance effectively deferred setting upgrading standards until after issuing an authorisation. A detailed upgrading timetable would be the subject of face-to-face, site-level negotiation.

Moreover, the deadline for meeting new process BATNEEC standards had been weakened. In the draft CIGNs, upgrading was to be done 'at the earliest opportunity and no later than the 1st May 1997'. The published CIGNs suggest Inspectors seek an upgrade 'generally no later than 1st May 1997'. Moreover, if upgrading would require a 'major change in process configuration' (HMIP, 1993, p.9) then there may be an extension to the upgrading period. ICI's environmental adviser, Mike Wright, told ENDS Report at the time that he thought such a provision would be widely used (ENDS, 1993, p.33).

This chapter began by explaining how processes in the organic chemical sector are often not as homogenous as in other industrial sectors. IPC Regulations[11] prescribed organic chemical processes according to their chemistry and not the technology they used. This presented problems, especially for firms carrying on a variety of chemical processes using the same equipment. The Regulations implied they would have to apply for an authorisation each time they operated a new class of chemical reaction on their plant. There would be more paperwork in preparing numerous applications, with detrimental effects upon manufacturing lead times.

Even bulk chemical companies were faced with a requirement to apply for several authorisations for what they considered to be, in a business sense, a single process. Integrated processes used an ensemble of chemistry. If some of these were inorganic processes then they would not need authorising until the later, inorganic chemical sector IPC application deadline (May-July 1994).

Consequently, IPC was causing uncertainty and fear of red tape amongst operators (ENDS, 1993c, p.20). As early as February 1991 operators and the CIA had lobbied the DoE's political leaders about the Regulations. Tony Baldry, Parliamentary Under Secretary of State for the Environment wrote that 'further consultation will be undertaken on detailed issues as appropriate' (Parliamentary Written Answers, 21st February 1991, Column 198). But the sheer political pace of IPC's introduction meant the Regulations were passed unaltered in April 1991, the majority of other industrial sectors having more straightforward processes for regulation.

Aware of the problem, HMIP issued an informal consultation paper amongst chemical operators in September 1991 (ENDS, 1991, p.29). It introduced the 'envelope' concept as a device for accommodating operators' needs for flexible process authorisations. The paper proposed granting a single authorisation for an 'envelope' of activities, which the operator would detail in an initial application. Switching between activities would merely require the streamlined notification of HMIP.[12]

Some enveloping was mutually beneficial to both policy actors. HMIP lacked the organisational resource to meet the persistent workload associated with hundreds of applications from the speciality chemicals sector. Envelopes could help contain the regulatory burden upon both policy actors - the question was, how wide should envelopes become? Industry welcomed the concept as an opportunity to secure the flexibility they desired. 'The approach still needs to be tested particularly from the point of view of the size of the envelope' (CIA, 1992b, p.7).

Propelling the envelope concept were events at the site-level. The next chapter covers the site-level implementation of IPC. Nevertheless, it is useful to enter briefly that territory here, since the envelope issue serves as a clear illustration of bottom-up influence upon IPC. As new or substantially changed organic processes came into IPC ahead of the timetable for existing processes (July 1993), so problems with the initial envelope approach became apparent. The diversity of processes allowed in each envelope was limited by the Regulations.

Operators wanted more flexible, wider envelopes, and renewed their lobbying. The CIA met Minister for the Environment and Countryside, David Maclean, on 24th February 1993. He wrote that, 'The industry believes that problems of process definition will result in unreasonable uncertainty and excessive cost for the industry in applying for authorisations under IPC and will delay the authorisation process' (Parliamentary Written Answer, 6th May 1993, Column 175). The CIA won participation in amending the legislation and were able to increase the flexibility with which processes were regulated.

On 6th May 1993 David Maclean announced an extension of the organic IPC application deadline to 31st October 1993.[13] This would allow time for the passage of amended Regulations[14] allowing greater flexibility over the definition of process envelopes. It also provided a valuable breathing space for operators struggling to get applications in on time (as reported by several operators interviewed). The Minister mentioned that 'a small working party comprising representatives of the industry and of HMIP has been looking into this problem' (DoE, 1993b). The reduction in prescription on other CIGN issues facilitated greater policy network integration in future, site-level negotiation. The envelope issue differed to the extent that industry was able to become integrated in the implementing network earlier on, at the central guidance level rather than the site-level.

It was a CIA-HMIP working party that approached the DoE with proposals for legislative change. A DoE civil servant recalled, 'it was fairly obvious that they wanted to be able to say, our process is an 'x' and we want one authorisation in the same way as everyone else ... It meant if HMIP agreed with the applicant that it was a coherent activity they would get an authorisation for it'. Envelope authorisations would now be set for the 'most apt' groups of process activities (HMIP, 1993d). Industry lobbyists successfully widened the flexibility further, to allow the inclusion of process heaters in an envelope, which hitherto had had to have their own (fuel and power) authorisation.

Moreover, the industry obtained a small batch envelope clause. This made process definitions completely flexible for plant producing small quantities of chemical product. Any chemical reaction, not just the most apt groupings, can be carried on these plant and only one authorisation is necessary. The DoE civil servant said, 'that came out of the end of what we were doing in terms of trying to make it easier to identify a process and give it an authorisation. We had fairly heavy lobbying from the small fine chemicals sector ... It doesn't matter whether the Inspector thinks its really one process or not, they get one authorisation'. An interviewed operator involved in that lobbying described it as 'the final coup, where you could have one application up to 250 tonnes per year where anything could go in'.

On the envelope issue, operators had secured a return to the collaborative participation enjoyed under BPM. The CIA believed their point had been demonstrated: 'We believe that the process of defining the problems and looking at potential solutions through a co-operative effort ... has proved its worth. We, therefore, support the proposal for the production by HMIP of appropriate guidance which is urgently needed. We consider that the involvement of the CIA in the process is imperative because of the greater knowledge the chemical industry, by definition, has of its own operations than does HMIP' (Written correspondence between CIA and DoE, 19th August 1993).

Amended Regulations were laid before Parliament on 5th October 1993, and guidance issued to Inspectors on the 17th October. This was barely two weeks before the application deadline. For the most part the envelope division of a site's prescribed activities had already been negotiated with the local Inspector. Operators generally wanted fewer envelopes because this meant fewer IPC charges. Inspectors, meanwhile, were concerned that their decisions were consistent with any central guidance and the decisions of their colleagues.

Industry's organisational resource enabled a case history of envelope decisions to be built up for use during site-level negotiation. Speciality firm Thomas Swan Ltd initially obtained validation from HMIP for a site-wide envelope application. This was later revoked and three envelopes negotiated. This did not stop a number of other operators trying to get similar site-wide envelopes. An Inspector said one multi-national had to have an unminuted meeting between its senior staff and HMIP's Director, David Slater, in order to resolve the issue.

The late finalisation of official envelope guidance removed earlier uncertainty. This multinational operator's experience of that uncertainty was typical amongst interviewees: 'It was like moving goal posts, because our Inspector, her understanding of the rules of the game about enveloping were changing all the time as well. She was new to the job, Slater was moving the goal posts every five minutes, and HMIP was under pressure from the CIA ... and what we did was we were eventually able to justify that we could have the chemistry that was involved in the epoxy additives manufacture all put under one generic title of condensation reactions, which is really stretching it'. HMIP removed earlier uncertainty by agreeing to widen the flexibility of its envelope concept.

Some operators took advantage of the changes by challenging earlier envelope decisions. As supervisory Inspector Peter Merrill wrote

It was evident that the basis for those challenges to the Inspectorate's interpretation of the amended [Regulations] were financial rather than technical issues. We have been, in the main, successful in avoiding confrontations by the deployment of admirable negotiating skills but are now committed to involving the CIA, representing the main industrial players, in the re-examination of our interpretations. We believe that we should see this as an opportunity to demonstrate our flexibility in that we may consider, and where appropriate accommodate, refinements to the definition of process such that it is of best utility in both regulation and control.
(HMIP, 1994b, p.17)

Operators admitted in interview that cost was an influential factor in wanting fewer envelopes. Some operators have sought variations to rationalise[15] the envelopes split across their site, usually in the light of experience of working with IPC. One operator was able to re-align his envelopes such that each contained a mixture of plant of different ages. This contrasted with the initial split which resulted in one envelope containing just old plant. 'There's a bit of a greying at the edges now, which in a way is to our advantage ... in that it gives us a bit more scope in justifying operating the older plant unit with one or two minor improvements rather than a major investment upgrade' (operator interview).

An indication of the flexibility HMIP allowed over envelope amendments is the reduction in IPC authorisations compared to initial estimates. Early in 1993, HMIP anticipated 650 organic chemical (envelope) processes requiring authorisation (DoE, 1994, p.5). Eventually, 481 applications were received (HMIP, 1995e, p.2) from 219 operators (Written correspondence with Minister for Environment and Countryside, David Atkins, via Sir Derek Spencer MP). That is, more flexible envelopes reduced the number of authorised 'processes' by approximately one quarter. This matches the experience amongst the operators interviewed.[16]

The overall picture gained from operator and Inspector interviews is that of site-level negotiation over how best to group processes into envelopes, based on loose definitions of process chemistry. When the Regulations and official guidance finally caught up with the issue, many envelope decisions had been agreed, though sometimes after several changes. Some operators used the new guidelines to modify those agreements and have since asked for variations to their authorisations. This was the key outcome of the whole envelope saga: it reduced the prescriptiveness with which Inspectors had to separate IPC applications, and formally deferred the definition of authorisable processes to site-level negotiation with operators.

Reduced elaboration of the meaning of 'substantial change'

Prescribed processes which undergo a 'substantial change' have to re-apply for an IPC authorisation.[17] This is taken to mean a change resulting in a substantial increase in substances released from the process. Draft CIGNs provided some examples of the types of substantial change warranting re-application. These included the addition of an exhaust gas incinerator using auxiliary fuel, or increasing the flow of scrubber liquor in order to enhance the capture of emissions. Both might lead to an overall increase in environmental releases. For similar reasons an increase in process throughput of five per cent or more was given as an example of a substantial change. These examples, particularly the last, were opposed by industrial respondents.

The published CIGN dropped all examples of substantial change. Indeed, it expanded the list of examples of non-substantial change to include conversion to purer feed-stocks. Inspectors were referred to DoE guidance for 'what constitutes a substantial change' (HMIP, 1993, p.14). Ironically, the DoE is of circumlocutory help: 'Guidance on what constitutes a substantial change for a particular class of process will be included in the relevant Chief Inspector's Guidance Note' (DoE, 1993, p.17).

Less detailed guidance on waste audits

In both the draft and published CIGNs HMIP suggests Inspectors should encourage operators to conduct waste audits for their processes.[18] The CIA thought this over-extended the scope of IPC, 'pushing IPC to the limits' (CIA's Diane Browne, quoted in ENDS, 1992, p.18) - even though the CIA advises companies to do audits under its Responsible Care programme. HMIP argued it was a valid 'management technique' in pursuing BATNEEC (HMIP, 1993e, p.52). Waste audits 'identify deficiencies in the data and information to be included in their applications; and also identify areas within their processes where reductions in the releases of substances ... may be accomplished' (HMIP, 1993, pp.6-7).

The draft CIGNs included quite a detailed list of exercises and items which a waste audit should consider.[19] The outcome should result in the identification of preferred cleaner process improvements in addition to the usual end-of-pipe measures.

What we tried to do was give a bit of advice on how you go about [a waste audit]. I think what we put in initially was too prescriptive about how it

155

should be done. Again it came across as being a bit overbearing, and HMIP telling people how to do things ... Again it was industry's concern that we were being prescriptive about how things should be done. Now all the time we were trying to say, this is a way of doing it. But we soon realised that it was putting people's backs up. So that's why we softened it dramatically, so that what we were saying is, in general this is what we need you to do, how you do it is up to you. But we had to make that clearer so that people weren't over concerned that we were trying to be prescriptive.
(Inspector interview)

In the face of industry pressure, published CIGNs offered a brief and general suggestion for release minimisation assessments, which 'do not seek to impose particular procedures' (HMIP, 1993, p.7).

Relaxing of the volatile organic compound classification

Draft CIGNs had set an emission limit of $20mg/m^3$ for all VOCs. Several operators were concerned at the all-inclusiveness of this limit. 'We are particularly concerned with the single figure limit (of $20mg/m^3$) set for emissions of organic chemicals into the air. It is known that different organic chemicals have substantially differing effects on living organisms and also, it has been predicted, widely different contributions to the creation of ozone in the lower atmosphere. Consequently, a limit which would represent BATNEEC for more critical organic chemicals at a larger scale could entail excessive costs in many other cases' (An operator's consultation comment).
So for VOCs, HMIP devised two categories with more or less stringent emission limits. Class A VOCs retained a $20mg/m^3$ emission limit, reflecting their higher potential for harm. Other, Class B VOCs were downgraded to a less severe $80mg/m^3$ (HMIP, 1993, p.11).
For air releases in general, there was concern that emission limits were expressed exclusively as concentrations. Some operators wished to see mass emission limits. Removing substances from exhaust gases can involve reducing the air flow rate, which has the perverse effect of raising substance concentrations even though the overall mass of substance released has been reduced. Consequently, the published CIGN included a statement alerting Inspectors to the option of setting emission limits as a mass limit per unit of product manufactured (HMIP, 1993, p.12).
This was one final element in a general reduction in prescriptiveness concerning CIGNs and their elaboration of BATNEEC standards. But was this reduction particular to the chemical industry?

Weakened CIGNs and abandonment of top-down regulation

The overall effect of the changes to organic chemical CIGNs was to defer regulatory standard setting until site-level implementation and thereby strengthen industrial influence over them. The guidance presented in CIGNs, concerning BATNEEC for new processes and the standards to which existing processes should upgrade, was not to be enforced uniformly by Inspectors; it was to be mitigated by site-specific factors.

The organic chemical CIGNs were the first CIGNs to do this. All earlier CIGNs did not contain the caveats emphasising the non-prescriptory nature of the guidance, that authorisation conditions 'depend on all the circumstances of an individual application' (HMIP, 1993, p.1). Moreover, the emissions standards listed in earlier CIGNs appeared more prescriptive: 'For all new plant the following concentration limits apply ...' (HMIP, 1992b, p.6).

CIGNs are made less prescriptive for all sectors

One might think that the complexities of the organic chemicals sector was the reason for a lack of prescription. But subsequent CIGNs for less complex industrial sectors show a similar retreat from prescription. The format for CIGNs was revised. Subsequent CIGNs, and the four yearly revisions to original ones, no longer claim to present uniform guidance on BATNEEC for new processes. Instead they provide 'guidance on the best available techniques and standards for the class of processes defined ... without any consideration of ... site-specific issues ... The achievable release levels[20] in this Note do not take into account site-specific considerations and they should not be used as uniform release standards' (HMIP, 1995d, p.1). Post-chemicals sector CIGNs make it clear: IPC regulatory standards are no longer an industrial sector-wide issue, they are a site-specific issue for Inspectors and operators.

The same is true for process upgrading. Early CIGNs specified a date by which 'all existing processes should be upgraded to achieve the standards in this Note for new plant' (HMIP, 1992c, p.5). The new format CIGNs are even less ambitious than organic chemical CIGNs: 'The state and design of existing plant may prevent operators from achieving the release levels given in this Note, even with improvements ... Improvement plans are a site-specific issue, therefore, no target dates are included in this Note' (HMIP, 1995d, p.2).

A return to familiar rules of the game

On the 24th May 1993, HMIP's Head of Policy, Douglas Bryce, announced officially HMIP's abandonment of its arms' length approach (ENDS, 1993b, p.30). Unofficially, the arms' length approach had begun to buckle much sooner. Inspectors were practising closer, pre-application consultation with operators and were negotiating authorisation standards with them. Keith Allot believes this began after 'the disastrous first round of IPC applications' (1994, p.ix). HMIP had to return all of the 88 applications for combustion plant processes to operators, along with a 98 point questionnaire in order to solicit information needed to determine an authorisation. This episode led to long and sometimes acrimonious negotiations and Appeals from the operators. The tight implementation timetable could not accommodate such delays for every sector, particularly the large organic chemicals sector. Thus some (unofficial) pre-application consultation and relaxing of arms' was practised by Inspectors simply to smooth the regulatory process (see chapter 6).

The information included in operators' applications was of poor quality (Allott, 1994), just as it had been in BAT reports. In both instances this lack of information made standard setting difficult for HMIP. It could not sustain the hierarchical, centralised approach. Operators and Inspectors were consulting and negotiating at the individual site-level. Bottom-up pressures were shifting the rules of the game back to those typical of the air regime: centrally set standards were being abandoned for Inspector judgement; formal decision making procedures had to be replaced with informal consensus seeking; and Inspectors worked more closely with operators rather than regulating at a distance. The transparency hoped for with IPC also began to cloud over.

So the announcement that HMIP was no longer pursuing an arms' length approach merely confirmed unofficial practice. The CIA was reporting the end of the arms' length approach to their members seven months ahead of the HMIP announcement, 'in order to make the process of obtaining an authorisation more efficient' (CIA, 1992b, p.2). The reduction in CIGN prescription reflected this too. Their role had changed with the rules of the game. The changing rules also made possible the re-creation of a policy community, the subject of chapter 6.

Summary and conclusions

CIGNs began as an articulation of process specific BATNEEC standards for Inspectors to seek from operators. They have become guidance on items to consider in the site-specific negotiation of regulatory standards. Lack of CIGN prescription was not unique to the complex organic chemical sector, CIGNs in general now emphasise the importance of site-specifics. Analysis of the production of the organic chemical CIGNs explains this trend. The central reason was HMIP's dependency upon operators for technical and economic information concerning BATNEEC. The opportunity cost required to reduce this dependency, in terms of the organisational effort and time needed to set robust standards, was too great.

Initially, there was a desire on the part of the HMIP leadership to make a break from past standard setting arrangements. The use of consultants to gather BAT information 'independently' angered industrial operators and representatives. They felt shut out of the sector-wide standard setting process and feared an arms' length HMIP would uniformly apply these standards. Policy network integration was breaking down. Yet operators were able to re-enter and influence the standard setting process because HMIP lacked the knowledge to set robust BATNEEC standards on its own. The production of organic chemical CIGNs involved conflict between two policy actors seeking to impose contrasting rules of the game for IPC's implementation. The distribution of resources meant industry was more successful than HMIP.

Industry wanted flexible regulatory standards such as those enjoyed under the air regime. Its opposition to prescriptive, sector-wide standards could not be answered by HMIP because the justifying evidence behind them was so scant. BAT could not be distinguished in terms of environmental releases because the techniques reviewed possessed insufficient release data. A historical lack of necessity meant many processes' environmental performance was unknown. HMIP were left with nothing with which to answer industrial critics other than to emphasise that the standards in CIGNs were non-prescriptive and that authorisation conditions would be set through consideration of site-specificities. The importance of local circumstances was the source of the air regimes flexibility, and now it appeared HMIP were reverting to similar flexibilities over IPC.

Industry had indeed influenced the policy process, successfully challenging the arms' length approach. The power to do this lay in industry's position as the source of information necessary to create (technology-based) BATNEEC standards. However, other factors helped their successful influence attempt. The sheer volume of work organic chemical operators presented HMIP meant that the regulator was conscious it had to balance its regulatory requests against keeping to the implementation timetable.

Moreover, an industry backed government deregulation drive was spotlighting IPC as a bureaucratic burden upon operators. Launched in 1993, this red tape cutting exercise critically examined all areas of business regulation. Its timing was most opportune for industry, coinciding with IPC implementation and providing it with an opportunity to alert Ministers at important Departments, such as the DTi, to operator grievances. The deregulation drive proved to be an important and influential pressure upon IPC. It facilitated further HMIP's retreat to site-specific regulation. For this reason it is the first topic of discussion in the next chapter, which analyses site-level implementation of IPC.

Notes

1　The chemicals may be feed-stock for the contractor's own process, or they may be contracting out the small scale development of a new chemical process ahead of full scale manufacture.

2　Multi-nationals have bought up small firms in order to obtain specialisms in particular areas of industrial organic chemistry - though the UK still has a thriving independent specialities sector.

3　All CIA members must be part of its Responsible Care scheme. Part of the scheme involves 'cells' of local chemical companies meeting to share experiences and so on.

4　Monitoring was also being done by the Petrochemical Industries Association, chlorine producers and fertiliser manufacturers (interview with field Inspectors).

5　The CIA had an IPC Implementation Task Force. As an example of its lobbying work, it submitted the results of a survey of members about IPC, particularly the costs, to the DTi and HMIP in October 1994. It concluded that 'the level of costs remains a serious concern' (estimated at £31m, of which £10m were on IPC fees), and that there was 'too much emphasis' on documentation and a 'high degree of bureaucracy was perceived' (CIA, 1994, p.12).

6　Under the Environmental Protection Act, 1990 local authorities had finally been given prior approval air pollution regulations for 'middle tier' industrial processes.

7　HMIP could seek an extension from operators, but this adds to the backlog of applications for determination.

8　A DoE survey into public attitudes toward environmental policies conducted in 1993 found that 96 per cent of respondents 'strongly supported' or 'tended to support' 'stricter controls on factory emissions to the air, rivers an sea' (DoE, 1994b, p.144).

9　Ammonia emission limits were reduced from $30mg/m^3$ to $15 \ mg/m^3$, and hydrogen chloride emission limits reduced from $30mg/m^3$ to $10mg/m^3$.

10   References in consultants' BAT reports do include such texts.

11   S.I. 1991/472 'Environmental Protection (Prescribed Processes and Substances) Regulations 1991'.

12   Section 11, Part I, Environmental Protection Act, 1990.

13   The original being 31st July 1993.

14   S.I. 1993/2405 'Environmental Protection (Prescribed Processes and Substances) (Amendment) (No.2) Regulations 1993'.

15   Reasons include to reduce IPC charges, to harmonise the split with business operations, to remove envelopes from overlapping a stack, thereby making monitoring easier, and so on.

16   On average, operators proposed three envelopes per site, Inspectors wanted eight per site. The final figure was an average of five authorisations per site (based upon evidence from interviewed operators).

17   Section 10(7), Part I, Environmental Protection Act, 1990.

18   Referred to as release minimisation assessments in the published CIGN.

19   Derived from Institution of Chemical Engineers and US EPA guidance documents.

20   Note the deliberate change in HMIP terminology, from 'release limits' to the less prohibitive sounding 'achievable release levels'.

6 Re-creating a policy community: site-level implementation of IPC

Introduction

Chapter 5 analysed the deferral of standard setting responsibility from central guidance (CIGNs) to the site-level. HMIP lacked the information needed to set prescriptive standards for their authoritative enforcement in the field. Instead, implementation would now involve the negotiation of individual standards in the field, at the site-level. The collapse of the arms' length approach was complete.

In this chapter, those site-level negotiations are analysed with the continued use of the organic chemicals sector for material. Empirical evidence draws upon interviews predominantly. The hypotheses being tested are that a re-created policy community deeply influenced IPC policy output, with respect to the actions required of regulators and operators, at this implementation stage (in accordance with the bottom-up policy making model). Moreover, industry's dominant position in that policy community meant policy output was weaker than anticipated.

There was an implementation deficit between what IPC actually delivered and what had been initially anticipated by HMIP. The detailed analysis of site-level implementation in this chapter examines the actions HMIP anticipated from operators (and related Inspector tasks), the actions negotiated and eventually delivered by operators (and related changes to Inspector tasks), and consequently the implementation deficit the gaps between the two represent.

The theme which is central to IPC implementation is industry's possession of important economic and information resources, and how these undermined the authority of a regulator struggling to meet the organisational demands of a tight implementation timetable. Industry's economic resource was deployed directly in 'NEEC' negotiations, but it was also deployed indirectly. A

163

government deregulation drive, aimed at boosting the competitiveness of UK industry, reinforced the importance of industry's economic position and denied HMIP political support for tough regulation. The chapter begins with an analysis of the deregulatory policy community which intervened in IPC implementation.

Following on from this is an assessment of the IPC implementation deficit. Essentially, industry failed to provide all the regulatory information which it should have done. The results of a content analysis of the IPC public register, presented in this chapter, measures the extent to which policy output, in terms of the information-providing activity of operators, fell short of HMIP expectations. IPC represented a step change in regulatory effort for both regulator and regulated. The remainder of the chapter addresses the process by which Inspectors and chemical operators secured IPC authorisations. In the event, both policy actors found informal pre-application meetings of mutual benefit to their IPC tasks. This interaction began the re-creation of a policy community at the site-level. HMIP authorised incomplete applications and negotiated site-specific authorisation improvements with operators. Throughout the chapter, the membership, balance of resources, and integration of this evolving policy community is addressed (see Figure 6.1).

In theory, HMIP could have been tough on operators and refused to authorise poor quality applications. The discussion moves on to consider the formal authority vested in HMIP. In practice, both HMIP and industry lacked the information resources necessary for HMIP to exercise this authority. Compounding the problem was HMIP's organisational inability to exert its full authority. The distribution of resources were such that it had to seek the co-operation of industry.

The compromises made over authorisation conditions are subsequently analysed. The discussion seeks to demonstrate the shift from HMIP ensuring operators have demonstrated they can meet BATNEEC standards, to operators influencing the pace and shape of improvements under IPC. IPC implementation has been stalled by industry's bottom-up dominance of this policy community - a policy community whose domain over IPC continues into its enforcement.

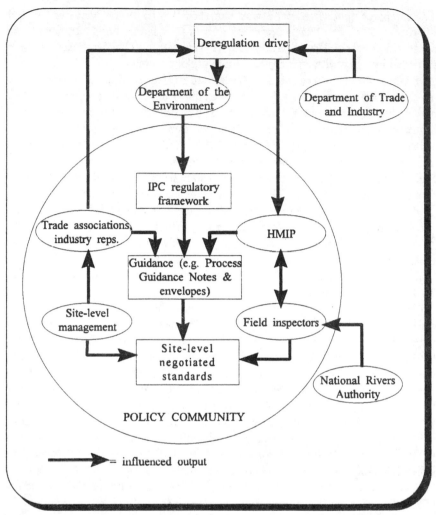

Figure 6.1 The IPC policy community and implementation of IPC

A deregulatory policy community and HMIP's political resource

HMIP's creation was triggered by the government's prevailing deregulatory ideology (chapter 4). Deregulation also influenced HMIP's implementation of IPC, and provided a context favouring the re-creation of a policy community. This section discusses this deregulatory context, and illustrates industry's ability to draw IPC to the attention of a deregulatory policy community co-ordinated by the DTi.

A campaign to cut red tape was launched by the Prime Minister on 2nd February 1993. The objective was to maintain and enhance the competitiveness of British companies (DTi, 1994). The deregulatory drive provided industry with an important lobbying opportunity.

In March 1993 the President of the Board of Trade, Michael Hesletine, set up seven deregulatory 'Task Forces' to examine all areas of regulation. They had six months to uncover 'priorities for the repeal or simplification of existing regulations and enforcement methods so as to minimise the costs on business' (Business Deregulation Task Forces, 1994, p.68). Task Force membership drew exclusively from the business community. The Chemicals and Pharmaceuticals Task Force[1] had senior staff from Wellcome, SORIS[2], Fine Organics, Shell Chemicals, Hickson Fine Chemicals, Hoechst, and ICI.

Of the 605 deregulatory recommendations made by the Task Forces, 35 were for IPC (6 per cent of the total). Their proposals sought familiar industrial objectives: that regulation has a clear 'scientific' basis; avoid uniformly set emission standards; earlier and closer consultation; and flexibility over regulatory requirements within a consistent approach (Business Deregulation Task Forces, 1994, pp.30-33).

The CBI flagged up IPC for special mention under its submission to the deregulation drive (CBI, 1993). It said businesses supported the need for environmental regulation and were behind the concept of IPC. But 'support broke down where the regulations were perceived to be unnecessary, counter-productive or too costly, compared to the benefits they might achieve' (CBI, 1993, p.1). In its survey of members 'IPC ... processes were identified by nearly half the correspondents as causes of over-regulation. Criticism focused upon inconsistent guidance and interpretation, regulatory clash, cost, inflexible time scales, and unnecessary regulation of small plants and processes' (CBI, 1993, p.1). The CBI argued the cost of IPC (in its present form) was excessive compared to any environmental benefit (see Downs, 1992, p.138).

In practice identifying the costs attributable to IPC is fraught with difficulty (Skea, Smith, Sorrell and van Zwanenberg, 1995, p.50). IPC charges can be calculated, with application fees running at £3,860 per process component in 1995/96 and an annual subsistence charge of £1,805 per component (HMIP, 1995l, pp.3-4). The costs associated with process improvements are more difficult to identify. Industrial forecasts on environmental expenditure have been too high in the past (see Allott, 1994, pp.171-172). CIA annual forecasts have been up to twice as high as the levels of investment which actually transpired. A study which attempted to cost IPC suggested it had added less than 1 per cent to operator production costs (Allott, 1994, p.175). Nevertheless, industrial figures appear to have been effective in generating concern about IPC's financial and bureaucratic burden.

Five of the Task Forces' IPC recommendations were specific to the chemical industry. No other sector got such singular treatment. The chemical industry was reported as having 'jumped at the chance to lobby for changes to IPC' (ENDS, 1993d, p.18). A DTi report found the chemical industry had benefited in the past from less tough environmental regulation compared to Swiss and German competitors, but that environmental regulation was beginning to impose serious problems on the industry (Bird, 1993, p.34). The report recommended this be taken into account in the DTi's deregulation work (Bird, 1993).

The deregulation drive secured commitments from the DoE. Reporting in January 1994, the DTi noted that action had already been taken to provide chemical operators with envelope authorisations. A deregulatory review of prescribed processes was already in hand: amendment Regulations passed in May 1994 reduced the number of IPC processes from approximately 5,000 to 3,000 (interview with HMIP and DoE policy staff; ENDS, 1993e, p.32; ENDS, 1994, p.33). The DTi also approved industry consultation on new CIGNs and for BATNEEC and BPEO methodologies (DTi, 1994, pp.36-40).

A government White Paper on competitiveness published in 1994 committed the DTi and DoE to funding an evaluation of the environmental and economic effects of IPC. It also committed HMIP to considering whether operators with independently verified management systems (such as BS7750[3]) could enjoy discounted IPC charges (HM Government, 1994, p.136). Further deregulatory pressure was brought to bear through the Deregulation and Contracting Out Act passed on 3rd November 1994. The Act gave any Minister the power to make Regulations to change the enforcement procedures used by regulators,[4] in addition to powers to repeal burdensome Regulations.[5]

Most of these proposals have subsequently come into force.[6] The Task Forces had meetings with the regulator, so HMIP would have known the deregulatory concerns in advance of DTi reports. Further lobbying by industry about the level of IPC charges (HMIP, 1995c) persuaded Ministers to appoint an HMIP Advisory Committee in July 1994 (interview with DoE civil servant; HMIP, 1994). The Committee, whose five strong membership contained four industrialists,[7] were to review whether HMIP was operating in an efficient and effective manner, keeping costs to a minimum (HMIP Advisory Committee, 1995, p.9).

One Inspector compared all this critical examination to working in a goldfish bowl. The deregulatory investigations have influenced the regulatory process. A great deal of flexibility and pragmatism has been forthcoming from HMIP. The deregulatory drive emphasised the importance of industry as a source of wealth creation and employment. This economic resource denied HMIP political support for a tough approach to IPC. Lacking this political resource meant, in turn, that HMIP had to be cautious about the strength of their regulatory demands. Industry's integration into more flexible IPC arrangements maintained a level of legitimacy for HMIP both with industry and government.

Developments show HMIP wishing to assuage industrial dissatisfaction with IPC. Collaboration was sought with industry with regard to developing a tool-kit of environmental assessment methods for use by operators (HMIP, 1994, p.6). HMIP has felt it necessary to conduct a joint assessment with chemical operator Allied Colloids in order to demonstrate some of the economic and efficiency benefits arising from IPC[8] (HMIP, 1995h, p.1). Announcing this initiative to the North West Branch of the CIA, HMIP's Director David Slater said 'I am sure that we would find that IPC is not, overall, as expensive as some might have us think and that it is in fact extremely good value for money' (HMIP, 1995h, p.1).

Bottom-up pressures were already influencing IPC implementation (see the discussion about envelopes in chapter five). The effect of the deregulatory drive was to reinforce these pressures with top-down directive. HMIP could not count on political support for any attempt to preserve its arms' length position on IPC. In the end it was a combination of bottom-up pressure and a lack of top-down support which brought about a return to flexibility and negotiation.

This section demonstrates how industry was able to manipulate a general deregulatory policy community[9] to include IPC in its ambit. The deregulation initiative had been launched by the Prime Minister, it was being sponsored by an important Whitehall Department sympathetic to industrial concerns (the DTi), its recommendations were to be acted upon. Individual operators could utilise the financial knowledge they possessed during BATNEEC negotiations with Inspectors; but the deregulation drive provided an opportunity to reinforce moves back to familiar rules of the game by which such negotiations were conducted. Analysis of these negotiations over IPC standards will benefit from prior knowledge of the eventual IPC policy output. The following section demonstrates that an implementation deficit arose, which subsequent sections seek to explain.

Evaluation of IPC policy output: an implementation deficit

IPC placed a duty upon operators to demonstrate that their process did not cause environmental harm, and that they were managing their process using BATNEEC and BPEO. The application document, from which legally binding authorisation conditions would be set by Inspectors, was supposed to carry this demonstration. This section draws upon interview evidence and, more importantly, an analysis of the contents of IPC applications and authorisations from 60 per cent of the organic chemical operators transferred from the air regime.

IPC legislation[10] and HMIP guidance, specifying the information which HMIP needed in operators' applications (HMIP, 1991), was sent to all operators. These information requirements are summarised in Table 6.1 below. The purpose of the content analysis is to measure the extent to which operators met these information requirements and to measure the types of condition placed in authorisations. Applications and authorisations record what actions operators and Inspectors have done under IPC, for example the quality of an operator's environmental assessment of their process. As such, the content analysis characterises IPC's overall policy output from the many hundreds of prescribed processes it regulates. This not only provides a measure of IPC policy output, but, by comparing it to HMIP's initial requirements, it enables the implementation deficit to be gauged.

Altogether, the content analysis makes apparent the poor quality of operators' applications and the types of condition which appeared in authorisations. In effect, Inspectors issued deemed consents to operators, allowing them to continue operating along pre-IPC lines whilst seeking future improvements. The overall objective of this section is to convey this feature before subsequent chapter sections explain the consequences of this turn of events: a return to policy community arrangements between Inspectors and operators.

Operators had to include information in their applications about their process, its environmental performance, and how it complied with the principles and standards of IPC. Each of these three areas (process, environment, compliance) is analysed in the following three sub-sections. The first presents the types of process information and the proportions of operators who included such information in their applications. For instance, how many operators provided HMIP with detailed process chemistry as opposed to very general chemical descriptions? The following sub-section focuses on the environmental information included in IPC applications: the proportions of operators supplying emission data; the proportions of operators who specified how they monitored their emissions; and the spread of different environmental assessment methods used by operators. In the final section attention turns to measuring the types of BATNEEC and BPEO demonstrations offered by operators. This section also examines the variety of process improvements offered by operators in their applications.

Table 6.1
Summary of information requested of IPC applications from HMIP

Process description	Abatement techniques	Monitoring
Map of plant and of release points. Purpose of plant/products. Operation times. Process flow diagram. Process chemistry (including by-products and wastes). Mass balance. Raw material specifications, storage and use.	Details of design and operation of: the process itself, how it is used to minimise releases; the recycling or use of wastes and by-products; end-of-pipe abatement; site air abatement; and effluent treatment plant.	How and when releases will be monitored. Details of sampling and analytic techniques used. Details of background environmental monitoring. Justification of monitoring programme on grounds of: records process operation; records releases; and records environmental effects of process.

Environmental releases	Environmental assessment	Proof of BATNEEC/BPEO
Specific and consistent units to be used. Media and point of release for each release. Release rates, concentrations and periods. Annual mass of releases. Maximum release rate. Air releases at STP and including % oxygen and exhaust velocity. Height of vents/chimneys and local topography. For discharges to water/sewer: BOD; COD; temperature; pH; SS.	For 'every release'. Transport of release through environment. Impact of release on the environment, ecosystems and organisms (local and further). Background concentrations of substances released. Details of models used and any assumptions made.	Justify fully that the process is BATNEEC. Alternative processes should have been considered. Process operated should be justified as BPEO. Existing process applications should include an upgrading timetable of proposed improvements toward new process standards.

[1]   BOD = Biological Oxygen Demand; COD = Chemical Oxygen Demand; SS = suspended solids; STP = Standard Temperature and Pressure.

Source: HMIP (1991)

The typical operator pattern for preparing applications was for the site Health, Safety and Environment Manager (or Site Director in small firms) to co-ordinate and negotiate IPC with HMIP. Either as a team or simply called upon when necessary, staff with expertise in the relevant area[11] would research and gather information for the application. Only a few interviewed operators used consultants. Apart from their continued use in specific tasks, such as dispersion modelling, operators who had used consultants said they would do IPC work in-house in future (see also Allott, 1994, pp.21-23). Three areas which an IPC application had to cover are analysed below: process information; environmental information; and demonstrating compliance with IPC.

Application process information

Process information was closest to the day-to-day activity of operators and consequently the area covered best in applications. However, gathering existing data was not always as simple as pulling information from the relevant process files. Operators of older processes had to re-learn how they operated their process. Iterative process improvements made through years of operating experience had not always been accompanied with updated documentation. Thus chemists and engineers would have to re-appraise the process for IPC - in some cases discovering room for further efficiencies as a result.

The results of the content analysis for existing organic chemical processes found that 38 per cent of applicants had failed to offer any justification of the way they carried on their process.Fifty-one per cent justified their process on commercial grounds, and 11 per cent on environmental grounds. 16 per cent had considered alternatives to the way they operated the process. The types of abatement equipment used by operators is presented in Table 6.2 below. Good process management and end of pipe equipment, such as scrubbers or bag filters, were the most common techniques. Process management included statements such as this one from Synthetic Chemicals' application, 'Some reduction [of VOCs] is possible which will be achieved by attention to operation and maintenance procedures rather than by substantial change in plant or process' (Application No. AJ9334). Process descriptions tended to be qualitative. Sixty-six per cent of applications provided such descriptions, 26 per cent contained some technical detail such as operating conditions, and the remainder provided no description or had commercial confidentiality.

Table 6.2
Percentage operators using various types of abatement technique

Abatement technique	Process management	End of pipe	Effluent treatment	Cleaner process
Percentage utilisation	50%	68%	36%	27%

Thirty-three per cent of operators included some sort of generic mass balance for their process. For envelopes, the 'worst case'[12] process or a typical reaction was usually chosen as an example in the application. Generic terms were commonly used in process chemistry.Thirty-two per cent provided specific chemical reactions(easier for continuous bulk processes).Only 6 per cent had sought commercial confidentiality for their chemistry, with 50 per cent using generic terms instead. Seeking confidentiality added delay to the process, particularly if HMIP's decision was not favourable and had to be Appealed upon, and even then there was the risk the information could still end up on the public register. These procedures took up time and resources for operators and Inspectors alike (see later). Avoiding such delay, by utilising generic terminology, benefited both regulator and regulated. By April 1995, only six commercial confidentiality Appeals out of a total of 1,728 IPC authorisations were lodged with the DoE, of which two were withdrawn and four determined (HMIPe, 1995, p.4).

The use of generic chemical descriptions offered another advantage to operators: generic terminology introduced greater flexibility into the application and subsequent authorisation. So, for example, 'hydrogenating a nitrile' covers all hydrogenation reactions of all nitriles irrespective of the chemical group attached to the nitrile. 'Once its down in your application and that is authorised, you're tied to those quantities. Whereas keeping things very generic and approximate gives us that operating flexibility that we need' (operator interview). Inspectors were pragmatic about this, feeling it better to have at least some information on the public register than lots of commercial confidentiality requests. They would advise operators to use generic terms if necessary, and keep confidentiality requests to a minimum. The public image of lots of withheld information suited neither HMIP nor operators.

The lack of requirement for operators to monitor their emissions under the air regulatory regime left them ill-equipped to report releases under IPC (see later), and also affected process information with respect to locating emission points. Emission points (vents) had tended to be added as plant expanded. For operators it proved a 'slog' simply identifying which emission points led from which reaction vessels, ancillary equipment, work areas and so on. Some operators had sites with hundreds of emission points. Flow diagrams and the identification of which points emitted which substances was a task operators were asked to carry out for IPC application. As with other issues, one multinational operator who already had engineering piping and instrument diagrams was reluctant to produce less commercially sensitive flow diagrams specifically for IPC. Under threat of Appeal, the Inspector accepted being shown the detailed flow diagrams in private with no diagram reaching the public register. Sixty-one per cent of applications did not contain a map of emission points.

Given their poor state of knowledge concerning emissions it is not surprising that operators generally failed to meet guidance on the environmental information needed in applications.

Due to both operator inertia and inability, physical monitoring was deferred until after authorisation in many cases. Data presented in the application was generally based upon theoretical calculation or approximations after limited monitoring. The tight IPC timetable prompted HMIP to direct its Inspectors to only ask for additional information if they believed the operator already possessed such information.[13] If that information needed to be generated by the operator, such as the emissions profile of a batch reaction, then it was to be deferred to an authorisation request. Many applications were authorised this way.

61 per cent of operators provided air emission concentrations. The same percentage provided annual mass emissions. 61 per cent of operators indicated they had done some physical monitoring; though, according to interview evidence, a majority of the data is based upon calculation and approximation.

Incomplete monitoring presented problems for statutory consultees. A civil servant at the Ministry of Agriculture, Fisheries and Food (MAFF), one of the statutory consultees, explained:

It is MAFF's experience that a lot of applications have not contained full environmental and stack release data. The control of the operation of the plant is HMIP's remit. Food safety is the remit of MAFF. Therefore, MAFF is interested in the emission inventory, quantities and release data. These data are necessary for modelling assessment carried out [for food contamination]. Where no such data are available MAFF has requested that a monitoring regime be instigated as part of the plant's improvement plan, and the data be supplied to MAFF when available.

(Written correspondence, 19th July 1994)

Out of all the statutory consultees, MAFF[14] made the most requests to HMIP (32 per cent of applications). The NRA was next, making requests for 25 per cent of applications, followed by sewage undertakers (i.e. the water companies) with 7 per cent.[15]

Most environmental assessments did not match HMIP guidance. In the Guidance Note to Applicants, HMIP request that an environmental assessment of the process:

should include an assessment of how the release is transported through the environment and how it effects the environment and the ecosystems within any relevant environmental medium. The assessment should be sufficiently detailed to identify the major effects of the releases, both locally and farther afield should there be any suspected effect at such distances away from the process[16]

(HMIP, 1991, p.5)

Here was the operator's opportunity to demonstrate the 'harmless' nature of their process.

Inspectors said they generally came across three types of assessment from operators:

1   Use dispersion modelling or calculations to estimate ambient concentrations attributable to the process, and compare these to 1/40th the Occupational Exposure Limits - a quotient as arbitrary as the 1/30th used by air Inspectors in the past (Mahler, 1967, pp.152-3).

2   Compare the process emission concentrations or annual mass released with those of a much larger emitter in order to suggest your process is not problematic.

3   Simply assert that your process is harmless. There are healthy looking trees around the site perimeter, for example.

Analysis of operators' applications discovered all three types of environmental assessment in common use. Table 6.3 presents the breakdown of the types of assessment conducted.

Table 6.3
Proportion of various types of environmental assessment conducted by operators

Type of assessment	Modelling	Concentration limits	Identify impacts	Dismiss impacts	None
Percentage operators	17%	39%	4%	17%	23%

Seventeen per cent of operators had done some dispersion modelling for the ambient concentrations arising from some of their releases. No operators had met HMIP guidance and considered the ecosystem effects of their releases. Instead ambient concentrations were compared against one-fortieth the Occupational Exposure Limit. The most common assessment was to compare emission concentrations either with the CIGN, if they were below the levels given as guidance, or to compare emissions with a bigger source or with data for the total national emission of that substance. In each case the operator's method was to demonstrate harmlessness by belittling their release rather than demonstrating its impact was harmless.

Some operators did identify the impacts associated with the substances they released, but dismissed the possibility of their releases causing such effects. Allied Colloids identified tropospheric ozone creation and stratospheric ozone depletion as problems associated with the substances they emitted. They dismissed these effects as unproblematic, given the small size of their emission (Application No. AK7256). Synthetic Chemicals did do some (unreferenced) dispersion modelling for their benzene emissions, finding that 'under C2 weather conditions this would be 1ppb, a small fraction of that experienced in normal traffic conditions'[17] (Application No. AJ9334).

The third type of environmental assessment was exemplified by Hicksons Fine Chemicals - that is, dismiss the possibility of any impact: 'Due to the large number of potential emissions it is difficult to give an accurate assessment of the emissions and hence their impact. Due to the careful management of the plant and the large scrubbing duty available it is expected that emissions and hence the effect on the environment is negligible' (Application No. AK9283).

A dismissive attitude toward process environmental impact might be justified had measurement of that impact been attempted. The issue though, is that operators have failed to publicly demonstrate why they are justified in assuming their processes are so benign. Such a demonstration is a statutory IPC requirement.

English Nature, another statutory consultee, recognised this situation: 'We are concerned with whether a process may impact on nature conservation ... In order to undertake such an assessment we generally need good information on the fate of pollutants in the environment. For many IPC applications this is lacking ... We do not ordinarily comment on operational issues. Our interaction with HMIP has assured us they are fully competent to do their job. However, they do lack expertise of environmental impact information and we see our role in that light' (Written correspondence, 15th July 1994). Yet English Nature's concern extends only to those processes which might impact on designated Sites of Special Scientific Interest. The content analysis found they made requests for 1 per cent of applications.

Compliance information covers operators' demonstrations that their process was using BATNEEC and is the BPEO, that their monitoring regime is able to check compliance with any authorisation limits, and that a programme of process improvements exists into the future. Like release monitoring and environmental assessment, operators' compliance demonstrations were disappointing.

Analysis of operators' BATNEEC and BPEO justifications are presented in Table 6.4. None of the applications provided a systematic BATNEEC[18] or BPEO appraisal of their process based upon technical and economic considerations (see Pearce and Brisson, 1993 for an example BATNEEC methodology, and HMIP, 1995f for BPEO). None of the justifications provided quantitative, comparable performance or economic data for using one type of abatement in preference to another. Demonstrations were qualitative, describing the abatement practised and how this might compare with other options in terms of the (unquantified) generation of more waste for land-filling and so forth. Some operators did refer to CIGN emission limits when their process was within them, as proof of BATNEEC.

Table 6.4
Proportion of operators demonstrating compliance with BATNEEC and BPEO

Type of demonstration	Qualitative	Asserted	None
BATNEEC	28%	51%	21%
BPEO	3%	54%	43%

14 per cent of operators provided justifications that their monitoring regime could demonstrate IPC compliance, such as the application from Courtaulds Chemicals listing the substances monitored, the sampling periods, and the techniques employed (Application No. AK3129).

Upgrading proposals from operators followed the same pattern. Thirty-eight per cent of operators failed to suggest any improvements. When improvements were offered in applications they were either timetabled actions , such as establishing monitoring protocols (that is, tasks for which the operator had committed herself to doing by a given date), or commitments to examine the feasibility of options (that is, examine but do not undertake tasks). The types of 'timetabled' and 'examined' improvements fell into three categories: monitoring; environmental assessment; and plant improvement. Interviewed operators said their improvement suggestions were based upon projects which they had been planning anyway - though IPC may have brought the timing forward - and areas where it was obvious they needed to make an effort, such as monitoring. The proportions of each of these improvements volunteered in applications is given in the top row of Table 6.5.

It should be borne in mind that these suggestions, and the applications generally, were the product of ongoing negotiation between operators and Inspectors. The improvements finally requested in the authorisations issued by HMIP are provided for comparison in the bottom row of Table 6.5.

Table 6.5
Proportion of types of improvement to organic processes appearing in IPC applications and authorisations

	Monitoring (T)	Monitoring (E)	EA (T)	EA (E)	Plant upgrade (T)	Plant upgrade (E)
Applicn.	13%	18%	0%	1%	28%	32%
Authsn.	46%	56%	19%	7%	33%	92%

Key: (T) = timetabled action; (E) = examine feasibility and report to HMIP; EA = environmental assessment.

HMIP authorisations

Applications generally failed to provide information to a level according with official HMIP guidance. Further work was required of operators to solicit missing regulatory information, and this became a key focus for the authorisations. Authorisation 'Improvement Programmes' became the most important element of IPC, in which specific operator tasks were set for completion by set dates. One Inspector characterised the authorisation objective becoming the requirement for operators to discover and convey their current environmental performance - which is what applications should have done. This had not occurred in the applications so had to be carried over into authorisation requirements. Any significant[19] process improvements became the subject of future negotiations.

Inspectors were directed by HMIP centrally to authorise what applicants had provided. Authorising the status quo meant that IPC was effectively stalled. As Inspector Peter Merrill wrote in HMIP's in-house magazine (HMIP, 1994b, p.17):

Much of that which might have been done now, particularly in addressing deficiencies in information supporting applications, has been translated into certificate reporting or improvement conditions. The future assessment of those reports which will come forward in response to these conditions, and which will for example quantify hitherto qualitative statements, may very well dictate a significant variation caseload.

In other words, once operators have supplied the information and assessments which should have been forthcoming in their applications, there will be a considerable task in varying the authorisation conditions to reflect these findings.

Release limits

Authorising the status quo meant that release limits set in the authorisation simply reflected the concentration or mass release levels reported by operators in their application. As one operator summed it, 'when they authorise it, if you say you emit ten parts per million of amines, then they will authorise it at ten parts per million'.

HMIP has not limited waste arisings destined for off-site landfill or incineration as tightly as air emissions and water discharges - quantities of 'land' releases are not specifically limited in authorisations.[20] Interviewed operators thought quantities of land releases could rise as air and water releases are diverted to this media. Research is needed to see if the lack of specific limits presents 'land' routes as the pollution path of least resistance, and to confirm or deny anecdotal evidence that drummed waste arisings are increasing.

In the absence of discharge levels (to water) in an application, Inspectors would 'grandfather' into authorisations the relevant discharge limits set by the NRA under the Water Act, 1989. Consent conditions for discharges to sewers were also grandfathered into IPC authorisations. Discharges to sewers had limits set by the sewage undertaker (the regional water company), which would base these on its own limits for the eventual discharge of sewers to water, set by the NRA. Therefore in both cases the limits imposed were effectively based on NRA environmental quality considerations, since this is the mechanism provided in the Water Resources Act, 1991. HMIP effectively relied upon the NRA for control of releases to water media.

Air limits were based upon emissions reported in applications. In some instances, operators' emission calculations proved over-optimistic. Consequently, some authorisation limits have had to be relaxed in the light of the results from physical monitoring. Five out of the nineteen operators interviewed had to have such variations made to their authorisations. One multinational anticipated this might happen, so they used emissions figures higher than calculated. This made it more likely that when actual values were measured, they would be comfortably below their authorisation limits and could be presented as an improvement to the process. It also avoided the poor image a relaxation in authorisation emission limits might present.

In implementing IPC, HMIP has not required a tightening of environmental releases in the round or otherwise. Rather, it sought a baseline from which to begin to regulate prescribed processes. The content analysis of existing process authorisations found 25 per cent of the processes were meeting the air emission levels provided in the CIGNs. Forty-three per cent of processes were emitting above these levels.For 32 per cent of processes no emission limits had been set, owing to a lack of release data on which to base them. Once the data is generated by operators then limits will be written into authorisation variations.

Overall, the content analysis presented in this section has shown operators failed to provide all the necessary regulatory information expected by HMIP. Inspectors were instructed to seek the missing information and operator actions (such as the installation of monitoring regimes) after authorisation. The mechanism for doing this was to request items in the authorisation's Improvement Programme: a timetabled list of actions expected from operators.

The significance of the authorisation Improvement Programme

IPC has not lived up to the initial expectations of either the DoE or HMIP, as outlined in their official guidance (DoE, 1993; HMIP, 1991). What IPC has achieved is the beginning of an improvement in industry's environmental management capability (Smith, 1996, p.85). Monitoring regimes are being put into place, more environmental assessments are being conducted, and processes are being examined with environmental improvements in mind (see Table 6.5). These authorisation requirements were written into Improvement Programmes, and it is these which are the most significant achievement of IPC to date. Industrial inertia resulted in this unforeseen (by the regulator) strategy being followed for IPC: reliance upon the Improvement Programme to try and make up an implementation deficit with respect to missing application information.

The content analysis shows that around half the organic chemical operators are having to examine and/or carry out further monitoring of their processes. The 33 per cent of actual process improvements requested in authorisations were for good housekeeping measures (such as bunding storage areas with impermeable concrete, or fitting flow meter alarms to scrubbers so that breakdowns will be noticed) rather than significant improvements. Ninety-two per cent of processes require an examination of the feasibility for environmental improvement and process upgrades.

One Inspector pointed out that a good applicant would not have required any authorisation Improvement Programme requests since all the information, including upgrading plans, would have appeared in their application. Authorisations for existing organic chemical processes had, on average, 8.5 Improvement Programme requests.

The Improvement Programme provided Inspectors with a second chance to solicit missing regulatory information from operators. More time could be allowed for these requirements. Improvement Programmes were recognised by all interviewed Inspectors as a useful regulatory tool for bringing process operators up to a suitable IPC baseline. HMIP may only have authorised what operators provided, in contrast to what HMIP had initially requested, but they argued that now operators were within the IPC legal framework it was possible to require operators to fill in the regulatory gaps. In effect, HMIP had provided deemed authorisations, and then sought to get operators into sufficient shape to begin their IPC demonstrations.

Ironically, former air Inspectors in HMIP had been rebuffed when they suggested this approach prior to IPC implementation in April 1991 (interview with Inspector). It was said to be too reminiscent of (air) scheduled process registration and out of step with the new, arms' length culture. In the event, industry inertia over applications forced a similar approach.

A step increase in operator organisation and information resources

The DoE argued that the organisational challenge which IPC presented industry, in terms of collecting information on releases and so forth, was generally no greater than under the previous fragmented system. Indeed, 'it would entail bringing together existing information on discharges to all media which may yield some small administrative savings for many firms' (DoE, 1988a, p.27). In practice, the organisational resources necessary to meet IPC proved to be greater than this. Generating regulatory information was a vital first step for site-level IPC implementation. HMIP authority and regulatory procedures depended upon this information. As the source of such information, industry possessed an influential resource.

Operators had not been required to conduct IPC demonstrations before, so some of their failure can be attributed to inexperience and lack of environmental expertise.[21] HMIP lacked such expertise too. Dispersion models and formulae were available to Inspectors to check the ambient concentration of process releases, but HMIP lacked the expertise to assess any resulting environmental and ecosystem impacts. They were in a poor position to offer advice to operators.

A broader regulatory focus: the whole industrial process

For operators (and Inspectors) used to the air regulatory regime, IPC presented a step change in regulation. In addition to the added burden of drafting applications and authorisations, overcoming confidentiality concerns, the administration of cost recovery charging and the public register, the unit of regulation was now much larger. It was more explicitly the whole industrial process (including the 'techniques' of process management and operator training), and it covered releases to all three environmental media.[22]

Under the air regulations, Inspector and operator concern was for emissions from the end of the emission point. With IPC this concern extended back to include the whole process. An example provided by one Inspector was a paint making process. Scheduled under air regulations, the regulatory unit had been the bag filter installed above a chute which poured lead solution. Prescribed under IPC, the whole paint making operation is the regulatory unit. Operators agreed, 'an Alkali Inspector would go and look at an HCl scrubber; he wouldn't be interested in the rest of the site'.[23]

New information requirements

Historically, very little monitoring had been carried out on scheduled processes. Emissions may have been checked during initial process commissioning or after the installation of abatement equipment, but very little routine monitoring was practised by operators. A multinational operator said about their emissions, 'prior to IPC we would have known very, very little. Post-IPC there are still areas where we know little, but there are areas where we know a lot more because we've carried out monitoring as part of IPC'.

The supply of process information and environmental assessments were other new operator requirements, as were BATNEEC/BPEO justifications and a programme of process improvements. All this was information HMIP deemed[24] to be necessary if Inspectors were to be able to determine an authorisation (HMIP, 1991, p.1). A Guidance Note sent to all applicants informed operators of these requirements (see Table 6.1), and other steps were taken by HMIP to inform applicants of their new IPC task.

Clarification of operator regulatory duties

Inspectors were notifying (air) scheduled process operators about the new IPC regime during inspection visits. The trade press had been informed by HMIP and was passing information on to industry in magazine and journal articles (see for example, Parfitt and Andreassen, 1992, pp.6-9, 'ENDS Report',

'Environment Business'). HMIP held regional seminars to which local operators were invited and IPC explained generally (HMIP, 1991d, p.61). Early seminars held in November 1991 'emphasised the need for a process operator to include an adequate level of detail in an IPC application and for any dialogue between HMIP and an operator to be open and thus publicly accountable' (HMIP, 1993e, p.38). Regional, sector specific seminars were also held closer to relevant application periods, those for chemical operators taking place in February and March 1993 (HMIP, 1993g, p.33). Trade and professional organisations were holding their own seminars too (Institution of Chemical Engineers, 1993). Some operators may have been reluctant to generate and supply regulatory information, but they could not argue they were ignorant of HMIP requirements.

Missing regulatory information

Despite being warned of their new, extended regulatory duties, operators were failing in this task. Other studies show that an implementation deficit was generic to IPC and not a chemical sector problem specifically. A survey of all IPC applications submitted up until 1st April 1993 found that application quality did not comply with official guidance (Allott, 1994). Only 37 per cent of the 328 applications had modelled the dispersion of their releases, with only 12.5 per cent including ambient pollution levels. 12.5 per cent of applications were considered to have 'offered any meaningful assessment of the [process] impact on the local environment and ecosystems' (Allott, 1994, p.x). The assessment of alternative process options, which must feature in any BPEO assessment, was absent in 51 per cent of applications. Twenty-four per cent of alternative assessments were brief, and only the remaining 30 per cent had given serious consideration to alternative processes or abatement options (Allott, 1994, p.x). Similar results arose from a study done in March 1995 (Skea, Smith, Sorrell, and van Zwanenberg, 1995).

Inspectors were aware of the poor quality of applications early on in the IPC timetable. Authorising processes on the basis of these applications was difficult, so Inspectors began holding unofficial pre-application and pre-authorisation meetings with individual operators in order to make the whole process smoother and easier. Closer integration eventually became officially accepted. Nevertheless, HMIP did have the authority to have forced IPC implementation along a different route, as the next section demonstrates. It could have refused to authorise the processes until applicants had come up with missing and more detailed information. However, the balance of resources and the circumstances were such that HMIP did not exercise its authority and pursue a different implementation route.

The authority of HMIP

The introduction of a consent based system of authorising processes increased the authority of HMIP (see chapter 4). Legally binding authorisation conditions defined more clearly when an offence had or had not been committed. But these conditions had to represent BATNEEC for the process, and establishing this involved the same resource interdependencies as under the air regime. CIGNs did not provide authoritative BATNEEC standards which could be used by Inspectors irrespective of the quality of individual applications. Instead Inspectors were being advised by their superiors that individual, site-specific circumstances had to be taken into account when setting standards. However, this was not HMIP's original intention.

Section 6(4) of IPC legislation requires HMIP to be certain that operators can meet the conditions set in an authorisation.[25] Initially, HMIP assumed operators' applications would be forthcoming with information relating to the environmental performance of their process, demonstrate that they met BATNEEC/BPEO, and would upgrade to meet new process standards (as in the relevant CIGN) (HMIP, 1991). Authorisation would involve transposing application information into legally binding authorisation conditions. Thus HMIP's initial interpretation of Section 6(4) was to advise Inspectors to refuse applications which they thought made spurious claims (HMIP, 1991c, pp.9-10). Moreover, if information was missing from the application, or insufficiently detailed, then HMIP could request that the operator furnish the information within a specified period in order to determine the authorisation.[26] If the applicant failed to provide the information then the Inspector could refuse to authorise[27] the process (DoE, 1993, p.7).

So, in theory, HMIP had the top-down authority to obtain from operators the regulatory information it needed. In practice, the bottom-up realities of implementation meant many processes were authorised with incomplete application information. HMIP's interpretation of Section 6(4) shifted to it exercising caution when imposing any conditions in an authorisation in the absence of relevant operator information. Without sufficient information Section 6(4) became a brake on the imposition of regulatory conditions. Inspectors were advised not to burden operators with authorisation conditions on which they could Appeal for 'NEEC' reasons (Inspector interviews).

There were several reasons why HMIP chose not to enforce its legal powers strictly. An important influence was the delay this would have imposed on IPC (Inspectors had, on average, 6.14 man-days to authorise each organic chemical application). A majority of applications failed to supply sufficiently detailed information for the type of straightforward authorisation procedure originally envisaged by HMIP. To have served all operators with requests for further information would have introduced severe delay into IPC implementation. The alternative, for Inspectors to impose BATNEEC authorisation conditions in the absence of information, may also have generated delay by provoking scores of Appeals.[28] Authorisation workload was already considerable - HMIP's in-house magazine had a Blitz-like spirit of shouldering this burden and the associated overtime with good humour (see, for example, HMIP, 1993i: 1). Appeals presented a considerable increase in workload to hard pressed Inspectors (Inspector interview).

Moreover, Inspectors have to answer Appeal claims. To answer these successfully required the Inspector to possess information which rigorously demonstrated that authorisation conditions represented BATNEEC for that process: the precise information Inspectors lacked. Appeals were out of the regulators hands and could be upheld, which would set awkward precedents for future regulatory decisions (Hawkins, 1984, pp.27-28). In practice the Appeal authority (the DoE) encouraged the Appellant and HMIP to go back and try to negotiate an agreement informally. This policy meant negotiating consensus authorisation conditions with operators in the first place seemed more sensible to Inspectors.[29]

So HMIP did not draw upon the full authority available to it. Some indication of the reasons behind this have already been given: a lack of political support (the deregulation drive); the implementation burden this would have presented; and Appeals could have set complicating precedents. HMIP lacked the political and organisational resource to exercise its full authority. A speciality chemical operator explained, 'They wouldn't accept draft applications but at the end of the day they didn't have much option but to discuss them with you, because what they were finding was that they were varying so much from company to company, and even within a company, that it got to the stage that they had to go out and issue guidance verbally - even though the written stuff [guidance] was there'.

The pressures of a tight implementation timetable and insufficient information were driving a bottom-up redefinition of the rules of the game. More informal, off-the-record discussion and negotiation was taking place. Moves back toward policy community arrangements were occurring because, under the circumstances, they were of mutual benefit to operators and Inspectors.

The mutual benefits of a policy community arrangement

An absence of explicit information makes hierarchical command-and-control relations difficult to sustain (Kenis and Schneider, 1991, pp.42-43; chapter 2). Non-prescriptive CIGNs, compounded by a lack of information amongst individual applications, encouraged policy community relations amongst Inspectors and operators. The anticipated arms' length procedure of an operator supplying the necessary regulatory information dissolved into site-level discussion with an Inspector over what would be sufficient for a 'valid' application and how deficits could be made up after authorisation.

Pre-application discussions began as a pragmatic response to poor quality applications (ENDS, 1992, p.19). As time went on, this bottom-up adjustment became institutionalised to the extent that central HMIP began advising Inspectors to allow between two and three pre-application meetings with applicants (Inspector interview). Circumstances were such that HMIP needed to avoid conflict and seek industry co-operation in order to keep IPC implementation on time. HMIP's future provision of missing regulatory information was secured in exchange for closer and more individual operator access to regulatory decision making.

Benefits to Inspectors from pre-application discussion

A driving benefit for Inspectors was that they could make perfectly clear to operators what information was required. Interviewed Inspectors acknowledged that whilst applications weren't perfect, pre-application meetings had led to some improvements.

A second advantage for Inspectors became the identification of obvious areas for improvement. The Inspectors knew in advance of submission the sort of conditions and improvement requests needed in the authorisation, such as installation of monitoring (cf. making requests for missing information in advance of issuing the authorisation). These could be flagged up and discussed with the operator. This helped smooth the whole authorisation process. Pre-application meetings also enabled Inspectors to gain familiarity with the process and its operation in advance of receiving the application. With the heavy workload, any early indication of unfamiliar areas which would require some research or consultation with colleagues was welcomed by Inspectors.

Particular to the chemicals sector, pre-application discussion facilitated the division of operations into envelopes for authorisation (see chapter 5). Negotiation over envelopes did not prevent preparation for applications. After all, envelopes are collections of chemical reactions carried out on plant. It is these reactions and plant which generate the releases, have the impacts, must utilise BATNEEC, and represent the BPEO. Enveloping merely affected the way these reactions and so on were grouped together. Overall, pre-application consultation smoothed this process and generally reduced the regulatory burden on hard pressed Inspectors.

Operators welcomed pre-application discussions with Inspectors. It fitted their perennial strategy of wishing to be integrated in the standard setting process. One multinational described it as a 'cultural reversion' to the discursive approach familiar to the air regime. Not only could application requirements be discussed, but some negotiation over authorisation conditions could take place too (for example, deferring monitoring until after authorisation).

Pre-application discussion meant negotiation could begin on a more open ended basis. A speciality operator contrasted the arms' length approach of 'you tell us what you're doing, if we don't like it we'll tell you', with the air regime in which operator and Inspector would 'discuss something in advance, agree on it and then put that forward, rather than the other way around. Now we're moving back to the way it was, in terms of mutual consent'. The rules of the game on standard setting were reversing away from formally consulting operators on pre-defined (HMIP) standards. Initial options were now more open to negotiation, the aim being to seek consensus.

Greater Inspector familiarity with individual operators' processes was of mutual benefit. 'That's an approach I'm very happy to go along with. We're very happy if he understands the process. It makes it easier, if something goes wrong, for him to appreciate why ... Because if you understand, there's much less scope for you to be at odds with us on something' (operator interview). Inspectors continued to be drawn from the same pool as operators. Combining this with an intimacy with site-level operations helped to reinforce the shared appreciative system concerning the most suitable approach to IPC. Inspectors acknowledged that there was a trend back to the private negotiations typical of the air regime, in which operators are more candid and there is co-operation between policy community members. Face-to-face discussion provided an opportunity for operators to shape standards into a pattern more to their suiting. This process of integration continued with negotiations over authorisation Improvement Programme conditions.

The negotiation of IPC Improvement Programmes

Pre-application discussions with operators had made apparent to HMIP the implementation deficit to be expected from applicants. Policy community integration was further enhanced by official consent to private negotiation over authorisation conditions. HMIP guidance introduced for the organic chemicals tranche, and continued for other tranches, instructed Inspectors to invite operators to comment upon draft authorisations (HMIP, 1993h, p.2). Like pre-application discussion, the benefit to HMIP was increased administrative efficiency in the authorisation process - by providing an opportunity for clarification of terms and prevent misunderstandings which might lead to unnecessary delay (or Appeal). It also provided operators with the opportunity to influence the standards by which their processes would be regulated.

Inspectors and operators became involved in informal negotiations in the sense that site-level meetings were unminuted, information was exchanged which remained off the public record, and transparency was attenuated to recording only the outcome - as conditions in the final authorisation document. This contrasts with aspiration under the arms' length regime whereby correspondence would be documented for the public register (ENDS, 1990) - like an 'audit trail' (RCEP, 1988).

Draft authorisations are not publicly available. Uncovering the influences and changes made to draft authorisation Improvement Programmes for this study has had to rely upon interview evidence. A negotiating pattern similar to the production of CIGNs emerges from this analysis. Prescriptive improvement actions required by Inspectors in their draft authorisations were, in the face of operator challenge, re-written into less prescriptive requirements for operators to examine and report on the feasibility of improvements. Any future upgrading decisions will rest upon the operators' findings. The authority of Inspectors' initial requests for action was, once again, undermined by a lack of information.

Inspectors' initial site-level determination of standards

Inspectors were conducting their regulatory task with a lack of political resource and a workload that challenged their organisational resources. Information resources sufficiently robust to enable the systematic imposition of BATNEEC improvement standards were unavailable. Chapter 5 demonstrated how the supportive prescription of their key regulatory aid, CIGNs, had been weakened. In these circumstances, Inspectors fell back on standard setting techniques similar to the air regime (chapter 3). Sector wide economic criteria and transparent decision making suffered as a result.

Inspectors did find CIGNs useful in some respects. They provided an introduction to process types with which they were unfamiliar. And even though standards in them were not prescriptive, they did provide a useful starting point for negotiation with operators. Some used them in setting draft authorisation conditions, initially asking operators to upgrade to the relevant CIGN as an improvement condition.[30] Process improvements would be drafted which would bring the most significant releases in line with BATNEEC. Other, less formal decision making aids were used in addition to CIGNs for prioritising and setting BATNEEC standards, and to ensure consistency across authorisations.

HMIP did not possess a data base of capital or operating costs, and Inspectors were chemists and engineers not economists (Inspector interviews). They did not possess the economic information or knowledge against which operator 'NEEC' justifications could have been compared, had such justifications been made. In the absence of operator justification and economic knowledge Inspectors had to resort to less explicit methods for determining if an imposed improvement requirement entailed excessive cost.

Inspectors sought a feel for what improvements could be achieved by seeing what competitor operators' environmental performance was like. Inspector colleagues with experience in the relevant industrial sector could be contacted and asked about the performance and improvement conditions they were placing on the same type of prescribed process.[31] Alternatively, Inspectors examined the IPC public register to check the environmental performance of similar processes. Finally, Inspectors could consult an Inspector from the relevant HMIP Industry Group for advice.

By these means Inspectors obtained an implicit yardstick for what sort of standards an operator should upgrade toward: CIGNs; Inspector experience; competitor processes on the public register; and Industry Groups. These BATNEEC determinations were written into Improvement Programme requirements as part of the draft authorisation presented to operators. Comparison with existing practice was thus a key decision making tool for Inspectors.

However, CIGNs were now advising Inspectors that BATNEEC was a site specific issue. The other sources of information carried little authority owing to their implicit nature and differences in context. Comparisons with others could prove a useful tool for levering more information from operators, 'so-and-so is meeting this limit, why can't you?'; but it was not a solid, demonstrable basis for the systematic derivation of site-specific standards. Inspectors were in no position to set BATNEEC standards which were legally 'enforceable' (Hawkins, 1984, pp.32-35). Consequently, operator opposition transformed many of the Inspectors' draft authorisation requirements for upgrading action into requirements for operators to examine the feasibility of such upgrades.

Operator participation in the site-level determination of standards

92 per cent of organic chemical authorisations for existing processes contain Improvement Programme requirements to examine the feasibility of upgrading (Table 6.5). These are not requirements to actually upgrade, simply to examine the potential for upgrading and report the findings to HMIP. Neither does this necessarily mean such upgrading will take place, operators' studies may find site-specific reasons for not doing so.

Operator opposition to draft Improvement Programme upgrading requirements were based upon three types of objection. First were the timetables provided by Inspectors for meeting new process BATNEEC standards. Second was the ability to finance the requested improvement actions. Finally, operators complained that the programme of work IPC imposed did not follow any site-wide rationale.

All three objections are related. Each stems from a general operator desire to manage the pace and pattern of environmental improvements. The argument coming from operators was not so much that they could not afford upgrades, but rather they couldn't afford them just yet given the programme for capital spending already put in place by their Board.

Operators argued that feasibility studies in place of upgrading requirements would ensure that capital became available for action in the future. As one multinational put it, the argument presented to HMIP was that a feasibility study 'enables us to internally flag up the issue with the people who hold the capital for improvement plans. We say, look, we're having to put in a feasibility study with HMIP on reducing VOC emissions from VC3 at the end of the year. That flags up the people with the purse strings to have the capital there in three or four years to put in the feasibility plan'.

The mutual benefits of feasibility studies

HMIP appeared happy to allow this delay. Inspectors were deferring their upgrading requests into the future, under operator assurances that then they would be more likely to take place voluntarily. The authority vested in Inspectors to do otherwise was undermined by their dependency upon other policy actors for resources. Key amongst these was their dependency upon operators for process and economic information. Feasibility reports from operators would generate such information. Delaying IPC improvements in this way was mutually beneficial. Interviewed Inspectors argued they would be in a better position to make regulatory decisions in the future. Equally, changing improvement actions into feasibility studies accorded with the new consensus rules of the game (Table 6.6).

Decision making was easier because feasibility requests prompted operators to come up with solutions to their own environmental problems. HMIP wanted industry to cultivate its own environmental management expertise and not be dependent upon regulator advice. This approach opens Inspectors up to less risk compared to HMIP prescribing solutions which subsequently fail - and which cannot be enforced because they derived from HMIP itself.[32]

Seeking voluntary or consensus improvements from operators bypassed HMIP's organisational inability to police large numbers of imposed regulatory conditions (see Hanf, 1993, p.100). HMIP's IPC inspection visits in 1994/95 were 45 per cent the level averaged by the air Inspectorate in the late 1970s,[33] who themselves sought voluntarism in order to overcome organisational constraints (chapter 3). This drop in inspection frequency is bigger than it appears since IPC has 64 per cent the number of processes as under the air regime.[34] Finally, HMIP's return to pragmatism and flexibility won some goodwill from operators, all of whom said in interview that the regulatory relationship was much improved compared to HMIP's arms' length approach to IPC.

Table 6.6
Feasibility studies reflect the policy community's 'consensus' rules of the game

HMIP prescribes improvement actions	Operator required to conduct feasibility studies for future negotiation	Operator allowed to carry on their process without looking to improve
HMIP favoured	HMIP agreed	HMIP opposed
Industry opposed	Industry agreed	Industry favoured

Operators benefited from being able to participate closely in standard setting. Operators with several authorisations were able either at the draft stage or through later variations (once all the authorisations were passed) to negotiate Improvement Programmes from a site-wide perspective more in harmony with their own priorities.

The appreciative system of the policy community was evolving. HMIP envisaged its role as encouraging improved operator environmental management generally, and seeking operator solutions to negotiated regulatory goals. This also suited operators, who enjoyed the flexibility and participation this approach to pollution control entailed. So whilst feasibility studies were a necessity owing to HMIP's organisational constraint and the (lack of) resource distribution in the policy community, under arms' length or otherwise, the studies actually suited the emerging appreciative system of goal-directed self-regulation.

Operator influence over Improvement Programme conditions

Not all Inspectors were immediately forthcoming with flexibility on Improvement Programmes. One speciality company explained that altering Improvement Programme timetables to suit their site priorities came after authorisation: 'Our main concern was we had seven authorisations which we didn't submit in any particular order. Their Improvement Programme they set for each authorisation with time-scales on, and we had a great deal of discussion about our resource to do that time-scale ... Right at the beginning we pointed out that their Improvement Programme had taken no account of the priorities on the site, nor would it do. We kept on arguing that, and they kept on ignoring us. They finally have now seen our point of view and the authorisations are currently being revised, as are the Improvement Programmes, to take account of that, to allow us to set out priorities at a site level'. One multinational operator described how this allowed them to 'align the regulatory requirements with the management system' for the site.

Another speciality operator told its Inspector that the time-scales for tasks in the Improvement Programmes amounted to too big a workload. Nonetheless, it tackled the requirements as best they could. However, HMIP was disappointed with the lack of detail in operator reports arising from the Improvement Programme. The operator acknowledged this, but argued it had met its statutory obligations and HMIP could expect little else given the time-scale allowed. This impasse was overcome by HMIP inviting the operators to draw up its own programme of improvements for the prescribed processes within a site-wide perspective. This suits the operator, who is now able to integrate a strategic review of the site's operations with IPC and some improvement requests from the sewage undertakers. Repeatedly, operator influence results from its position as the source of necessary IPC regulatory information.

In some cases operators were embarking upon improved environmental performance independently of IPC. Those relevant to the prescribed processes were included in applications and Improvement Programmes. One specific example was an operator's switch from solvent-based chemistry: 'Without HMIP, although HMIP will take credit for this, 33 per cent of our solvent loss will disappear this year because we've moved one of our processes from a solvent route to an aqueous route ... Its a very spurious entry, but it suits them'. Other operators reported similar practice, with one arguing that 80 per cent of his Improvement Programme reflected tasks that would have happened anyway, albeit not so rapidly. Another summed up the rationale behind this, 'Some of the improvements that we put forward were planned anyway. But it can't do us any harm to put them down as proposed improvements in the actual document'.

Even when operators change their plans, it appears they can seek changes to their IPC requirements to reflect these changes. One example was provided by a multinational operator concerning the monitoring of one of its effluent streams. Physical monitoring had been planned by the operator prior to IPC as a means to check the accuracy of effluent charges made by the sewage undertaker. Fitting monitoring equipment was consequently written into the

IPC Improvement Programme. However, one month before the deadline in the Improvement Programme, the operator decided the equipment was too expensive and opted against its installation. It sought a variation from HMIP to reflect this change of mind. The Inspector was happy to change the Improvement Programme request from - 'Suitable equipment shall be installed, used and maintained at Outfall 5 in order to measure and record , at all times, the instantaneous rate of flow and the total daily flow of effluent at that point' - to - 'A report detailing how the volume of liquid effluent discharged via Outfall 5 is calculated together with an analysis of the accuracy of the calculation shall be submitted by 28th February 1995'. The operator had discussed the matter with the Inspector and justified the change, the variation was simply a formal reflection of private negotiations.

All the operators interviewed had achieved revisions either to draft authorisations or variations to existing authorisations. Operators sometimes won influence over an Inspector by bringing more senior management to meetings to make assurances about honouring improvements in the future. At the time of interviewing, operators were working on these feasibility studies, having put initial Improvement Programme effort into monitoring and so forth.

One operator said the site-wide perspective meant it anticipated no change in the level of expenditure from what would have been required to meet the Inspectors initial requirements. However, feasibility studies meant the expenditure would be spread over a longer period and improvements across the site more co-ordinated. Another multinational was deliberately pro-active in calling for a site-wide approach from the outset. The operator said the Inspector was pleased with this co-operative approach and consequently invited the operator to set the improvement timetables across the site's authorisations. Another said 'HMIP has never asked us to do anything which we think we cannot do. The reason for this is that we have got an environmental policy, we are part of the Responsible Care programme, we are expecting accreditation under BS7750, we've got a commitment from our Board to improve on a regular basis our environmental performance'.

This pragmatism from Inspectors is reminiscent of air pollution enforcement policy. Interviewed Inspectors confirmed that the operator's attitude was important to them, and indeed there are indications this is becoming official policy. HMIP's head of Environmental Technology and Management, Martin Bigg, has suggested environmental management systems (such as BS7750) were a useful indication of an operator's ability to comply with IPC (Bigg, 1994, p.6). David Slater, HMIP's Director, told a CIA conference of his belief in the complementarities between voluntary environmental management systems and his aspirations for IPC (HMIP, 1995i, p.6). In April 1995, HMIP consulted on a system for determining the effort spent checking operator IPC compliance which takes operator environmental management systems into account (HMIP, 1995j, p.4). HMIP has shifted its strategy from arms' length adjudicators to pragmatists willing to be flexible if operators appeared to be committed to making some sort of improvement in the future.

The general picture which emerges from interview evidence is one of operators managing IPC regulation and standard setting. This is reflected in the high proportion of feasibility study requests in authorisations on the public register. Had operators submitted good quality applications, complete with the information necessary for an Inspector to set authorisation standards, then operators would have found themselves in a zero-sum game. HMIP would have benefited by being able to prescribe standards as it had originally envisaged. Operators would not have obtained any benefit. In the event, IPC implementation became more of a positive-sum game for operators. HMIP will eventually get their desired regulatory information, but operators will now benefit too by being more integrated into future regulatory decision making, and ensuring these are suitable to their individual operations.

This was done by promoting improvement feasibility studies from a site-wide perspective. Standard setting was deferred into the future, based upon the outcome of operator feasibility reports; which means future standards are not going to be imposed without their close participation. In other words, operators regained the flexibility and participation which had characterised the air regime. The rules of the game were now more favourable to operators too. Negotiation was accepted, consensus and co-operation would be sought, and involvement was exclusive to operators and Inspectors.

The ongoing IPC policy community

The pattern by which IPC was implemented re-created policy community arrangements between HMIP and industry. But IPC was not a once off authorisation process. The policy community of Inspectors and operators is involved in continuing negotiation as a result of the initial implementation deficit. In addition, IPC imposes the routine regulatory duties of monitoring and reporting emissions by operators, and site Inspections by HMIP.

Routine regulatory activities are not discussed in this book. Suffice to say that both were beginning to become established at the time of writing, once the turbulence of initial IPC implementation had subsided. Operators and Inspectors had agreed suitable monitoring protocols, and HMIP was beginning its programme of site inspections, including check monitoring using contractors (HMIP, 1995, p.15). The purpose of paying some attention here to activities beyond IPC implementation is to make clear the extent and nature of the policy community that has been re-created. Three elements are briefly examined: amendments to the legislation in the light of the bottom-up practice of post-authorisation feasibility studies; HMIP's enforcement policy; and development of environmental assessment tools.

Bottom-up influence on legislation

Much of the above analysis related to the organic chemicals tranche. However, interviews with Inspectors about IPC revealed that the pattern of site-level implementation was repeated for other types of process. Such a pattern was not anticipated by the DoE. The Regulations stating which documents are to be placed on the public register did not foresee feasibility studies (interview with civil servant). As a consequence, resulting operator reports do not go on the public register, thereby rendering upgrading negotiations private. The outcome of Inspector-operator negotiations, based upon feasibility study findings, will become public only after a variation reflecting the outcome is made to the original authorisation.

On 1st April 1996 the government amended the Regulations[35] to include operator feasibility reports on the public register (ENDS, 1996, p.41). The amendments do not provide for the retrospective inclusion of feasibility reports. This means that the entire first round of IPC authorisations (1991-1996) will not include on the public register those items missing in original applications and requested in the Improvement Programme: details of compliance monitoring arrangements; environmental assessments; and upgrading feasibility studies.

The amendments are another bottom-up policy development (like envelopes). The amended Regulations formalise two features of the way prescribed processes are controlled. First, regulating for public access to operator reports is official acknowledgement that operators can and will submit poor quality IPC applications. The regulators are institutionalising site-level practices which allow for operators to obtain authorisations after incomplete justifications of their processes. Second, the Regulations are tacit acceptance that IPC will involve ongoing negotiations dominated by Inspectors and operators. This is in contrast to the initial public authorisation of processes with its mechanism for consultation.

Improvement Programme negotiations based upon feasibility reports leading to substantial[36] variations will provide an opportunity for other interested parties to comment upon their adequacy. However, such public access is effectively at the whim of the policy community of Inspectors and operators negotiating variation conditions. It is they who will decide the topics and contents of feasibility studies requested in future variation notices, if any. Non-substantial proposals are not open to comment from third parties or statutory consultees. Negotiating improvements to a process' environmental

194

performance will continue to be exclusive to Inspectors and operators, even though feasibility reports will become public in the future.[37]

Transparency will begin to drip into the IPC system through variations to authorisations placed on the public register (reflecting the decisions made during ongoing Inspector-operator negotiations). Improvement requests in these variation notices will require some subsequent reporting from operators, which should also reach the public register.

It has not been possible to assess the variations arising from ongoing IPC negotiations. Analysis of the public register took place in 1994, too soon after authorisation for operator reports and authorisation variations. Without an analysis comparing Improvement Programme feasibility requirements with subsequent variation notice conditions it is not possible to draw confident conclusions about IPC's eventual policy output and outcomes. Nor is there an established time series of environmental release data from processes to check for improved process performance.[38] Of course, this does not affect the initial conclusion that the IPC application-authorisation process, and IPC as originally intended, has suffered a significant implementation deficit.

In this instance then, bottom-up pressures have influenced a re-formulation of the IPC legislative framework. Feasibility studies arose from operator inertia with respect to submitting good quality applications. Proposed amendments will bring some transparency to future policy community negotiations without improving access to them. IPC can thus be characterised as the air regime with a glass lid on: more transparent but no more accessible.

IPC enforcement policy

Legally binding authorisation conditions widen the opportunities open to HMIP for strict enforcement and prosecution. However, a fundamental prerequisite for any enforcement policy is a monitoring regime capable of ensuring compliance and detecting any transgression. Under the air regime inspection visits were the key regulatory tool for this task. However, programmed inspection visits for IPC remain at the low levels which contributed to falling confidence in the air regime - 3,642 for 1994-95 (HMIP, 1995, p.131).

HMIP's policy is to rely upon industrial self-monitoring for following compliance performance (HMIP, 1995, p.15). HMIP is seeking public confidence in this aspect of self-regulation through a system of certification for emission monitors (ENDS, 1996, p.34), continued visits by Inspectors, and periodic check monitoring by sub-contractors. This check monitoring has had a slow start. The establishment of check monitoring programmes intended in 1993 was not possible owing to financial constraints upon HMIP (DoE, 1994, p.10). Contracts finally began to be placed from August 1994 onwards

(HMIP, 1995k, p.14). Moreover, 'HMIP said in 1995 that it could only find the staff for fewer than three out of five necessary site visits to ensure compliance with regulation by industry' (Friends of the Earth, 1996 citing DoE, 1995).

However HMIP chooses to monitor IPC, its approach to enforcing IPC seeks co-operation from operators and not conflict. There are administrative and legal options open to Inspectors wishing to correct operator transgression. Enforcement Notices and Prohibition Notices are administrative measures provided for in the legislation.[39] Both Notices specify the remedial actions necessary from the operator to ensure compliance. The latter is more significant than the former in that it revokes the authorisation[40] until the action is carried out. The legal remedy is to seek prosecution.

HMIP enforcement policy is to relate the severity of the action to the environmental consequence of the offence and the operator culpability (HMIP, 1995, p.4). To date this policy has produced the results conveyed in Table 6.7.

Table 6.7
HMIP's record on enforcement action

Enforcement action	1992-93	1993-94	1994-95
Enforcement Notices	-	43	92
Prohibition Notices	1	2	3
Prosecution	14	13	15

Source: HMIP (1995e, p.7)

The level of enforcement activity in Table 6.7 is comparable with that pursued by the air Inspectorate in the 1970s (Table 3.3). Further comparison can be made in the sense that enforcement action follows similar rules of the game: the decision of the Inspector is related to the attitude struck by an operator. If both members are co-operative, then no formal action will result.

Unauthorised releases[41] and other instances of non-compliance do not automatically generate formal enforcement action. Operators have to report unauthorised releases to HMIP within 24 hours. During the content analysis, such reports were found on the public register without any formal enforcement. A letter from the Inspector may ask for a report into the causes of the incident, but it appears that Enforcement Notices arise in instances where failures could lead to recurrences or more serious pollution events.

An example is an Enforcement Notice served against ICI Chemicals & Polymers for spilling surfactants into the River Tees on 22nd May 1995. The Inspector reported that 'there had been two previous releases from the alkoxylation process to the River Tees, on 10 March and 4 April. These had resulted from reactor systems releases and had been partly due to operational errors and partly due to human error. HMIP formally warned the company about the inadequacies revealed then' (HMIP, 1995i, p.17).

A review of enforcement case histories for chemical operators, derived from HMIP's in-house magazine, shows three chemical operators have received Prohibition Notices for the 'imminent risk of serious pollution' (DoE, 1993, p.18) since January 1993. Four chemical operators have been prosecuted, and Table 6.8 classifies the causes for Enforcement Notices issued to chemical operators between January 1993 and November 1995.

Table 6.8
Enforcement Notices against chemical operators Jan 1993 - Nov 1995

Incident prompting an Enforcement Notice	Lack of documentation	Unauthorised release	Failure to improve	Lack of training/poor practice
Enforcement Notices	2	33	9	7

Source: 'HMIP Bulletin'

The evidence suggests HMIP's enforcement policy bears certain resemblance to the air Inspectorate's. A key difference is that HMIP is far more open about its formal enforcement action. Operators are named and the incidents responsible are described by HMIP. Such public chastisement strengthens the significance of formal enforcement action as a device of last resort. Inspectors said they were reluctant to issue Enforcement Notices if an operator was generally co-operative, tending to be reserved for 'wilful' breaches of compliance. Confrontation hardens operators and tends to solicit unhelpful 'yes' or 'no' answers to questions. One Inspector said he expected operators to breach their limits, and would be suspicious if they did not. Rather, it was the circumstances under which breaches arose that were important.

However, the similarity between HMIP's and the air Inspectorate's enforcement policies and enforcement statistics suggests IPC will come in for public criticism in the future. Indeed, there were 107 unauthorised releases from prescribed processes at ICI's site in Runcorn between January and July

1996. None of these prompted formal enforcement action from Inspectors (ENDS, 1996, pp.3-5). Inspectors may feel that informal approaches seeking consensus and co-operation may be more productive, just as their air pollution predecessors did, but third party analysts may interpret the extent of this informality as evidence of the regulator being soft on polluters.

Accounting for operator attitude is becoming part of HMIP's official enforcement policy more generally. HMIP wishes to promote responsible environmental management amongst operators with schemes such as reducing Inspection frequency and possibly reducing IPC charges to those operating an accredited EMS.

The development of environmental assessment tools

There is evidence that the integration of industry into a policy community with HMIP is extending beyond the negotiation and enforcement of individual, site-level IPC standards. The policy community is also collaborating in the development of a 'tool-kit' of environmental assessment methodologies for application in IPC.

The idea behind the collaboration is to provide standardised techniques for use by operators and Inspectors when conducting environmental assessments for IPC (HMIP, 1994c, p.6). It was first put forward by HMIP in September 1994, followed by a seminar on the subject in January 1995. Over 50 companies are involved in the collaborative projects that have been established (ENDS, 1995d, p.10). Industry has participated from the start, researching and solving problems of mutual benefit in ways reminiscent of BPM Note production.

HMIP is also involved in developing other regulatory tools that will help improve IPC regulation in the future. Beginning in 1991, HMIP developed a methodology which attempts to enable the systematic determination of BPEO (HMIP, 1992d; HMIP, 1995f; see also Hartnell, Skea, Smith and Stirling, 1994). Early development was done solely by HMIP's Pollution Policy Division (HMIP, 1992d). Development was similar to CIGNs, with draft documents sent out for formal consultation (HMIP, 1994d). Later development has involved the collaboration of operators with piloting and refining the BPEO assessment methodology (Inspector interview). The reason for raising this work here is to indicate how the pattern of HMIP-industry interaction at 'policy' level has changed with time; and how the 'formal consultation' route taken in the early 1990s contrasts with more recent approaches using participative collaboration. The latter is true for environmental assessment tools but also for other projects, such as assessing IPC's financial benefits for operators (HMIP, 1995h) and new CIGNs.

So more recent developments on guidance and regulatory tools have tended to involve industry, following similar rules of the game to those at the site-level. Whether these new tools improve application quality and authorisation decisions remains to be seen, although they are arriving too late for authorising the majority of the country's most complex and polluting processes.

Summary and conclusions

This chapter has analysed how IPC policy output was predominantly determined at the site-level implementation stage. Release limits reflect what operators were releasing prior to IPC: there has been no 'integrated' balancing of process releases to all three environmental media. IPC implementation has brought about improvements in operator ability to monitor environmental performance, some process improvements, and examinations into the feasibility of carrying out more process improvements.

For the most part though, bottom-up (and some top-down) pressures resulted in IPC implementation being different to that originally envisaged by HMIP. There was a significant implementation deficit in the sense that much of the work operators should have done for their applications was not carried out. This has had the affect of delaying full IPC implementation, as operators meet authorisation requirements to conduct monitoring/environmental assessments. Moreover, it has enabled operators to negotiate flexible, site-specific improvements more in line with their business priorities. The result has been that IPC fits the bottom-up model of policy making, and is the domain of a policy community whose membership is exclusively HMIP and industry.

Industry enhanced its degree of integration within the policy community and increased its influence over IPC. The intensity of Inspector-operator interaction increased.[42] Industry was able to do this owing to the distribution of resources between the two members.

An important factor was HMIP's organisational inability to allow delays to IPC implementation - it lacked the manpower to exercise its authority and request missing information before authorising processes. Industrial influence also derived from the absence of regulatory information in applications. HMIP lacked both environmental performance data and financial data to impose site-specific standards.

Industry was the source for such site-specific information and was able to use this resource imbalance to get HMIP to follow rules of the game more to industry's liking. HMIP's willingness was enhanced by the prevailing political climate which valued industry's economic resource and was seeking targets for deregulation. In total, the policy community appears similar to that controlling the old air pollution regime. Membership was the same. Similar resource interdependencies prevailed. And an equivalent level of integration has re-emerged. Consensus agreements were sought and members were expected to co-operate. Negotiations were pragmatic and flexible, seeking IPC standards for individual site-level circumstances, particularly over the important authorisation Improvement Programme. The dimensions of the IPC policy community are summarised in Table 6.9, along with a comparison with the preceding air policy community dimensions (also compare Figures 6.1 and 4.1).

Table 6.9
Comparison of air and IPC policy communities

Dimension	Air regime	IPC regime
Membership	Inspectorate and Industry	HMIP and Industry
Resource distribution	Inspectorate	HMIP
	Authority: Inspectors must demonstrate the process meets BPM. The vague nature of this statutory principle undermined this resource. Have the authority to register processes - which operators must obtain.	Authority: Inspectors authorise prescribed processes. Specific authorisation conditions are legally binding. However, these conditions still depend upon a vague statutory principle (BATNEEC).
	Knowledge: Inspectors have knowledge of legal requirements and of pollution control techniques.	Knowledge: Inspectors have knowledge of legal requirements and of pollution control techniques.
	Industry	Industry
	Information: Operators are the source of information concerning process emissions, and the financial data necessary for assessing the 'practicability' of controls.	Information: Operators are the source of information concerning process emissions, and the financial data necessary for assessing the level at which costs become 'excessive'.
	Economic: Industry is a source of wealth and employment.	Economic: Industry is a source of wealth and employment, given political support by the deregulatory drive.
	Organisation: It is industry which innovates pollution control techniques, and	Organisation: It is industry which innovates cleaner

	operators who install them.	processes, and operators who install them.
	Money: Operators fund improvements in air pollution control.	*Money:* Operators fund improvements in processes' environmental performance.
Integration	Interaction: Inspectorate and operators participate in the formulation of central guidance. Inspectors and operators exercise discretion in negotiating site-level standards. Appreciative System: Pollution control is a technical issue. Inspectors are the experts, disseminating advice and good practice amongst operators concerning specific pollution problems. Rules of the Game: - primacy of industrial activity; - policy community members co-operate; - standards negotiated at site-level; - seek consensus not conflict; - confidentiality; - informal agreements; - voluntarism sought; and - formal enforcement is device of last resort.	Interaction: Interaction has increased. Formal operator consultation over central guidance has shifted to collaboration and negotiation between members. Inspectors and operators exercise discretion in negotiating site-level standards. Appreciative System: Pollution control is a technical issue. Inspectors ensure operators pursue good environmental management, and pursue goal-directed self-regulation. Rules of the Game: - primacy of industrial activity; - policy community members co-operate; - standards negotiated at site-level; - seek consensus not conflict; - output of negotiations should be transparent; - output of informal negotiation recorded in formal conditions; - voluntarism sought; and - formal enforcement is device of last resort.

Like other policy communities, there were mutual benefits from a shift away from the contentious arms' length approach. By being flexible and pragmatic, and by granting greater operator access to decision making, HMIP won operator goodwill, was promised improvements in the future, and was generally able to keep IPC implementation to its statutory timetable. Policy community arrangements continue with the ongoing enforcement of IPC.

There are, however, some important differences between the air and IPC policy communities. The first is the transparency with which these communities shape policy. The IPC policy community is more transparent, but to only a limited extent. Process releases are now publicly available, as are site-specific process standards. However, there is no public exposure to the reasons why a particular standard is considered BATNEEC for a given circumstance.[43] Moreover, unlike other forms of government consultation, industry comments upon draft CIGNs are not publicly available. Nor are draft authorisation conditions. Negotiations remain private to HMIP and operators. And, to date, operator feasibility reports remain off the public register.

IPC maintains the British 'policy style' evident under the air regime, whereby the 'preference is for the particular over the general, the concrete over the abstract and the commonsensical over the principled' (Weale, 1992, p.81). However, some changes are evident along the integration dimension. The appreciative system has transformed from Inspectors offering advice on specific problems, into Inspectors seeking evidence of more general environmental management competence from operators; and so operators generate proposals for meeting negotiated regulatory goals: goal-directed self-regulation.

Thus the penultimate hypothesis to this book is confirmed with qualification: IPC is the domain of a policy community reminiscent of its air predecessor though the appreciative system now reflects the new roles expected of Inspector and operator. IPC policy output may be more formal and transparent, but within this framework occurs informal negotiation and opaque standard setting. Environmental improvements are being prompted by IPC, most immediately to the environmental management capability of operators - monitoring and environmental assessment. Some process improvements are promised in the future, but only after a negotiated consensus has been reached between Inspectors and operators. The final hypothesis raised by policy networks' power dependency theory - that industry's information and economic resources place it in a powerful position - has been confirmed with the empirical identification and characterisation of the IPC policy community. Operators are having to make some improvements, but they dominate the pace and shape of those improvements.

Notes

1   The other Task Forces were for: Retail, Tourism and Other Services; Food, Drink and Agriculture; Construction; Engineering; Financial Services; and Transport and Communications.

2   Specialised Organics Information Service Ltd.

3   The British Standards Institute accredited environmental management system.

4   Part I, Chapter I, Section 5, Deregulation and Contracting Out Act, 1994.

5   Part I, Chapter I, Section 1, Deregulation and Contracting Out Act, 1994.

6   A draft BPEO Methodology was published in August 1995 (HMIP, 1995f), consultation on a revised IPC charging scheme considers reductions for operators with a suitable EMS (ENDS, 1995c), as does HMIP's April 1995 consultation on new Inspection policy (HMIP, 1995g), and a scoping study for the evaluation of IPC took place in March 1995 (Skea, Smith, Sorrell and van Zwanenberg, 1995).

7   The fifth was an editor of ENDS Report, an environmental policy magazine.

8   Note also that the first round of IPC authorisation has generally resulted in the creation of monitoring regimes, identification of significant process releases and an examination of options for their reduction. Significant improvements have yet to arise. The expense and effort in securing application has yet to show significant environmental benefits to balance against the regulatory costs. This makes IPC ripe for deregulatory criticism. However, I would argue this is a lag effect. Now that operators are establishing environmental management systems under IPC's influence and requirement, then benefits could arise in the future (depending upon the rigour with which HMIP reviews authorisation conditions).

9   The Institute of Directors were also calling for deregulation, and the Sunday Telegraph launched its campaign against red tape, including a feature on HMIP, in January 1993.

10 Statutory Instrument No. 507 'The Environmental Protection (Applications, Appeals and Registers) Regulations 1991'.

11 For example, chemists may present data on the process chemistry, chemical engineers would produce piping and instrumentation diagrams or explain the abatement techniques used, and so on.

12 This was also advice offered by NEDC - Specialised Organics Sector Group (NEDC -SOSGN, 1992, p.3).

13   Thirty-eight per cent of applicants received official requests for further information.

14   Or the Welsh Office's Agricultural Science Adviser in Wales.

15   Note that the public register does not record comments from non-statutory consultees, such as local communities or NGOs.

16   The Guidance Note explicitly said that this should include the ambient concentration of the release, and the increase in background concentrations of the substance attributable to the release. This should be examined in the context of the effect on susceptible organisms. Guidance to field Inspectors said that any modelling done by operators should be referenced or its methods and assumptions described in the application (HMIP, 1991c, p.4).

17   Their plant is in the countryside, eight or nine miles outside Wolverhampton.

18   HMIP guidance explained 'it is not sufficient to describe excessive costs in absolute terms without reference to the cost of the product. The applicant must be able to demonstrate that the increased cost of the product produced by the best available technique is grossly disproportionate to any environmental benefit likely to occur from that method of production. The extra cost must represent a significant fraction of the cost of the finished product' (HMIP, 1991c, p.3).

19   Significant improvements are taken to be those which reduce environmental releases.

20   Authorisations contain a standard statement for releases to land or incineration. It issues a general duty for operators to have a management procedure that ensures releases are BATNEEC and are stored, handled and disposed of 'in the most appropriate manner and that contamination of land is avoided' (see for example, Authsn. No. AN2331, Thomas Swan Ltd).

21   Although consultants could have been commissioned. This was part of the arms' length objective, to force operators to obtain environmental expertise.

22   In practice, HMIP's concern with releases to land (such as drummed toxic effluent sent for landfill) has been less than for the other two media. Control of land disposal is regulated by other authorities under different statutes. In authorisations, HMIP does not limit quantities to land and defers disposal requirements to control by other authorities.

23   In addition to this were IPC prescribed processes without prior regulation under the air regulations.

24   Supplying this information was also a statutory requirement.

25   Part I, Section 6 (4), Environmental Protection Act, 1990.

26   Schedule 1, Part I, Paragraph 1 (3), Environmental Protection Act, 1990.

27   Schedule 1, Part I, Paragraph 1 (4), Environmental Protection Act, 1990.

28   The Appeal delays generated by the Fuel and Power IPC tranche were an early lesson for HMIP's arms' length approach and could not become universal to IPC.

29   Up to 28th October 1994, 34 Appeals had been lodged against HMIP authorisation decisions in England, of which 23 had been withdrawn and 10 were still current. Only one had been determined (Written correspondence with DoE civil servant).

30   Existing process operators were finally set conditions such as: 'Prepare proposals based on the data obtained in Section 2, for discussion with the Chief Inspector, to bring the emissions into line with the New Plant standards as defined in the Chief Inspectors Guidance Notes' (Robinson Brothers' authorisation no. AK6438). Thus standards in the CIGN are written into statutory requirements, albeit to help focus operator feasibility studies.

31   HMIP's professional field staff is relatively small and this facilitates informal consultation amongst colleagues.

32   A problem under the air regime.

33   IPC visits: 6,615 (HMIP, 1995e, p.131). Average air Inspections: 14,817 (Table 3.2).

34   IPC frequency: 3.8 visits per process per year (calculated from data in HMIP, 1995e). Air frequency: 5.5 visits per process per year (calculated from data in chapter 3).

35   S.I. 1996 No. 667 'The Environmental Protection (Applications, Appeals and Registers) (Amendment) Regulations 1996'.

36   Guidance between substantial and non-substantial change is vague (chapter 5).

37   Note that these reports are likely to contain many confidentiality requests since any BATNEEC demonstrations of sufficient detail will need to consider information concerning the operators' production costs.

38   One should expect improvements, given the poor starting point from which many operators were brought into IPC. Given their lack of knowledge concerning their process releases, it can be expected that many operators will be able to find some inexpensive room for improvement from their sub-optimal starting points. Interviews with operators found many had discovered areas ripe for improvement. In some instances these were new discoveries, others had been recognised before IPC. IPC provided the impetus to overcome inertia.

39   Sections 13 and 14 of Part I of the Environmental Protection Act, 1990 respectively.

40   This makes operation of the process illegal.

41   That is, beyond the limits set in the authorisation.

42   Manifest in the shift from consultation to negotiation.

43   IPC diverges from DoE guidance to the extent that the DoE suggest 'that BATNEEC is determined and applied in a transparent, rational and consistent way'. (DoE, 1993, p.13).

7 Conclusion

Introduction

Two research questions have driven the research presented in this book: why was the IPC regime introduced in Britain; and how has IPC been implemented? In addressing this latter question, IPC was contrasted with its air predecessor, along with an examination of how regulatory standards were established and an assessment of IPC policy output. Analysis used theories of policy making from the policy networks literature and insights from implementation studies. Thus the IPC policy process was analysed by focusing upon the networks of policy actors attempting to influence the outcomes of decisions arising during that process (chapter 2).

Policy networks can be characterised and analysed along three dimensions: their membership; the pattern of resource distribution and interdependence between members; and the degree of integration amongst the membership. This latter dimension is very different to 'integration' as understood for IPC. The integration dimension of a policy network relates to the shared appreciative system and the rules of the game which develop between members and which mediates their interaction with one another. To avoid confusion, this chapter reserves the term 'integration' for the policy network dimension and uses the term 'IPC' when referring to systems of pollution control which regulate environmental releases in the round.

The theoretical background of chapter 2 was used to generate five hypotheses concerning the IPC policy process: (1) the preceding air regime was the domain of a policy community of Inspectors and operators; (2) the shift to IPC was driven by policy actors in an issue network external to this policy community; (3) IPC policy output, in terms of the action required of regulators and operators, has been influenced the most during its implementation; (4) this implementation is the domain of a policy community exhibiting characteristics similar to the air predecessor; (5) industry is an influential policy community member and has been able to weaken IPC policy output.

Chapters 3, 4, 5 and 6 tested these hypotheses and answered the two initial research questions. Chapter 3 analysed the industrial air pollution regime and discussed the discontent with this arrangement that came from some quarters in the early 1970s. In the following chapter the disruptions of the 1980s which finally led to a switch to IPC were the focus of study. Finally, chapters 5 and 6 sought to explain implementation of the new IPC regime.

The purpose of this concluding chapter is threefold. First, the accuracy of the hypotheses is assessed and consideration given to whether IPC represents a fundamental shift in UK environmental policy. Second, an assessment is made into the adequacy of the policy networks framework as a tool for analysing the policy process. Finally, the future prospects for IPC are discussed.

The IPC policy process

Change and continuity in industrial pollution regulation

Analysis has confirmed the first hypothesis, that industrial air pollution policy was the domain of a policy community. The membership of Inspectors and operators regulated emissions in an exclusive partnership. The organisationally constrained Inspectorate had the authority to ensure operators pursued the vaguely defined BPM principle. Operators possessed the information needed to elaborate this principle and the wherewithal to apply it. This resource interdependency bound the policy community together.

For over one hundred years the policy community brought the same appreciative system to pollution control and regulated emissions using the same rules of the game (see Table 6.9 for a summary). It perceived pollution control as a technical issue, to be solved in partnership between the exclusive membership, who worked co-operatively and confidentially towards consensus on solutions to specific pollution problems. Air pollution policy was thus dominated by conservative, professional and economic interests.

One has to look outside the policy community to its critics in order to identify the source of the IPC policy issue. Criticism was a particular reflection of widespread environmental concern in the late 1960s and early 1970s. An issue network of public interest policy actors, such as Social Audit, felt the exclusive and confidential manner in which Inspectors and operators arrived at pollution controls was unaccountable, and that it did not serve the public interest. Standards were not publicly available and enforcement was informal. The appreciative system of the air policy community clashed with the appreciative system of the issue network. The latter wanted more publicly

208

accountable standards and tougher enforcement within a less exclusive framework. It was this vocal issue network which prompted the RCEP investigation into industrial air pollution policy.

The RCEP's 1976 report provided a cogent case for IPC reform and endowed the issue with respectability. It touched upon the issues of wider participation and accountability, but it was their scientifically-based criticism of single medium pollution controls which became the RCEP's main concern. The RCEP recognised that fragmented pollution controls simply shunted pollution between environmental media. It recommended IPC reforms and a single regulator to administer them.

Even with the issue raised and the case for reform made, IPC did not automatically proceed to the policy formulation stage. The political saliency of this issue faded away with the general dimming of environmental issues in the late 1970s (Pepper, 1986, p.18). Moreover, the creation of the HSC/E in 1975 meant industrial air pollution policy was linked to a wider industrial health and safety policy network whose stability had significance for government in other, more important policy sectors. This linkage acted against government intervention. In addition, industrial members of the air policy community, under the CBI, were happy with this new administrative arrangement. The government replied to the RCEP's IPC recommendations in 1982: they rejected them and supported the fragmented status quo.

When formulation of reforms finally began, it was initially because EC intervention was challenging the appreciative system of the air policy community. Directives were being negotiated in Brussels which would require incorporation into domestic law and appeared to portend more uniform and formal European regulations. Factors external to the policy community were propelling change. The policy community opened up into an issue network seeking to manage these external pressures. Members wanted to see credibility restoring measures which would defend the British tradition of operator involvement in setting site-specific, flexible standards from a perceived European threat. Industrial leaders began arguing for the return of the technically expert Inspectorate to the DoE, where it could more effectively support Britain's policy position. The DoE favoured such change too.

At the same time, the Inspectorate's distinct identity and role was under threat. The HSE was proposing to incorporate its functions into general health and safety units, which would weaken the autonomy and technical position of domestic air pollution policy. This furthered other issue network members' desires for the Inspectorate to be returned to the DoE. The membership lacked the authority to remedy this situation, and an appeal was made to government to take some action over domestic air pollution policy. A Cabinet Office Efficiency Scrutiny was launched as a result. It was their deregulatory findings which finally prompted government intervention and the creation of HMIP under the DoE. This intervention put reforms onto an IPC trajectory.

Meanwhile, the DoE was proposing single-media reforms, incorporating EC requirements into British air pollution control practice. However, it could not proceed without the government's authority resource to pass primary legislation (that is, the Clean Air Bill); this was turned down by government. Parliamentary time was found eventually after the government's 1988 populist recognition of growing public concern for the environment. The IPC legal framework eventually introduced in the ensuing Environmental Protection Act, 1990 drew upon the work done for the Clean Air Bill and EC requirement. It introduced more formal and transparent procedures for the regulation of industrial releases. These were to be administered by HMIP, who would also be responsible for setting regulatory standards based upon the BATNEEC and BPEO principles.

Thus the second of the research hypotheses is only partially correct. It is true that policy change arose due to external pressures upon the policy community. An interplay of EC pressure and HSC/E administrative manoeuvre were key drivers. But it was members of the policy community, reacting to these pressures, which sought reforms and began debating domestic reform of industrial pollution policy. They drew suitably resourced policy actors into an issue network as they were needed. Policy change was managed by an issue network, including air policy community members, reacting to external pressure (see Figure 4.1).

When it came to implementing IPC, HMIP unilaterally imposed its own rules of the game. They decided to deepen IPC's formality by introducing an arms' length approach to regulation. This arms' length approach meant policy network membership during implementation would be less integrated and more hierarchical. Regulatory standards were to be established centrally by HMIP, independent from industry. Operators would have to demonstrate compliance with fixed standards rather than negotiate standards. This approach clashed with the rules of the game expected by industry, who felt excluded.

Industry was able to thwart HMIP's initial desire to change the rules of the game. The creation of HMIP and IPC's more formal framework had not altered the resource interdependency fundamental to technology-based pollution regulation. The regulator may have had the authority to require improvements, but HMIP remained dependent upon industrial resources if BATNEEC standards were to become a reality. The information asymmetry was such that Inspectors could not impose BATNEEC pollution control standards authoritatively. Operators were the source of the technical, environmental and economic information that was needed to set those standards.

When HMIP embarked upon this task with CIGNs it was forced to modify their function (chapter 5). HMIP began emphasising the lack of prescription about CIGNs, that they were merely for general guidance purposes. Standard setting was deferred to the site-level instead, where the same resource interdependency (information versus authority) existed. Without industry's information HMIP was unable to exercise its authority. HMIP's organisational constraints and lack of political support made this information dependency more acute. So when operators submitted poor quality applications with insufficient information for Inspectors to set standards in authorisations, HMIP had to abandon its arms' length policy. A return to site-specific flexibility and the participation of operators in standard setting took place.

Compared to original HMIP aspirations, IPC has suffered a significant implementation deficit. Many of the tasks HMIP wished to see operators undertake in advance of submitting their applications have had to be deferred to authorisation conditions and operator feasibility studies. The quantification of releases, assessment of environmental impacts, and development of improvement programmes are now all post-authorisation activities. But at least some improved environmental management of the processes is beginning to take place.

So analysis has found the third hypothesis to be correct: that IPC implementation fits the bottom-up model. Policy output has been decisively influenced at this late, site-level stage. It is the domain of a policy community which, whilst possessing a few differences, remains broadly reminiscent of the air policy community, as suggested by the fourth research hypothesis.

Output of Inspector-operator negotiations is more transparent under IPC, and the application-authorisation framework within which they take place has more formality about it than its air predecessor. Nevertheless, negotiations still take place in private between Inspectors and operators at the site-level. It is these which determine IPC policy output, that is the environmental controls and improvements to processes, and operators enjoy considerable influence over them.

The air and IPC policy communities have the same membership and resource dimensions. The integration dimension includes the same rules of the game as for the air regime, but has a slightly different appreciative system (Table 6.9). The appreciative system still perceives pollution control as a technical issue for Inspectors and operators; but nowadays Inspectors seek demonstration of competent environmental management from operators. In the past Inspectors were perceived as technically competent individuals encouraging operators to do their best over specific pollution problems. Under IPC, operators are perceived as adopting environmental management skills themselves, with HMIP holding a watching brief and negotiating with operators the improvements to be made and auditing progress to that end.

211

Given the resource distribution, HMIP came to realise that site-level negotiation had advantages. IPC implementation was not a straightforward case of reluctant capitulation by HMIP to industry - though this did take place, and demonstrates the final hypothesis that industry has been a dominant policy community member. Given industrial inertia over IPC, HMIP came to realise that the policy community arrangements that developed were of mutual benefit, even if they were not what it had initially desired. The IPC policy community has enabled HMIP to keep to its implementation timetable and avoid criticism from political masters, whilst industry has been able to win influential access to standard setting.

The persistent British tradition

Overall, this analysis has shown the IPC policy process to be long and incremental; which confirms the characterisations made by O'Riordan and Weale (1989, p.292) and Jordan (1993, p.405). Both their studies suggest IPC presents evidence of a shift in UK environmental policy. The former claim that 'No longer can the British hide behind plant-specific emission controls linked to broad, non-statutory, environmental quality targets' (1989, p.291). For Jordan, IPC fits an 'emerging style' which 'is likely to be more transparent, increasingly formalised and structured, participative, timetabled and more strictly enforced; [and] the administrative structures are likely to be more centralised, integrated and possibly more technocratic and managerial' (1993, p.411).

Both studies view Europe as a driving force behind these changes. O'Riordan and Weale argue a process of 'purposive adaptation' was occurring in the late 1980s, whereby a more formal European approach was having to be accommodated by the informal British tradition (1989, p.292). Pearce and Brisson (1993, p.39) believed a more formal, sector-wide, systematic approach to standard setting was essential for IPC; any return to the traditional 'case-by-case' approach would be a 'retrogressive step'.

This study has been able to improve upon these insights thanks to the passing of a few years of IPC implementation. The formality they forecast has been found to be ambiguous. A formal, arms' length approach, out of step with the British tradition, was adopted by HMIP not long after publication of the O'Riordan and Weale paper. But difficulties in its application led to informally set, plant-specific emission controls, albeit within more formal and transparent procedures than the air regime.

O'Riordan and Weale (1989) are nevertheless correct to characterise IPC as the British tradition working within a more formal EC legal framework. By analysing IPC implementation this book has been able to elaborate upon these characteristics and has argued that elements of the British tradition persist with more depth than previous studies anticipated (see also Skea and Smith, 1996). The statutory framework - which brought formality to regulatory procedures, which divided regulatory duty between applying operators and authorising Inspectors, which introduced transparency through a public register, which made authorisation conditions legally binding, and which required upgrading timetables - simply follows European Directive (see Table 4.2). But the negotiations by which BATNEEC standards are established, including the pattern by which improvements are pursued, remain informal, seek consensus, and are deeply influenced by industry. By extension, it can be concluded that IPC does not present evidence of a fundamental shift in domestic environmental policy.

Policy networks and the policy process

In this section the objective is to reflect upon the study of IPC and to draw conclusions regarding the utility of policy networks for analyses of the policy process. The approach taken is to answer the question: how successfully do policy networks explain the policy process, from issue creation to policy implementation (Figure 2.2) and its eventual policy output?

In chapter 2 it was pointed out that the literature identified policy networks' conservative affect upon the policy process. That discussion also pointed out that non-incremental policy change tended to be driven by factors exogenous to policy networks. This IPC analysis has confirmed both of these observations.

Policy networks and conservatism in the policy process

After criticism of the air regime in the 1970s, and disturbances in the 1980s, this study has found that in the 1990s we are left with an IPC regime similar to its air predecessor. The key strength of policy network analysis has been its ability to characterise (see Table 6.9) and explain (chapters 5 and 6) this similarity. Policy network analysis has indeed been able to explain a significant aspect of the IPC policy process: its conservatism.

Policy networks 'both constrain and facilitate policy actors and policy outcomes' (Rhodes and Marsh, 1994, p.11). Chapter 2 explained how they are constituted from resource interdependent policy actors (the resource dimension) and evolve appreciative systems and rules of the game concerning interaction between members and with the outside world (the integration dimension). The more integrated the policy network the more likely it is to constrain policy innovation and to facilitate the status quo, particularly if economic or professional interests are dominant (Rhodes and Marsh, 1992, p.196).

It was during IPC implementation that there was a return to an informal, flexible, and consensus seeking approach to setting pollution control standards. IPC policy formulation had created a more formal and transparent regulatory framework, but within this beats the heart of the air regime. The source of policy networks' success in explaining this rests upon the power dependency theory at the centre of this analytical approach, and the ultimate importance of resources during implementation.

This study has shown that when a policy network member wishes to alter a network's integration dimension, their success is limited by the resources they possess and by those upon which they are dependent. HMIP has had to accept that IPC does not meet its initial anticipation regarding their relationship with operators and the policy output that took place. In this respect, the characteristics of the IPC policy network have influenced the policy process significantly.

Analysis demonstrated how HMIP was unable to change the rules of the game of the policy network responsible for IPC implementation because there had been no concomitant redistribution of the necessary regulatory resources. Policy network analysis identified the sources of these resources: the authority to allow processes to operate (HMIP); the necessary information to set standards (operators); the financial and organisational resources to make improvements (operators); the organisational resources to enforce these improvements (HMIP); and underlying political and economic resources (political support, wealth and job creation) (operators). The balance favoured operators, who were able to influence policy output and the process by which future output would be negotiated.

HMIP was unable to exercise its full authority without possessing industrial information. The eventual provision of information by operators was exchanged for access to standard setting. It was through the process of negotiation that the policy community was not only constituted but also developed its appreciative system and rules of the game: the resource dimension can explain the degree of integration which developed. Thus power dependence theory can account for events during implementation, reflected and reinforced by the appreciative system and rules of the game that develop.

It is unsurprising that policy networks most successfully explain the policy process during the implementation stage, where concrete tasks must be delivered and resources are required most. But policy network analysis was also shown to be useful during the issue creation stage. In this instance, it was the properties of the integration dimension which were analytically useful, though the resource dimension also had to be evoked to explain the limited success of the 1970s issue network.

The public interest issue network, including Social Audit, possessed an appreciative system at odds with the practices of the air policy community. If

214

the air policy community had been perceived as unproblematic - that is, more inclusive and transparent - it is unlikely that a policy issue would have arisen. The power dependency theory explained why the issue network was unable to push through desired reforms. Its membership did not have the authority resources to force organisational or procedural change. They could only make vocal their concerns in the hope that this would raise the political saliency of industrial air pollution policy, and prompt the intervention of sufficiently authoritative policy actors.

Paradoxically, this episode in the early 1970s demonstrates how policy communities, which establish routines and de-politicise issues, can become a focus of external politicisation - owing to the exclusion of contrary interests which internal de-politicisation involves. Policy networks can consequently make an important contribution to the study of issue creation by explaining why and how certain policy actors are included or excluded from a policy sector. Moreover, with members of a policy community tending to possess resources most pertinent to the policy problem, policy network analysis can also explain why external politicisation of the issue will fail to make changes unless it can attract the intervention of policy actors with more authoritative resources.

The integration dimension of policy networks helped explain some of the events during IPC policy formulation too. In this instance it was the clash between the appreciative systems of the air policy community and the EC. The comparative analysis of these appreciative systems explained why some members of the policy community were galvanised into lobbying for defensive reforms as a bulwark against European encroachment. Recognition of the importance to analysis of this integration dimension has come relatively late to the policy network literature.[1]

Despite the conservatism of policy networks, a process of policy change did take place in the 1980s. IPC does provide a different legal framework to its air predecessor. However, explaining the drives behind these changes required an examination of exogenous factors - which brings us to the second element of this section.

Policy networks and exogenous sources of policy change

Being conservative entities, recourse has to be made to factors outside policy communities to explain policy change. Chapter 2 pointed out that there were four sources of exogenous policy change: economic; ideology; new knowledge/technology; and new institutional arrangements. Policy network analysis can explain how policy network members interact with these exogenous factors. However, the point made here is that policy network analysis cannot explain these exogenous factors themselves. With the above sub-section concluding that policy network analysis provides useful explanations for incrementalism and conservatism, this sub-section concludes that it is not so useful for explaining the sources of policy change.

The challenge to the air policy community certainly came from outside. Recourse had to be made to the heightened environmentalism in the late 1960s and early 1970s. Policy network analysis was still useful, since it was upon the air policy community that general environmental concern became particular. But a more complete explanation of the origins of the IPC issue would need to account for this wave of environmental concern (see, for example, Pepper, 1986).

The RCEP's Fifth Report became a respected, new knowledge resource concerning the drawbacks of fragmented, single-medium pollution control systems. However, this alone was insufficient to prompt policy change. The introduction of IPC reforms in the 1980s was motivated by two different types of exogenous factor: new institutional arrangements; and ideology.

The new institutional factor was the enhanced authority of the EC. The EC made necessary some reform to domestic air pollution regulation. The Cabinet Office Efficiency Scrutiny triggered a switch to IPC reforms owing to the fact its conclusions resonated with the government's deregulatory ideology. To account more fully for IPC one would have to explain the growth of the EC as a policy-making institution, the political ascendancy of the deregulatory New Right, and to a lesser extent the episodes of heightened public environmentalism in the late 1980s.[2]

Exogenous factors are an important element in explanations of policy change. Power dependency theory and the appreciative system concept are sources for hypotheses concerning the way a policy network is likely to interact with given exogenous factors. However, policy networks cannot explain these factors themselves. It is in this sense that policy networks fail to provide a complete theory of policy making. The problematique for this book was primarily substantive - explaining the IPC policy process. It was not intended that the study should develop theories of the policy process and so this will not be pursued here.[3] This book has simply tested the utility of the policy networks concept in its current state.

In summary, policy network analysis has improved understanding of the IPC policy process. It has been able to explain the continuities in industrial pollution regulation. The changes to regulation which did take place, however, have their origins in factors external to the policy community traditionally responsible for pollution control. Whilst policy network analysis can explain interaction with these exogenous factors, it is unable to explain the origins of these factors.

Future IPC developments

In this penultimate section consideration is given to IPC's future prospects. There are two events which could impact upon IPC's future development, and the likelihood of any change from these events is discussed below. These two events are: HMIP's incorporation into the new Environment Agency (a non-departmental public body) in April 1996; and the future requirement to incorporate the EU's Integrated Pollution Prevention and Control Directive (IPPC) into domestic practice. Since neither address the resource interdependency fundamental to IPC, it is unlikely that IPC will experience any significant changes.

The Environment Agency

The Environment Agency could impact upon IPC in two ways. The first is the influence of the former NRA's regulatory culture within the new Environment Agency (of which HMIP and the NRA are components), and the second is a general, statutory cost-benefit duty upon Environment Agency decisions. This cost-benefit duty is likely to dampen any NRA-influenced moves toward a more legalistic approach to enforcement.

The Environment Agency's creation echoes that of HMIP - an amalgam of pre-existing regulators whose creation was driven by multiple motives: a more integrated approach; improved technical effectiveness; and similar deregulatory desires (Gallagher, 1996; Carter and Lowe, 1994). There are 1200 fewer NRA staff going into the Environment Agency than was expected two years ago (Gallagher, 1996), and there have been reports of 'tough budgetary constraints and staff cuts' at HMIP's Technical Guidance Branch - responsible for CIGNs - when it enters the Environment Agency (ENDS, 1996: 38).

The NRA, HMIP and the Waste Regulatory Authorities (WRAs) have been brought together in the Environment Agency. Just as HMIP's creation initially led to RCI domination of its regulatory culture, so the NRA could repeat this in the EA. Over 7,000 of the Environment Agency's 9,000 staff come from the NRA, compared to 430 staff from HMIP (Environment Agency, 1995). Eleven of the top fifteen Environment Agency posts have gone to former NRA staff, including the Chief Executive, Ed Gallagher (ENDS, 1995e, p.3). Former HMIP Director, David Slater, remains responsible for IPC. He has stated that the Environment Agency facilitates a site-wide approach to pollution regulation. He has expressed an interest in building upon the NRA's 'catchment management' approach to water pollution control, using it as the basis for controlling releases to all media (Slater, 1996).

An elevation of environmental quality factors in decision making is one of the potential NRA/Environment Agency influences upon IPC - (see Environment

Agency, 1996). The NRA's catchment management approach derived environmental quality targets and priorities for a water catchment through consultation with community, commercial and conservation interests. It drew upon these environmental quality targets when setting discharge limits (grandfathered by HMIP into IPC authorisations).[4]

The NRA also had a higher public profile and was more independent than HMIP, disagreeing with government if necessary[5] (see NRA, 1991; NRA, 1995, p.6). The NRA's approach to enforcement was more legalistic than HMIP's[6] (see NRA, 1993, p.23). However, any 'NRA effect' in this respect is likely to be mitigated or even negated by the second aspect of the Environment Agency's impact: their cost-benefit duty.

The Environment Act, 1995, formally creating the Environment Agency, places upon it a duty to take into account the 'likely costs and benefits' when deciding whether or not to exercise its authority.[7] Draft DoE guidance suggests the duty applies to all decision-making levels - policy, strategy, and individual enforcement (ENDS, 1995f, p.25).

IPC already has cost-benefit criteria in BATNEEC, but the new duty enables industrial interests to use judicial review to challenge more strategic aspects of IPC (such as HMIP's BPEO methodology). Thus the Environment Act ,1995 formalises further the deregulatory pressures upon IPC. Industry's information resource will remain important for any cost-benefit appraisals sought by the Environment Agency, just as it was for BATNEEC appraisals. So overall, whilst there is potential for the Environment Agency to change regulatory approach over IPC, the realities of the cost-benefit duty are likely to maintain policy community arrangements and discourage vigorous regulation.

Integrated pollution prevention and control

Another future influence upon IPC will be the introduction of an Integrated Pollution Prevention and Control Directive (IPPC) by the EU. It has principles and procedures in common with IPC; indeed UK experience fed into the EU negotiations which shaped IPPC. Both systems are technology-based permit schemes which set similar conditions in pursuit of the integrated control of pollution from industrial processes (or 'installations' in the Directive's parlance). The DoE is proposing to incorporate IPPC within the existing IPC framework.

Official discussion on IPPC began in spring 1991. A draft Directive was eventually agreed by the Council of Ministers in June 1995. This needs the European Parliament's approval before being formally adopted by the Commission. At the time of writing (April 1996) the Directive had not been passed, and even when this does happen there will be a further three year period to allow it to be brought into domestic law. So IPPC will not impact upon IPC until summer 1999 at the earliest. Nevertheless, we can anticipate some of the Directive's likely impacts, which is the objective of this section. Deriving from the EU, one might expect IPPC to introduce more formality and uniformity to pollution control. But there is little to suggest this will be the case. IPPC has more similarities to IPC than dissimilarities (see Skea and Smith, 1996).

BAT versus BATNEEC, uniform versus site-specific standards. Early draft Directives spoke of processes having to prevent and minimise releases using the Best Available Techniques (ENDS, 1992c, p.31). This was promoted by northern Member States with a tradition for uniform technology standards. New processes should meet the BAT standards and existing processes would have to upgrade to BAT. However, the final draft agreed by the Council of Ministers requires regulators to continue to set permit conditions based on the BAT principle, but 'taking into account costs and advantages' (Article 2.10), 'thus preserving the UK's site-specific approach to authorisations' (DoE, 1995b). Site-specific factors are given further emphasis with a requirement to take into account 'the technical characteristics of the plant concerned, its geographical location and the local environmental conditions' (Article 8.2a).

European uniform emission standards. Germany pushed negotiations for a system whereby the Commission could adopt uniform standards for IPPC processes. The UK, amongst other Member States, objected to this (ENDS, 1995g, p.39). Negotiations resulted in Article 17a, which empowers the European Commission to propose 'Community emission limit values', based upon information it receives on BAT from Member States. For such uniform emission limit values to be adopted, the Commission's proposal must receive Qualified Majority Vote by the Council of Ministers. IPPC could, potentially, deliver uniform European emission standards. However, such powers already exist, under the Air Framework Directive for instance, and have rarely been exercised. The issue of uniform standards has been an issue for some time in European environmental policy and, given past experience, IPPC appears no closer to making such an approach a reality.

An increase in the number of processes regulated. The Annex I list of processes requiring a permit under IPPC is greater than the list of prescribed processes under IPC. Up to 5,000 processes could be added to IPC by the Directive (ENDS, 1995g, p.38). The main additions in the draft Directive are intensive livestock units, the food and drink industry, and processes in manufacturing industry. The DoE tried to negotiate an IPPC list of processes matching IPC, and it encouraged industrial operators in the new sectors to follow its example and lobby the European Parliament to amend the draft

Annex I list (DoE, 1995b). Intensive livestock operators have already secured specific cost effectiveness and practicability clauses mitigating the stringency of any controls placed upon them (Articles 8.2 and 8.3).

Even if further lobbying activity proves unsuccessful, the DoE has stated it will consider the scope for interpreting certain caveats in the Directive such that they will not require the new processes to be brought directly under IPC.

Two caveats are understood to offer potential. The first concerns the equivalence between single-media pollution controls administered by separate regulatory bodies and an integrated pollution control system. Article 6 allows separate controls to continue so long as a co-ordinated approach is taken and has an effect equivalent to integrated controls. Thus operators of processes currently outside IPC but whose emissions and discharges are already regulated under different regulations[8] need not be brought into IPC and can avoid the associated application-authorisation burden.

The second caveat concerns some installations which can, in certain circumstances, be issued permits with general binding rules rather than specific permit (authorisation) conditions (Article 8.6). Effectively, this caveat allows whole classes of processes to be authorised collectively. The DoE 'will be looking into the extent to which it can make use of this flexibility for some of those processes which do not currently need an IPC permit' (DoE, 1995).

An increase in prescribed substances. The scope for the DoE to keep non-prescribed processes outside IPC could be limited for two reasons. Firstly, the draft Directive has a list of prescribed substances requiring BAT controls which is much broader than the IPC list of 23 items. As such all processes, whether currently prescribed or not, could be effected if they release IPPC substances. Secondly, some domestic regulations for discharge to water, even if extended to include the new IPPC substances, follow controls based upon environmental quality standards rather than the BAT requirement. Thus operators may have to be brought into IPC even though they are regulated separately for emissions and discharges, because the latter are not equivalent to an integrated application of the BAT principle. In other words, the DoE may find itself having to extend the scope of IPC to fit IPPC after all, and so increase the number of processes regulated by the Environment Agency.

More IPC processes will have significant resource and staff implications for the Environment Agency. New guidance notes will have to be prepared which will elaborate BAT or BATNEEC for the new types of process introduced by IPPC. The number of processes regulated could increase from the current 3,000 up to as many as 8,000 processes. All of these will require inspection visits. Each will be submitting monitoring returns and paying annual fees for administration by the Environment Agency. No doubt many processes will have improvement programmes, progress upon which will need checking.

Those improvement programmes and initial authorisation will need negotiating. So IPPC will stretch the Environment Agency's limited resources even further, though the exact magnitude of this is unclear. Obviously any expansion of prescribed process or substance categories without a commensurate increase in Environment Agency resources will exacerbate current IPC problems concerning its limited and indulgent enforcement policy (see chapter 6).

Limited public register. Staff at DoE said many of the lessons of IPC implementation fed into IPPC negotiations and drafts of the Directive. Yet IPPC provisions for public access repeat the mistakes made for IPC, that is they do not allow for the public provision of feasibility reports from operators made in response to authorisation requests. With IPPC set to bring in processes and operators new to IPC, it is likely that such feasibility reports will be necessary. Domestic IPC legislation now covers this contingency[9] and such reports will in future reach the public register. The point is that the IPPC Directive does not require this for other Member States. UK operators may object to having to make commercial confidentiality requests and so forth when submitting feasibility reports if European competitors do not have to worry about such transparency during negotiations with their regulatory bodies.

Upgrading timetables. An earlier draft Directive published in September 1993 suggested all existing processes coming under IPPC should meet BAT standards by 30 June 2005 at the latest (Article 4). During negotiations periods for existing process BAT improvements as long as fourteen and even twenty years were discussed (ENDS, 1995g, p.39). The final Directive allows an eight year period for existing processes to be authorised, after the three year period for bringing the Directive into domestic force, and within this period they must also meet BAT. This pacified some British industrialists' concerns that IPC upgrading was more stringent than IPPC.

However, the opposite effect may result. That is IPPC may actually mean more stringent upgrading in some instances. There are several reasons for believing this. Firstly, IPC legislation does not include a specific upgrading period for existing processes. It merely requires the Environment Agency to 'review' authorisation conditions every four years. Secondly, many operators are privately negotiating improvements with Inspectors, based upon their post-authorisation feasibility studies. It is unclear how quickly these processes will have to upgrade and to what standards. Finally, recent Chief Inspector's Guidance Notes on BATNEEC state that reaching new process standards may not be possible and should not necessarily be sought (HMIP, 1995d, p.2). So it could transpire that the IPPC eight year limit for existing processes meeting

221

BAT could actually be more stringent. However, one has to bear in mind the site-specific caveats associated with BAT. In practice, the contemporary pattern for negotiating improvements may well continue.

Overall then, the EU's IPPC Directive does not look set to steer UK regulatory practice in a more formal and uniformly applied direction. Indeed, the only significant difference between IPPC and IPC is the number of processes covered. Whilst it is unclear what this precise increase will be, it is clear that it will impact upon the Environment Agency's resources.

Conclusion: opening the IPC policy community

The authority-information resource interdependency is fundamental in contemporary industrial pollution policy. The creation of the Environment Agency and IPPC's introduction, just like HMIP and IPC before them, fail to address the asymmetry of regulatory information between operators and Inspectors typical for any technology-based regulatory system (Weale, 1992, p.177; Davies and Davies, 1975, p.227). More general economic resources (that is, wealth creation and employment) and political resources (support and legitimacy) can modify the balance of the authority-information resource interdependency. With IPC this modification currently favours industry over the regulator. The Environment Agency's cost-benefit duty could tilt the balance further in industry's favour.

Weale (1992, p.177) suggests a way around the dilemma of information asymmetry is to regulate operators for standards of responsible environmental management, compared to regulating processes. There are signs that the Environment Agency is incorporating this into IPC, though for different motives (assuaging industry-driven deregulatory pressures). The Environment Agency is examining how the regulatory burden can be reduced for operators with accredited environmental management systems (Bigg, 1994, p.6; HMIP, 1995i, p.4). The policy community's appreciative system now views the pollution control task as goal-based self-regulation. But these goals are still negotiated in private between Inspector and operator.

The bilateral and technocratic nature by which IPC goals are negotiated needs challenging. Indeed, some NGOs are beginning to criticise the regime (see Friends of the Earth 1996, 1996b). Regulatory standards may be more open under IPC, but regulatory standard setting remains opaque and undermines the legitimacy of those standards[10] (Smith, 1996, p.85). Operator freedom to 'self-regulate' must take place within fully accountable regulatory goals. The flexibility for operators to manage their environmental performance by means suitable to their individual business requires some means for checking its adequacy with respect to improving the environment. In other words, if a diversity of environmental management is to be tolerated then it

222

must be shown to be meeting legitimate regulatory goals. And that legitimacy requires the opportunity for wider public participation than at present.

As Weale points out, 'the legitimacy of rules from this perspective depends upon the participation of interested parties in a process and not upon the presumed superior expertise of a superior authority' (1992, p.176). How one arrives at a regulatory goal becomes as important as the goal itself.

The RCEP recognised the diversity of factors (technical, economic, environmental and social) and the inevitable value judgements behind pollution control decisions (also Blowers, 1984; Davies and Davies, 1975, p.4). For these reasons the RCEP called for wide participation in standard setting (e.g. the scientific community, amenity groups, local authorities and the general public) (RCEP, 1976, p.4; RCEP, 1988).

Moreover, if regulatory attention is to emphasise environmental management rather than tight controls on individual processes, then perhaps the regulatory unit should also change. Perhaps the integrated prevention of pollution from industrial sites would be a better approach to regulation. Focusing upon releases from the site facilitates wider participation during negotiations - local communities are more concerned about pollution levels attributable to a site than with the BATNEEC for, say, the manufacture of hexamethylenediamine. A site focus makes the technical and financial minutiae of individual processes less central, whilst consideration of the overall impact upon public health and the environment is elevated.

Site-wide targets deliver operators their cherished combination of flexibility and certainty. They can manage their activities however they wish, so long as they do not exceed their site limits - for which strict enforcement should apply. Indeed, regulatory goals for the site should follow the precautionary principle, with the negotiation of ambitious reduction targets based upon the objective of forcing operators into innovating closed-loop production systems on their sites, and institutionalising industrial ecology techniques into their business, research and design functions.

Of course the advantages and disadvantages of any proposed reform needs much more careful consideration than that taken here. But this book has shown that the need for such consideration is as great now as it was in the early 1970s. The value judgements concerning society's control of industrial releases remain buried under the technical decisions of an exclusive IPC policy community.

Notes

1   Rhodes and Marsh (1994, pp.13-14) and Dowding (1995, pp.147-150) both suggest Sabatier's advocacy coalition model could offer theoretical

advancement in this area (Sabatier, 1987; Sabatier and Jenkins-Smith, 1993).

2   A series of comparative national studies into policy networks in the water policy sector found two of these exogenous change agents to be important: the welfare state crisis/New Right; and the environmental challenge (Bressers and O'Toole, 1994, p.206).

3   See Smith (1993, p.7) and Rhodes and Marsh (1992, p.201) for the suggested linking of policy networks to theories of the state as a solution, and Mills and Saward (1994, pp.87-90) for a similar approach using meta-theories such as functionalism, materialism (in the Marxist sense), game theory, and structuration theory.

4   The Environment Agency has, for instance, been considering toxicity based release limits for IPC, to be used as a complement to the current practice of relying upon concentration limits. Toxicity limits have the potential for improved environmental protection against operator discharges which have a complex cocktail of chemicals released in combination. Traditional concentration limits do not give such assured protection since they can miss synergistic impacts and do not include effects arising from unknown chemicals in the release.

5   The NRA has, for instance, lobbied government since 1991 to activate powers in the Water Resources Act 1991 to create Statutory Water Quality Objectives (SWQOs). A pilot scheme for SWQOs finally began in 1996 (Environment Agency, 1996b, p.9).

6   In 1994/95, the NRA prosecuted 3.6% of consent holders (excluding sewage treatment works), compared to HMIP's 0.52% of IPC processes (for which the scope for infringement is broader).

7   Section 39, Part I, Chapter III, Environment Act 1995.

8   Such as Local Authority Air Pollution Controls and discharges regulated under the Water Resources Act.

9   S.I. 1996 No 667, 'The Environmental Protection (Applications, Appeals and Registers) (Amendment) Regulations 1996'.

10   Once IPC standards are set, avenues for third party challenge are limited to judicial review.

References

Adams, J. (1996), 'Cost Benefit Analysis: The Problem, Not the Solution', *The Ecologist*, Vol. 26, No. 1, pp.2-5.

Aldrich, H. E. (1979), *Organizations and Environments*, Prentice-Hall: Englewood Cliffs, New Jersey.

Alkali Inspectorate (1964), *Annual Report of the Alkali Inspectorate for 1963*, HMSO: London.

Alkali and Clean Air Inspectorate (1974), *Annual Report of the Alkali and Clean Air Inspectorate for 1973*, HMSO: London.

Allott, K. (1994), *Integrated Pollution Control: The First Three Years*, Environmental Data Services: London.

Ashby, E. and Anderson, M. (1981), *The Politics of Clean Air*, Clarenden Press: Oxford.

Atkinson, M.M. and Coleman, W.D. (1989), 'Strong States and Weak States: Sectoral Policy Networks in Advanced Capitalist Economies', *British Journal of Political Science*, Vol. 19, January, pp. 47-67.

Bachrach, P. and Baratz, M. S. (1970), *Power and Poverty*, Oxford University Press: Oxford.

Baldwin, D.A. (1978), 'Power and Social Exchange', *The American Political Science Review*, Vol. 72 , pp.1229-1242.

Barrett, S. and Fudge, C. (1981), 'Examining the Policy-Action Relationship', in Barrett, S. and Fudge, C. (eds), *Policy and Action: Essays on the Implementation of Public Policy*, Methuen: London.

Barrett, S. and Hill, M.J. (1981), *Report to the SSRC Central-Local Government Relations Panel on the 'Core' or Theoretical Component of the Research on Implementation*, unpublished.

Benson, J. K. (1980), 'A Framework for Policy Analysis' in Roger, D. L. and Whetten, D. A. (eds) *Interorganizational Co-ordination: Theory Research and Implementation*, Iowa State University Press: Ames.

Bernstein, M. H. (1955), *Regulating Business by Independent Commission*, Princeton University Press: Princeton, New Jersey.

Bigg, M. (1994), 'Reducing the Environmental Impact of Industry', *61st NSCA Environmental Protection Conference* 24th-27th October, Blackpool.

Bird, J.M. (1993), *Competitiveness in the UK Chemical Industry. An Assessment of the Reasons for the Success of the Chemical and Pharmaceutical Industries in the UK: A Study Commissioned by the Chemicals and Biotechnology Division of the Department of Trade and Industry*, Department of Trade and Industry: London.

Blowers, A. (1984), *Something in the Air: Corporate Power and the Environment*, Harper and Row: London.

Boehmer-Christiansen, S. and Skea, J. (1991), *Acid Politics: Environmental and Energy Policies in Britain and Germany*, Belhaven Press: London.

Boehmer-Christiansen, S. (1994), 'The Precautionary Principle in Germany - Enabling Government', in O'Riordan, T. and Cameron, J. (eds), *Interpreting the Precautionary Principle*, Earthscan: London.

Bressers, H., O'Toole, L. J. Jr. and Richardson, J. (1994), 'Networks as Models of Analysis: Water Policy in Comparative Perspective', *Environmental Politics*, Vol. 3, No. 4, Winter, pp.1-23.

Bressers, H., Huitema, D. and Kuks, S. M. (1994), 'Policy Networks in Dutch Water Policy', *Environmental Politics*, Vol. 3, No. 4, Winter, pp.24-52.

Bressers, H. and O' Toole, L. J. Jr. (1994), 'Networks and Water Policy: Conclusions and Implications for Research', *Environmental Politics*, Vol. 3, No. 4, Winter, pp.197- 217.

Brown, P. (1996), 'Industry Pressure Halts Ozone Curb', *The Guardian*, 5th March .

Bugler, J. (1972), *Polluting Britain: A Report*, Penguin: London.

Bulmer, M. (1983), *Royal Commissions and Departmental Committees of Inquiry: The Lessons of Experience*, Royal Institute of Public Affairs: London.

Business Deregulation Task Forces (1994), *Deregulation Task Forces Proposals for Reform*, Department of Trade and Industry: London.

Cabinet Office (1985), *Lifting the Burden*, HMSO: London.

Campbell, A. (1991), 'How Does the UK Legislation Fit in With the European Viewpoint?', *Proceedings of the National Conference on IPC for the Process Industries*, 20th-21st November.

Carter, N. and Lowe, P. (1994), 'Environmental Politics and Administrative Reform', *Political Quarterly*, pp.263- 274.

Chemical Industries Association (1992), *Services to Members*, CIA: London.

Chemical Industries Association (1992b), *IPC Authorisations: Further Advice for Member Companies*, Letter to CIA Member Companies, 25th August.

Chemical Industries Association (1994), *CIA Survey on Integrated Pollution Control*, CIA: London.

Chemical Industries Association (1995), *UK Chemical Industry Facts*, CIA: London.

Coleman, T. (1992), 'Integrated Pollution Control: Too Much to Bear an Too Much to Bare?', *Keynote Address to BICS Conference*, 9th December.

Coleman, W. and Grant, W. (1984), 'Business Associations and Public Policy: A Comparison of Organisational Development in Britain and Canada', *Journal of Public Policy*, Vol. 4, No. 3 , pp.209-235.

Collins, B. (1987), 'The Rayner Scrutinies', in A. Harrison and J. Gretton (eds), *Reshaping Central Government*, Transaction Books: Oxford.

Committee of Public Accounts (1992), *Sixteenth Report - Controlling and Monitoring Pollution: Review of the Pollution Inspectorate*, HMSO: London.

Committee on Safety and Health at Work (1972), *Report of the Committee of Safety and Health at Work*, HMSO: London.

Confederation of British Industry (1979), *Release of Environmental and Technical Information*, CBI Statement No. T559 79: London.

Confederation of British Industry (1980), *British Industry and the Environment*, CBI Statement: London.

Confederation of British Industry (1984), 'Agenda For Enterprise: CBI National Conference Report', *CBI News Special*, No. 56.

Confederation of British Industry (1986), *Clean Up - Its Good For Business*, CBI: London.

Confederation of British Industry (1993), *Deregulation and the Environment: Submission to the Government's Deregulation Unit*, CBI: London.

Crenson, M. A. (1971), *The Unpolitics of Air Pollution*, Johns Hopkins Press: Baltimore.

Crump, A. (1991), *Dictionary of Environment and Development: People, Places, Ideas and Organisations*, Earthscan: London.

Cunningham, C. (1992), 'Sea Defences: A Professionalised Network?' in Marsh, D. and Rhodes, R.A.W. (eds) *Policy Networks in British Government*, Clarendon Press: Oxford.

Dahl, R. A. (1957), 'The Concept of Power', *Behavioural Science* Vol. 2.

Davies, J.C. and Davies, B. (1975), *The Politics of Pollution*, Pegasus, 2nd Edition: Indianapollis.

Dearlove, J. and Saunders, P. (1984), *Introduction to British Politics*, Polity Press: London.

Department of the Environment (1976), *Press Notice 37 - Report on Air Pollution Control*, DoE: London.

Department of the Environment (1982), *Pollution Paper No. 18 - Air Pollution Control: The Government Response to the Fifth Report of the Royal Commission on Environmental Pollution*, HMSO: London.

Department of the Environment (1984), *Pollution Paper No. 22 - Controlling Pollution: Principles and Prospects*, HMSO: London.

Department of the Environment (1986a), *Inspecting Industry: Pollution and Safety - Action Plan*, HMSO: London.

Department of the Environment (1986b), 'Government to Create a Unified Pollution Inspectorate: HM Inspectorate of Pollution', *DoE Environment News Release* No. 439.

Department of the Environment (1986c), *Air Pollution Control in Great Britain: Review and Proposals - A Consultation Paper*, DoE: London.

Department of the Environment (1986d), *Pollution Paper No. 23 - Public Access to Environmental Information*, HMSO: London.

Department of the Environment (1988a), *Integrated Pollution Control Consultation Paper*, DoE: London.

Department of the Environment (1988b), *Air Pollution Control in Great Britain: Follow-up to Consultation Paper Issued in 1986*, DoE: London.

Department of the Environment (1990), *MINIS 11: 1989-90*, DoE: London.

Department of the Environment (1991), *MINIS 12: 1990-91*, DoE: London.

Department of the Environment (1993), *Integrated Pollution Control: A Practical Guide*, HMSO: London.

Department of the Environment (1993b), 'Integrated Pollution Control: Application for Certain Chemicals Extended', *Environment News Release 319*, DoE: London.

Department of the Environment (1994), *HMIP Directorate Return - MINIS 15 Part 4: Environmental Protection Group*, DoE: London.

Department of the Environment (1994b), *Digest of Environmental Protection and Water Statistics No. 16*, HMSO: London.

Department of the Environment (1995), *HMIP Directorate Return - MINIS 16 Part 4: Environmental Protection Group*, DoE: London.

Department of the Environment (1995b), 'EC Integrated Pollution Prevention and Control Directive', *Written Correspondence to DoE Consultees*, 19th September.

Department of the Environment (1996), *Indicators of Sustainable Development for the United Kingdom*, HMSO: London.

Department of Trade and Industry (1994), *Deregulation: Cutting Red Tape*, Business Deregulation Unit of the DTi: London.

Diver, C. S. (1980), 'A Theory of Regulatory Enforcement', *Public Policy*, Vol. 28, No. 3, pp.257-299.

Dowding, K. (1995), 'Model or Metaphor? A Critical Review of the Policy Network Approach', *Political Studies*, Vol. 43 , pp.136-158.

Downing, P.B. and Hanf, K. (1983), 'Modelling Environmental Regulation' in Downing, P.B. and Hanf, K. (eds), *International Comparisons in Implementing Pollution Laws*, Kluwer-Nijhoff: Boston.

Downs, J. (1992), 'Who Pays What?', in O'Riordan, T. and Bowers, V. (eds), *IPC: A Practical Guide for Managers*, Dotesios: Trowbridge.

Dunsire, A. (1990), 'Implementation and Bureaucracy' in Younis, T. (ed) *Implementation in Public Policy*, Dartmouth Publishing: Aldershot.

Dunsire, A. (1978), *Implementation in a Bureaucracy*, Martin Robertson: Oxford.

Efficiency Scrutiny (1986), *Inspecting Industry: Pollution and Safety*, HMSO: London.

Elmore, R. (1980), 'Backward Mapping: Implementation Research and Policy Decisions'. *Political Science Quarterly*, Vol. 94.

Environment Agency (1995), *Briefing Note: The Environment Agency - Opening for Business Soon*, Environment Agency: Bristol.

Environment Agency (1996), *The Environment of England and Wales - A Snapshot*, Environment Agency: Bristol.

Environment Agency (1996b), 'River Quality Targets May Soon Be Legal', *Environment Action*, Vol. 1, April/May, p.9.

Environmental Data Services (1985), 'Fears for Future of Air Pollution Inspectorate', *ENDS Report*, No. 120, January.

Environmental Data Services (1985b), 'Opening Shots in Whitehall Battle Over New Pollution Control Agency', *ENDS Report*, No. 129, October.

Environmental Data Services (1986a), 'New Fears for Air Pollution Inspectorate' *ENDS Report*, No. 141, October.

Environmental Data Services (1986b), 'Industry's Agenda for New Pollution Inspectorate', *ENDS Report*, No. 143, December.

Environmental Data Services (1986c), 'Waldegrave Gets Half A Loaf With Unified Pollution Inspectorate', *ENDS Report*, No. 139, August.

Environmental Data Services (1987), 'New Round of Consultation Begins On Air Pollution Controls', *ENDS Report*, No. 154, November.

Environmental Data Services (1987), 'Environment Top Priority, Says Chemical Industry Chief', *ENDS Report*, No. 154, November.

Environmental Data Services (1989), 'EC Air Quality, Industrial Air Pollution Directives Implemented', *ENDS Report*, No. 170, March.

Environmental Data Services (1989b), 'The Uncertain Road Towards Integrated Pollution Control', *ENDS Report*, No. 178.

Environmental Data Services (1990), 'Upsets on the Road to Integrated Pollution Control', *ENDS Report*, No. 186, July.

Environmental Data Services (1991), 'HMIP Consults on IPC for Contract Chemicals Sector', *ENDS Report*, No. 200, September.

Environmental Data Services (1992), 'Integrated Pollution Control and the Organic Chemicals Industry', *ENDS Report*, No. 207, April.

Environmental Data Services (1992b), 'Early Lessons in IPC for Speciality Chemicals Sector', *ENDS Report*, No. 205, February.

Environmental Data Services (1992c), 'EC Proposals on Integrated Pollution Control Comes Closer', *ENDS Report*, No. 207, April.

Environmental Data Services (1993), 'IPC Guides for Organic Chemicals', *ENDS Report*, No. 217, February.

Environmental Data Services (1993b), 'Organic Chemicals Industry Wins Time for IPC Revisions', *ENDS Report*, No. 220, May.

Environmental Data Services (1993c), 'Drawing the Battle Lines in the Deregulation Debate', *ENDS Report*, No. 217, February.

Environmental Data Services (1993e), 'Deregulatory Thrust for Pollution Control Rules', *ENDS Report*, No. 227, December.

Environmental Data Services (1993d), 'Drawing the Battle Lines in the Deregulation Debate', *ENDS Report*, No. 217, February.

Environmental Data Services (1994), 'Stronger Deregulatory Thrust in Revised Pollution Control Rules', *ENDS Report*, No. 232, May.

Environmental Data Services (1995), 'In Search of the Best Practicable Environmental Option', *ENDS Report*, No. 249, October.

Environmental Data Services (1995b), 'A Department in Distress', *ENDS Report*, No. 250, November.

Environmental Data Services (1995c), 'HMIP Takes Another Look at IPC Charging Scheme', *ENDS Report*, No. 245, June.

Environmental Data Services (1995d), 'Environmental Assessment Toolkit for IPC Applicants Takes Shape', *ENDS Report*, No. 244, May.

Environmental Data Services (1995e), 'NRA Staff Dominate Top Posts in Environment Agency', *ENDS Report*, No. 247, August.

Environmental Data Services (1995f), 'Cost/Benefit Duty, Contaminated Land Remain Leading Issues in Environment Bill', *ENDS Report*, No. 243, April.

Environmental Data Services (1995g), 'IPPC Directive to Force Major Changes in IPC', *ENDS Report*, No. 245, June.

Environmental Data Services (1996), 'HMIP Breaks New Ground in Draft Incinerator Guidance', *ENDS Report*, No. 254, March.

Environmental Data Services (1996b), 'Progress on Toxicity-based Consents', *ENDS Report*, No. 255, April.

European Communities (1983), 'Action Programme of the European Communities on the Environment (1982 to 1986)', *Official Journal of the European Communities*, No. C 46/3, 17/2/1983.

Fischer, K.and Schot, J. (eds) (1993), *Environmental Strategies for Industry*, Island Press: Washington, D.C.

Fischer, S., Dornbusch, R. and Schmalensee, R. (1988), *Economics*, McGraw-Hill, 2nd Edition: New York.

Francis, J. (1993), *The Politics of Regulation*, Blackwell: Oxford.

Frankel, M. (1974), *The Alkali Inspectorate: The Control of Industrial Air Pollution*, Social Audit: London.

Friends of the Earth (1989), *The Environment: The Governments Record*, Friends of the Earth: London.

Friends of the Earth (1996), 'FoE Comment on Environment Agency', *FoE Press Release*, London.

Friends of the Earth (1996b), 'Government Keeps New Agency on a Short Lead', *FoE Press Release*, 6th February, London.

Gallagher, E. (1996), 'Environment Agency Chief Executive's Speech: The Agency - Its Aims and Objectives', *The Environment Agency - Framework for the Future Briefing*, QEII Conference Centre, 6th February.

Grant, W. (1984), 'Large Firms and Public Policy in Britain', *Journal of Public Policy*, Vol. 4, No. 1, pp. 1-17.

Grant, W., Patterson, W. and Whitston, C. (1988), *Government and the Chemical Industry*, Clarendon Press: Oxford.

Gray, T.S. (ed) (1995), *UK Environmental Policy in the 1990s*, Macmillans: Basingstoke.

Haigh, N. (1989), *EEC Environmental Policy and Britain*, Longman, 2nd Edition Revised: London.

Haigh, N. (1994), 'The Introduction of the Precautionary Principle into the UK', in O'Riordan, T. and Cameron, J. (eds), *Interpreting the Precautionary Principle*, Earthscan: London.

Haigh, N. and Lanigan, C. (1995), 'Impact of the European Union on UK Environmental Policy Making', in Gray, T.S. (ed), *UK Environmental Policy in the 1990s*, Macmillans: Basingstoke.

Ham, C. and Hill, M. (1993), *The Policy Process in the Modern Capitalist State*, Harvester Wheatsheaf, 2nd Edition: Hemel Hempstead.

Hancher, L. and Moran, M. (1989), 'Organising Regulatory Space', in Hancher, L. and Moran, M. (eds) *Capitalism, Culture, and Economic Regulation*, Clarendon Press: Oxford.

Hanf, K. (1978), 'Introduction', in Hanf, K. and Scharpf, F.W. (eds) *Interorganisational Policy Making*, Sage: London.

Hanf, K. (1982), 'Regulatory Structures: Enforcement As Implementation', *European Journal of Political Research*, Vol. 21, No. 1-2, pp.163-181.

Hanf, K. and Downing, P. B. (eds) (1983), *International Comparisons in Implementing Pollution Laws*, Kluwer-Nijhoff: Boston.

Hanf, K. and O'Toole (1992), L. J. Jr, 'Revisiting Old Friends: Networks, Implementation Structures and the Management of Inter-organisational

231

Relations', *European Journal of Political Research*, Vol. 21, No. 1-2 , pp.163-181.

Hanf, K. (1993), 'Enforcing Environmental Laws: the Social Regulation of Co-production', in Hill, M. (ed), *New Agendas in the Study of the Policy Process*, Harvester Wheatsheaf: London.

Hargrove, E.C. (1975), *The Missing Link*, The Urban Institute: Washington, D.C.

Hargrove, E. C. (1983), 'The Search for Implementation Theory', in Zeckhauser, R.J. and Leebaert, D. (eds) *What Role for Government? Lessons from Policy Research*, Duke Press Policy Studies: Durham, North Carolina.

Hartnell, G., Skea, J., Smith, A. and Stirling, A. (1994), *Environmental, Economic and BPEO Assessmet Principles for Integrated Pollution Control: A Response to the HMIP Consultation Document*, Unpublished Science Policy Research Unit Document, Brighton.

Hawkins, K. (1984), *Environment and Enforcement: Regulation and the Social Definition of Pollution*, Oxford University Press: Oxford.

Health and Safety Commission (1982), *Health and Safety Commission Report 1981-1982*, HMSO: London.

Health and Safety Commission (1987), *Health and Safety Commission Annual Report 1986*, HMSO: London.

Health and Safety Executive (1977), *Health and Safety: Industrial Air Pollution 1975*, HMSO: London.

Health and Safety Executive (1978), *Health and Safety: Industrial Air Pollution 1976*, HMSO: London.

Health and Safety Executive (1979), *Health and Safety: Industrial Air Pollution 1978*, HMSO: London.

Health and Safety Executive (1980), *Health and Safety: Industrial Air Pollution 1979*, HMSO: London.

Health and Safety Executive (1982), *Health and Safety: Industrial Air Pollution 1981*, HMSO: London.

Health and Safety Executive (1984), *Health and Safety: Industrial Air Pollution 1982*, HMSO: London.

Health and Safety Executive (1986), *Health and Safety: Industrial Air Pollution 1985*, HMSO: London.

Heclo, H. (1978), 'Issue Networks and the Executive Establishment' in King, A. (ed), *The New American Political System*, American Enterprise Inc.: Washington, D.C.

Heilman, J.G., Johnson, G.W., Morris, J.C. an O'Toole, L.J.Jr. (1994), 'Water Policy Networks in the United States', *Environmental Politics*, Vol. 3, No. 4, Winter, pp.80-109.

Hemenway, D. (1985), *Monitoring and Compliance: The Political Economy of Inspection*, JAI Press: Greenwich, Connecticut.

Hennessey, P. (1986), *Cabinet*, London: Basil Blackwell.

Hennessey, P. (1987), Article in *The Independent*, 21st December.

Her Majesty's Inspectorate of Pollution (1989a), *Notes on Best Practicable Means: BPM 11/89 - Incineration Works Chemical*, Department of the Environment: London.

Her Majesty's Inspectorate of Pollution (1989b), *First Annual Report 1987-88*, HMSO: London.

Her Majesty's Inspectorate of Pollution (1990), *Forward Look 1990-91 to 1994-95*, HMIP: London.

Her Majesty's Inspectorate of Pollution (1991), *Guidance Note to Applicants*, HMIP: London.

Her Majesty's Inspectorate of Pollution (1991b), *Third Annual Report 1989-90*, HMSO: London.

Her Majesty's Inspectorate of Pollution (1991c), *Determining Applications Made Under IPC: A Guidance Note*, HMIP: London.

Her Majesty's Inspectorate of Pollution (1991d), *Fourth Annual Report 1990-91*, HMSO: London.

Her Majesty's Inspectorate of Pollution (1992), *First Draft Chief Inspector's Guidance Notes - Process Guidance Note IPR 4/5 - Batch Manufacture of Organic Chemicals in Multipurpose Plant*, HMIP: London.

Her Majesty's Inspectorate of Pollution (1992b), *Chief Inspector's Guidance Note - Process Guidance Note IPR 5/1 - Merchant & In House Chemical Waste Incineration*, HMSO: London.

Her Majesty's Inspectorate of Pollution (1992c), *Chief Inspector's Guidance Note - Process Guidance Note IPR 1/3 Combustion Processes: Compression Ignition Engines 50 MW(th) and Over*, HMSO: London.

Her Majesty's Inspectorate of Pollution (1992d), *The Environmental Assessment of Releases from Prescribed Processes*, HMIP: London.

Her Majesty's Inspectorate of Pollution (1993), *Chief Inspector's Guidance Notes - Process Guidance Note IPR 4/5 - Batch Manufacture of Organic Chemicals in Multipurpose Plant*, HMSO: London.

Her Majesty's Inspectorate of Pollution (1993b), *Annual Report 1991-92 - Research Review*, HMSO: London.

Her Majesty's Inspectorate of Pollution (1993c), *Annual Report 1992-93 - Research Review*, HMSO: London.

Her Majesty's Inspectorate of Pollution (1993d), 'Communiction-PIC: IPC - Practical Requirements of S.I. 472 as Amended', *OPS-PIC No. 32*, HMIP: London.

Her Majesty's Inspectorate of Pollution (1993e), *Annual Report 1991-92*, HMSO: London.

Her Majesty's Inspectorate of Pollution (1993f), *A Review of the Available Techniques for Pollution Control in the Manufacture an Use of Nitrogen-Containing Organic Compounds - Research Report No. 93/025*, HMIP: London.

Her Majesty's Inspectorate of Pollution (1993g), *Annual Report 1992-93*, HMSO: London.

Her Majesty's Inspectorate of Pollution (1993h), *Standard Authorisation Format Ref: 2/93 - Guidance Issued by Regulatory Procedures Branch*, HMIP: London.

Her Majesty's Inspectorate of Pollution (1993i), 'The IPCIS Long Weekend', *HMIP Bulletin*, No. 26, December.

Her Majesty's Inspectorate of Pollution (1994), 'New Committee to Help Ensure Efficiency of Pollution Inspectorate', *HMIP Bulletin*, July.

Her Majesty's Inspectorate of Pollution (1994b), 'My God, More! Productions Presents ... Chemical Tranche 1 - A Documentary Drama', *HMIP Bulletin*, July.

Her Majesty's Inspectorate of Pollution (1994c), 'Co-operative Development of Tools for Environmental Analysis', *HMIP Supplement*, July.

Her Majesty's Inspectorate of Pollution (1994d), *Environmental, Economic and BPEO Assessment Principles for Integrated Pollution Control: Consultation Document*, HMIP: London.

Her Majesty's Inspectorate of Pollution (1995), *1994-95 Annual Report*, HMSO: London.

Her Majesty's Inspectorate of Pollution (1995b), *Technical Guidance Branch Publications List*, HMIP: Bristol.

Her Majesty's Inspectorate of Pollution (1995c), 'Open Forum on IPC Charging Scheme', *HMIP Bulletin*, July.

Her Majesty's Inspectorate of Pollution (1995d), *Chief Inspector's Guidance Notes - S2 1.03 - Combustion Processes: Compression Ignition Engines 50 MW(th) and Over*, HMSO: London.

Her Majesty's Inspectorate of Pollution (1995e), *Fourth Quarterly Report 1994-95*, HMIP: London.

Her Majesty's Inspectorate of Pollution (1995f), *Technical Guidance Note E1 - Environmental, Economic and BPEO Assessment Principles for Integrated Pollution Control - Draft*, HMIP: London.

Her Majesty's Inspectorate of Pollution (1995g), *Operator and Pollution Risk Appraisal (OPRA)*, HMIP: London.

Her Majesty's Inspectorate of Pollution (1995h), 'The "3E's?" Emissions, Efficiencies and Economics', *HMIP Bulletin*, March.

Her Majesty's Inspectorate of Pollution (July 1995i), 'Dr Slater Urges Place for Eco-management in Environmental Control', *HMIP Bulletin*, 38.

Her Majesty's Inspectorate of Pollution (1995j), *Operator and Pollution Risk Appraisal (OPRA)*, HMIP: London.

Her Majesty's Inspectorate of Pollution (June 1995k), 'A Further Monitoring Contract for Fuel and Power Processes', *HMIP Bulletin*, No. 37.

Her Majesty's Inspectorate of Pollution (July, 1995l), 'HMIP To Carry Out In Depth Audits at Major Companies', *HMIP Bulletin*, No. 38.

Her Majesty's Inspectorate of Pollution (1995l), *Fees and Charges for Integrated Pollution Control 1995-96*, HMIP: London.

Hill, M. (1982), 'The Role of the British Alkali and Clean Air Inspectorate in Air Pollution Control', *Policy Studies Journal*, Vol. 11, No. 1, pp.165-174.

Hjern, B. and Hull, C. (1982), 'Implementation Research as Empirical Constitutionalism'. *European Journal of Political Research* Vol. 2, pp.105-115.

Hjern, B. and Porter, D.O. (1981), 'Implementation Structures: A New Unit of Administrative Analysis', *Organization Studies*, Vol. 2, No. 3, pp.211-217.

HM Government (1994), *Competitiveness: Helping Business to Win*, HMSO: London.

HMIP Advisory Committee (1995), *Interim Report, February 1995*, DoE: London.

Hogwood, B. W. and Gunn, L. A. (1984), *Policy Analysis for the Real World*, Oxford University Press: Oxford.

Hogwood, B.W. (1995), 'Public Policy', *Public Administration*, Vol. 73, No. 1, pp.59-73.

Holdgate, M.W. (1979), *A Perspective on Environmental Pollution*, Cambridge University Press: Cambridge.

Hood, C.C. (1976), *The Limits of Administration*, Wiley: London.

Hutter, B.M. (1986), 'An Inspector Calls: The Importance of Proactive Enforcement in a Regulatory Context', *British Journal of Criminology*, Vol. 26, No. 2, pp.114-128.

Institution of Chemical Engineers - North Western Branch (1993), 'Environmental Technology BATNEEC II', *Symposium Papers 1993 No. 8*, Wilmslow, 1st-2nd December.

Irwin, F., 'Introduction to Integrated Pollution Control', in Haigh, N. and Irwin, F. (eds) (1989), *Integrated Pollution Control in Europe and North America*, The Conservative Foundation: Washington, D.C.

Jenkins, W. (1978), *Policy Analysis: A Political and Organisational Perspective*, Martin Robertson: London.

Jordan, A. (1993), 'IPC and the Evolving Style and Structure of Environmental Regulation in the UK', *Environmental Politics*, Vol. 2, No. 3, Autumn, pp.405-427.

Jordan, G. and Schubert, K. (1992), 'A Preliminary Ordering of Policy Network Labels'. *European Journal of Political Research*, Vol. 21, No. 1-2 , pp.7-27.

Kassim, H. (1994), 'Policy Networks, Networks and European Union Policy Making: A Sceptical View', *West European Politics*, Vol. 17, No. 4 , pp.15-27.

Kaufmann, F. X. (1986), 'Introduction', in Kaufmann, F.X., Majone, G. and Ostrom, V. (eds), *Guidance, Control and Evaluation in the Public Sector*, de Gruyter: New York.

Kenis, P. and Schneider, V. (1991), 'Policy Networks and Policy Analysis: Scrutinizing a New Analytical Toolbox', in Marin, B. and Mayntz, R. (eds) *Policy Networks: Empirical Evidence and Theoretical Consideration*, Campus Verlag: Frankfurt.

Kingdom, J. (1991), *Government and Politics in Britain: An Introduction*, Polity Press: Cambridge.

Knoepfel, P. and Weidner, H. (1982), 'Formulation and Implementation of Air Quality Control Programmes: Patterns of Interest Consideration', *Policy and Politics*, Vol. 10, No. 1, pp.85-109.

Levitt, R. (1980), *Implementing Public Policy*, Croom Helm: London.

Lewins, F. (1992), *Social Science Methodology*, Macmillan Education: Melbourne.

Liardet, G. (1994), 'Public Opinion and the Chemical Industry', *Chemistry and Industry* 18th February, pp.118-123.

Lipsky, M. (1980), *Street-level Bureaucrats: Dilemmas of the Individual in the Public Services*, Sage: New York.

Lowe, P. and Goyder, J. (1983), *Environmental Groups in Politics*, George Allen and Unwin: London.

Lowi, T.A. (1972), 'Four Systems of Policy, Politics and Choice', *Public Administration Review*, Vol.32.

Lukes, S. (1974), *Power: A Radical View*, Macmillan: London.

Lyons, G. (1992), *A Review of Part I of the Environmental Protection Act and Its Implementation*, World Wide Fund for Nature: Godalming.

Mahler, E.A.J. (1967), 'Standards of Emission Under the Alkali Act', *Paper presented to the International Clean Air Congress, London, October, 1966 and reproduced in the 103rd Annual Report of the Alkali Inspectorate*, HMSO: London.

Maloney, W.A. and Richardson, J. (1994), 'Water Policy-Making in England and Wales: Policy Communities Under Pressure?', *Environmental Politics*, Vol. 3, No. 4, Winter, pp.110-138.

Marin, B. and Mayntz, R. (eds) (1991), *Policy Networks: Empirical Evidence and Theoretical Considerations*, Campus Verlag: Frankfurt.

Marsh, D. and Rhodes, R. A. W. (eds) (1992a), *Implementing Thatcherite Policies: Audit of an Era*, Open University Press: Buckingham.

Marsh, D. and Rhodes, R. A. W. (eds) (1992b), *Policy Networks in British Government*, Clarendon Press: Oxford.

McCormick, J. (1991), *British Politics and the Environment*, Earthscan: London.

McLeod, R.M. (1965), 'The Alkali Acts Administration, 1863-84: The Emergence of the Civil Scientist', *Victorian Studies: a*, Vol. IX, No. 2 , pp.85-112.

Metcalfe, L. and Richards, S. (1987), *Improving Public Management*, Sage: London.

Mills, M. (1992), 'The Case of Food and Health and the Use of Network Analysis' in Marsh, D. and Rhodes, R.A.W. (eds) *Policy Networks in British Government*, Clarendon Press: Oxford.

Mills, M. and Saward, M. (1994), 'All Very Well in Practice, But What About the Theory? A Critique of the British Idea of Policy Networks' in Dunleavy, P. and Stanyer, J. (eds), *Contemporary Political Studies 1994 Proceedings of the Annual Conference of the Political Studies Association*, Political Studies Association: Belfast.

Mitchell, J.C. (1983), 'Case and Situation Analysis', *The Sociological Review*, Vol. 31, pp.187-210.

Mitnick, B. M.(1980), *The Political Economy of Regulation: Creating, Designing and Removing Regulatory Forms*, Columbia University Press: New York.

Mol, A.P.J. (1995), *The Refinement of Production: Ecological Modernisation Theory and the Chemical Industry*, CIP-Data Koninklijke Bibliotheek: Den Haag.

Morehouse, W. (1994), 'Unfinished Business: Bhopal After Ten Years', *The Ecologist*, Vol. 24, No. 5 , pp.164-169.

Mountjoy, R. S, and O'Toole, L. O. Jr. (1979), 'Towards a Theory of Policy Implementation: An Organisational Perspective', *Public Administration Review*, Vol. 39, No. 5.

National Audit Office (1991), *Control and Monitoring of Pollution: Review of the Pollution Inspectorate*, HMSO: London.

National Economic Development Council - Specialised Organics Sector Group (1992), *The Chemistry for a Better Environment*, NEDC: London.

National Rivers Authority (1991), *Annual Report and Accounts 1990/91*, National Rivers Authority: London.

National Rivers Authority (1993), *Annual Report and Accounts 1992/93*, National Rivers Authority: London.

National Rivers Authority (1995), *Annual Report and Accounts 1994/95*, National Rivers Authority: London.

Nilsson, S. and Pitt, D. (1994), *Protecting the Atmosphere: The Climate Change Convention and Its Context*, Earthscan: London.

O'Riordan, T. (1988), 'The Politics of Environmental Regulation in Great Britain', *Environment*, Vol. 30, No. 8 , pp.5-9 & pp.39-44.

O'Riordan, T. (1989), 'BPEO: A Case Study in Partial Bureaucratic Adaptation', *Environmental Conservation*, Vol. 16, No. 2 , pp.113-122.

O'Riordan, T. and Weale, A. (1989), 'Administrative Reorganisation and Policy Change: the Case of Her Majesty's Inspectorate of Pollution', *Public Administration*, No. 67, Autumn.

O'Riordan, T. (1992), 'The Environment', in Cloke, P. (ed), *Policy and Change in Thatcher's Britain*, Pergamon Press: Oxford.

O'Riordan, T. and Cameron, J.(eds) (1994), *Interpreting the Precautionary Principle*, Earthscan: London.

Owens, S. (1989), 'The Unified Inspectorate and Best Practicable Environmental Option in the United Kingdom', in Haigh, N. and Irwin, F. (eds), *Integrated Pollution Control in Europe and North America*, The Conservation Foundation: Washington, D.C.

Painter, C. (1989), 'Thatcherite Radicalism and Institutional Conservatism', *Parliamentary Affairs*, Vol. 42, No. 4 , pp.463-484.

Parfitt, A. and Andreassen, L. (1992), 'Get Those Applications Right', *The Chemical Engineer*, 29 October.

Pearce, D. and Brisson, I. (1993), 'BATNEEC: The Economics of Technology Based Environmental Standards', *Oxford Review of Economic Policy*, Vol 9, No. 4 , pp.24-40.

Peltzman, S. (1976), 'Toward a More General Theory of Regulation', *Journal of Law and Economics*, Vol. 19, No. 2 , pp.211-241.

Pepper, D. (1986), *The Roots of Modern Environmentalism*, Routledge: London.

Peterson, J. (1994), 'Policy Networks and Governance in the European Union: the Case of Research and Development' in Dunleavy, P. and Stanyer, J. (eds), *Contemporary Political Studies 1994 Volume 1: Proceedings of the Annual Conference of the Political Studies Association*, Political Studies Association: Belfast.

Platt, J. (1988), 'What Can Case Studies Do?', *Studies in Qualitative Methodology*, Vol. 1, pp. 1-23.

Pressman, J. L. and Wildavsky, A. (1973), *Implementation*, University of California Press: Berkely.

Purdue, M. (1991),'Integrated Pollution Control in the Environmental Protection Act 1990: A Coming of Age of Environmental Law?', *The Modern Law Review*, Vol. 54, July, pp.534-551.

Read, M. (1989), 'The Politics of Tobacco', *DPhil Thesis*,University of Essex.

Read, M. (1992), 'Policy Networks and Issue Networks: The Politics of Smoking' in Marsh, D. and Rhodes, R.A.W. (eds), *Policy Networks in British Government*, Clarendon Press: Oxford.

Reynolds, D. (1993), 'The Environmental Protection Act - Two Years Experience of Integrated Pollution Control', *Paper presented at Institution of Chemical Engineers North Western Branch's Symposium on Environmental Technology - BATNEEC II*, Wilmslow, 1st-2nd December.

Rhodes, G. (1981), *Inspectorates in British Government: Law Enforcement and Standards of Efficiency*, Allen and Unwin: London.

Rhodes, R. A. W. (1981), *Control and Power in Central-Local Government Relations*, Gower: Farnborough.

Rhodes, R. A. W. (1986), *The National World of Local Government*, Allen and Unwin: London.

Rhodes, R. A. W. (1988), *Beyond Westminster and Whitehall*, Unwin Hyman: London.

Rhodes, R. A. W. (1990), 'Policy Networks: A British Perspective', *Journal of Theoretical Politics*, Vol. 2 , pp.293-317.

Rhodes, R. A. W. and Marsh, D. (1992), 'New Directions in the Study of Policy Networks', *European Journal of Political Research*, Vol. 21, pp.181-205.

Rhodes, R. A. W. and Marsh, D. (1994), 'Policy Networks: 'Defensive' Comments, Modest Claims and Plausible Research Strategies', *Paper to the Political Studies Association Annual Conference, University of Swansea*, 29-31 March.

Richardson, J. J. and Jordan, G. (1979), *Governing Under Pressure: The Policy Process in a Post-Parliamentary Democracy*, Martin Robertson: Oxford.

Richardson, J. J., Maloney, W. A. and Rudig, W. (1992), 'The Dynamics of Policy Change: Lobbying and Water Privatisation', *Public Administration*, Vol. 70, Summer, pp.157-175.

Rose, C. (1990), *The Dirty Man of Europe: The Great British Pollution Scandal*, Simon and Schuster: London.

Royal Commission on Environmental Pollution (1976), *Fifth Report - Air Pollution Control: An Integrated Approach*, HMSO: London.

Royal Commission on Environmental Pollution (1984), *Tenth Report - Tackling Pollution: Experience and Prospects*, HMSO: London.

Royal Commission on Environmental Pollution (1988), *Twelfth Report - Best Practicable Environmental Option*, HMSO: London.

Royal Commission on Environmental Pollution (1993), *A Guide to the Royal Commission and Its Work*, RCEP: London.

Rudig, W. and Kraemer, A. (1994), 'Networks of Co-operation: Water Policy in Europe', *Environmental Politics*, Vol. 3, No. 4, Winter, pp.52-79.

Sabatier, P. (1986), 'Top-down and Bottom-up Approaches to Implementation Research', *Journal of Public Policy*, Vol. 6, pp.21-48.

Sabatier, P. A. and Pelkey, N. (1987), 'Incorporating Multiple Actors and Guidance Instruments Into Models of Regulatory Policymaking: An Advocacy Coalition Framework'. *Administration and Society*, Vol. 19, No. 2 , pp.236-263.

Sabatier, P. and Jenkins-Smith, H.C. (eds) (1993), *Policy Change an Learning: An Advocacy Coalition Approach*, Westview Press: Boulder, Colorado.

Saward, M. (1992), 'The Civil Nuclear Network in Britain', in Marsh, D. and Rhodes, R.A.W. (eds), *Policy Networks in British Government*, Clarendon Press: Oxford.

Sayer, A. (1992), *Method in Social Science: A Realist Approach*, Routledge, 2nd Edition: London.

Scharpf, F. (1978), 'Inter-organisational Policy Studies: Issues, Concepts and Perspectives', in Hanf, K. and Scharpf, F. (eds) *Inter-organisational Policy Making: Limits to Co-ordination and Central Control*, Sage: London.

Scharpf, F. (ed) (1991), *Games in Hierarchies and Networks: Analytical and Empirical Approaches to the Study of Governance Institutions*, Westview Press: Boulder, Colorado.

Schmitter, P. (1974), 'Still the Century of Corporatism', *Review of Politics*, Vol. 36.

Schuck,P. H. (1981), 'The Politics of Regulation', *Yale Law Journal*, Vol. 90, No. 3, January, pp.702-725.

Simmons, P. and Wynne, B. (1993), 'Responsible Care: Trust, Credibility and Environmental Management', in Fischer, K. and Schot, J. (eds), *Environmental Strategies for Industry*, Island Press: Washington, D.C.

Skea, J. (1995), 'Acid Rain: A Business-as-Usual Scenario', in Gray, T.S. (ed), *UK Environmental Policy in the 1990s*, Macmillans: Basingstoke.

Skea, J., Smith, A., Sorrell, S., and van Zwanenberg, P. (1995), *The Availability of Data Necessary to Evaluate Integrated Pollution Control: Report to the Department of the Environment*, Unpublished SPRU Report, Brighton.

Skea, J. and Smith, A. (1996), 'Integrating Pollution Control: European Directives, British Practice', in Lowe, P. (ed), *Britain in Europe: National Environmental Policy in Transition*, Routledge: London.

Slater, D. (1996), 'Pollution Prevention and Control', *The Environment Agency - Framework for the Future Briefing*, QEII Conference Centre, 6th February.

240

Smith, A. (1996), 'Voluntary Schemes and the Need for Statutory Regulation: the Case of Integrated Pollution Control', *Business Strategy and the Environment* Vol. 5, No. 2, pp.81-87.

Smith, M.J. (1993), *Pressure, Power and Policy*, Harvester Wheatsheaf: Hemel Hempstead.

Specialised Organics Manufacturers Eastern Region (1994), 'SOMER Reference Guide', *Speciality Chemicals*, March/April.

Stigler, G. (1971), 'The Theory of Economic Regulation', *Bell Journal of Economics and Management*, Vol. 2, Spring.

Stirling, A. (1993), 'Environmental Valuation: How Much is the Emperor Wearing?', *The Ecologist*, Vol. 23, No. 3 , pp.97-104.

Stone, A. (1982), *Regulation and Its Alternatives*, Congressional Quarterly Press: Washington, DC.

Thrasher, M. (1983), 'Exchange Networks and Implementation', *Policy and Politics*, Vol. 11, No. 4, pp.375-391.

Tinker, J. (1972), 'Britain's Environment: Nanny Knows Best', *New Scientist*, Vol. 53, No. 786, 9 March, p.530.

Tunnicliffe, M.F. (1977), 'The United Kingdom Approach and its Application by Central Government. Standards of Emission for the Scheduled Processes', *Paper presented to the International Clean Air and Pollution Control Conference, 1975 and reproduced in Health and Safety Executive Industrial Air Pollution Annual Report 1975*, HMSO: London.

Van Meter, D. and Van Horn, C.E. (1975), 'The Policy Implementation Process, A Conceptual Framework', *Administration and Society*, Vol. 6, No. 4.

Van Waarden, F. (1992), 'Dimensions and Types of Policy Networks', *European Journal of Political Research*, Vol. 21 , pp.29-52.

Vickers, G. (1965), *The Art of Judgement*, Chapman and Hall: London.

Viscusi, W.K. and Zeckhauser, R.J. (1979), 'Optimal Standards With Incomplete Enforcement', *Public Policy*, Vol. 27, No. 4 , pp.437-456.

Vogel, D. (1986), *National Styles of Regulation: Environmental Policy in Great Britain and the United States*, Cornell University Press: Ithaca.

von Moltke, K. (1988), 'The Vorsorgeprinzip in West German Environmental Policy', in RCEP, *Twelth Report - Best Practical Environmental Option*, HMSO: London.

Ward, H. and Samways, D. (1992), 'Environmental Policy', in Marsh, D. and Rhodes, R.A.W. (eds), *Implementing Thatcherite Policies: Audit of an Era*, Open University Press: Buckingham.

Weait, M. (1989), 'The Letter of the Law? An Enquiry Into Reasoning and Formal Enforcement in the Industrial Air Pollution Inspectorate', *British Journal of Criminology*, Vol. 29, No. 1, pp.57-70.

Weale, A. (1992), *The New Politics of Pollution*, Manchester University Press: Manchester.

Wheal, C. (1993), 'Pollution Law Collapses as Applications Swamp Inspectors', *The Engineer*, 11th February.

Wilks, S. and Wright, M. (eds) (1987), *Comparative Government-Industry Relations*, Clarendon Press: Oxford.

Wilks, S. and Wright, M. (eds) (1991), *The Promotion and Regulation of Industry in Japan*, Macmillan: Basingstoke.

Williams, W. (1980), *The Implementation Perspective*, University of California Press: Berkely, California.

Wilson, J. Q. (ed) (1980), *The Politics of Regulation*, Basic Books: New York.

Wright, M. (1993), 'Policy Networks in British Government, and Policy Networks: Empirical Evidence and Theoretical Considerations - Book Review', *American Political Science Review*, Vol. 87, No. 2, pp.529-530.

Wyburd, G. (1992), 'Case Study: Industry', in Berry, R.J. (ed), *Environmental Dilemmas - Ethics and Decisions*, Chapman and Hall: London.

Younis, T. (ed) (1990), *Implementation in Public Policy*, Dartmouth Publishing: Aldershot.

Younis, T. and Davidson, I. (1990), 'The Studyof Implementation', in Younis, T. (ed), *Implementation in Public Policy*, Dartmouth Publishing: Aldershot.

Index